Legacy of the Seventies

Experiment, Economy, Equality, and Expediency in American Higher Education

Lewis B. Mayhew

Legacy of
the Seventies

 Jossey-Bass Publishers

San Francisco • Washington • London • 1977

LEGACY OF THE SEVENTIES
Experiment, Economy, Equality, and Expediency in American Higher Education
Lewis B. Mayhew

Copyright © 1977 by: Jossey-Bass, Inc., Publishers
615 Montgomery Street
San Francisco, California 94111
&
Jossey-Bass Limited
28 Banner Street
London EC1Y 8QE

Library of Congress Catalogue Card Number LC 77-82070

International Standard Book Number ISBN 0-87589-344-9

Manufactured in the United States of America

JACKET DESIGN BY WILLI BAUM

FIRST EDITION

Code 7743

The Jossey-Bass Series
in Higher Education

Preface

Laurence R. Veysey (1965) points out that a revolution took place between 1870 and 1910, in the form, structure, and processes of American higher education. The classical curriculum of the colonial colleges, taught through recitation and detailed study of texts, gave way to the elective principle, the lecture, the seminar, the laboratory experiment, and professional study based on rigorously established scientific principles and conducted in multipurpose institutions. Veysey speculates that it is just possible that in the 1970s a new revolution may be underway. At the time he was writing, dissatisfaction with the conventions of American higher education was widespread, and many experiments and innovations with curricula, styles of teaching, modes of organization, and methods of testing seemed to be evidence of attempts to find a new format.

Now, it seems clear that the last years of the 1960s did indeed constitute a dividing point in the evolution of higher education and that a second revolution was actually begun. In *Legacy of*

the Seventies I seek to examine the origins, themes, and consequences of this recent watershed period and to offer some suggestions about the future based on the experience of this past decade.
Future historians will be able to put the past ten years and our
current conditions in better perspective, but the time is ripe for at
least a first appraisal of this important revolution.

The power of traditional academic structures, practices, and
values is great. Established pacesetting institutions and national
organizations have begun to question or restrain the more radical
educational reforms and institutions of this movement. Regional
accreditation has begun to enforce compliance with older standards
of quality. State governments have begun to question unlimited
public support for new kinds of programs and to impose tighter
budgetary limits on existing programs. Congressional leaders have
begun to question the value of much educational experimentation,
and the new federal administration, which is not unsympathetic to
higher education, is not likely to favor educational expansionism.
Thus, the prevailing attitude throughout the country with respect
to higher education seems comparable to that regarding energy:
We are realizing that resources are finite and that they must be
deployed in prudent ways. In short, the current period of questioning and hesitation affords an opportunity to sort out the accomplishments and the false starts of the last decade before committing ourselves either to further transformation or to earlier traditions. The
following chapters are intended to help in this reassessment.

The organization of this book is straightforward. It presents
the themes that have long characterized higher education in the
United States and then examines six major parts for which significant change has either been urged or attempted: nontraditional
study, new kinds of institutions being created, curricular and instructional experiments in established institutions, organization and
governance, educational technology, and methods and theories of
finance. The evidence presented comes from the author's visits to
many campuses since 1968, reviews of several hundred institutional
self-studies, the growing polemical and research literature, and the
various state and federal provisions for higher education. The mode
of analysis is eclectic, using an historical context within which to
critically examine psychological, sociological, and economic studies

and data. The point of view is that of an experienced, concerned, and sympathetic but skeptical observer of higher education since the end of World War II. The underlying assumption is that the large and complex system of higher education is conservative and changes little but that the experimentation and innovation taking place have the potential for modifying it. The research quest was to discover persuasive evidence of realization of that potential.

I hope that educators, political leaders, and the concerned public will learn from the examples and analysis presented to ponder seriously proposed changes, relative costs and benefits, and competing social and educational needs as a prelude to deciding educational policy for the 1980s and beyond, years that promise to be qualitatively different than the recent past. To help them do so, a variety of new, as well as older, information is examined, from what is hopefully a fresh perspective, a view somewhat different from previous writings. These new descriptions, criticisms, and predictions lead to the presentation of desired courses of action.

Appreciation and thanks go to many different people who allowed their institutions to be studied. Special thanks go to Frederick deW. Bolman who commissioned over 100 site visits during seven years, to Kay Andersen of the Western College Association who made visits to complex new institutions possible, and to Phyllis Anderson who typed and retyped the manuscript to meet my compulsively impossible deadlines. As always, love and thanks go to my wife, Dorothy C. Mayhew, who provides the environment necessary for sustained work.

Stanford University   LEWIS B. MAYHEW
August 1977

Contents

The Author

Lewis B. Mayhew is professor of education and chairman of the Committee on Administration and Policy Analysis in the School of Education, Stanford University. After five-and-one-half years in the U.S. Army during World War II, he spent twelve years at Michigan State University (1947–1958), three years at the University of South Florida (1959–1962), and fifteen years at Stanford (1962–present). For seventeen years (1957–1974) he served as part-time director of research at Stephens College in Columbia, Missouri. He received his bachelor's and master's degrees from the University of Illinois (1938 and 1947, respectively) and his Ph.D. in history from Michigan State University (1951).

He has written about many parts of higher education in the United States (over 20 books and 200 articles), consulted widely (over 500 institutions), and served on many different regional and national committees, such as the Educational Testing Service Board Committee on Test Development and the Senior Commission of the

Western College Association. He was consultant to the White House Conference on Education during Lyndon B. Johnson's administration, president of the American Association for Higher Education, and rated one of the 44 most influential leaders in higher education in the *Change* magazine survey of 1974.

Included among his publications are *General Education: Explorations in Evaluation* (with Paul L. Dressel, 1954), which demonstrated that complex educational outcomes could be reliably measured. *The Smaller Liberal Arts Colleges* (1962) anticipated the financial plight those institutions would face. *Arrogance on Campus* (1970) correctly gauged the end of student protest in the early summer of 1970. *Contemporary College Students and the Curriculum* (1969) became a major reference for faculty curriculum study groups throughout the South, and *The Carnegie Commission on Higher Education: A Critical Analysis of the Reports and Recommendations* (1973) assessed the impact of the commission's effort and placed it in a realistic perspective. *Higher Education as a Field of Study: The Emergence of a Profession* (with Paul L. Dressel, 1974) attempted to evaluate programs of higher education. Two books written with Patrick J. Ford, *Changing the Curriculum* (1971) and *Reform in Graduate and Professional Education* (1974), evaluated the many curricular reforms attempted during the 1960s.

Lewis Mayhew has been married for thirty-eight years to Dorothy C. Mayhew, and has three children, Lewis B., Jr., Madeline, and Robert. In addition, he and his wife have informally adopted a second daughter, Trudy. The Mayhews live on the Stanford campus and enjoy swimming, biking, and taking trips in their motor home.

To the children who must help shape
the future I have tried to predict:
Lewis B. and Kathy Mayhew,
Madeline Mayhew,
Robert Mayhew and Valrie Massey,
and Trudy Growe

Legacy of the Seventies

Experiment, Economy, Equality, and Expediency in American Higher Education

ONE

Evolution and Transformation

This book argues a thesis. It contends that from the end of World War II until 1968 the substance of American higher education changed remarkably little and remained consistent with its prewar intellectual traditions but that between 1968 and 1970 it began to change in such radical ways that if these changes persist American higher education will soon be profoundly different from what it has been in the past.

Some observers believe, of course, that during the 1950s and 1960s American colleges and universities underwent enormous change. The Carnegie Foundation for the Advancement of Teaching, for example, considers that great changes are illustrated by the community college movement, the transformation of state colleges into comprehensive universities, and the enlargement of professional schools (1976). And certainly the number and size of institutions and the cost, complexity, and variety of their programs increased dramatically. But, apart from these increases, careful examination of trends between 1945 and 1968 and reflection on their significance suggests that they represented no significant departure from long-existing tendencies.

Thus, until 1968, although fluctuations can be noted, the higher education community largely believed that higher education was rational and intellectual. It was an "academic" activity provided to a growing, but still limited, segment of the population for the quite specific purposes of screening these young people into preferred positions; enculturating them into at least a portion of the high intellectual tradition of the society; and preparing them, through a stress on meritocratic achievement, to enter the major professions and assume leadership in a complex and technological society. Egalitarian sentiments were expressed, to be sure, and egalitarian efforts were made; but as new kinds of students enrolled in college they were expected to conform to the orthodox and traditional practices of a residential—or simulated residential—campus. Although vocationalism was never excluded from their curriculum, there was a general faith that the essential core of collegiate education was the liberal arts and sciences. And while debate concerning the nature of education was no more absent than in previous times, there was nonetheless tacit agreement as to what was and what was not higher education. Colleges and universities were staffed with highly trained faculty members, long since socialized into a specific set of shared beliefs, who held closely to dearly cherished academic values. Grossly stated, higher education was simply what established institutions did.

But between 1968 and 1970 profound changes were both strongly advocated and actually put into operation on a large scale. These changes, which were sharply at variance with the ideals, values, and practices of the past, severely challenged the existing consensus in almost every respect. Rationality and intellectuality, meritocracy, selectivity, collegiality and shared authority, campus autonomy, professorial expertise and training, and the primacy of professors in instruction and evaluation—all were called into question by the 1970s. These new developments included efforts to serve new kinds of students with nontraditional modes of instruction and new types of institutions, the creation of centralized state control of institutions, the unionization of the faculty, the intrusion of courts into institutional affairs, and greater and greater reliance on tuition as the principal financial base for both public and private higher education.

All of these concepts and presumed needs had been available earlier, but for the most part had been ignored. Thus blacks and other minorities, as well as underprepared students, had been expected to conform to orthodox academic arrangements; independent study was available as an expensive enrichment process rather than as a primary mode of education; and the use of part-time and academically uncredentialed faculty was judged to be a necessary modification of quality rather than as an ideal medium of instruction.

Not insignificantly, these changes in serving new students, using nontraditional modes of instruction, creating new kinds of institutions and statewide systems of control, and searching for low-cost delivery systems became popular at exactly the same time that higher education began to encounter serious financial difficulties. While these developments derive from a number of forces, they all seem to have been chiefly responses of institutions and educators to the problem of surviving economically in a depressed and changing time while simultaneously serving the egalitarian wishes of many different people to obtain the credentials and values that higher education had to offer.

What emerged to assure institutional and professional security was a paradoxical juxtaposition of academic marketplace behavior and extreme academic egalitarian rhetoric; and, since professional security and egalitarianism are frequently antithetical, attempts to respond to both produced some highly unusual practices. New students were sought so that their needs could be met, but they were typically served by the least expensive modes of education. New institutions were created to serve the poor, in the hope that the poor could pay full tuition to maintain the institutions. Nontraditional methods of instruction were urged to accommodate an enormous variety of individual differences, yet for the most part they were considerably more expensive than the traditional campus-based techniques. State systems of public institutions became more centrally controlled to ensure greater access to higher education, yet they encouraged the shifting of greater costs to students, through tuition increases. Federal policy stressed egalitarian postsecondary education rather than conventional higher education, but it advocated greater use of student loans rather than lower tuition. And professional organizations such as the American Association of University Professors and the National Education Association theorized about professional values and better education, but they sought new members and dues through collective bargaining and guarding the economic interests of professors.

After only a decade of transformation and paradox, it may still be too early to predict with much accuracy the long-term consequences of these changes. But it is not too soon to put these changes in perspective by viewing them in the context of the past three decades. Nor is it too soon—in terms of trying to untangle the paradoxes and choose among competing options—to analyze the forces that produced these recent changes, gauge their present significance, and anticipate their possible future.

Post-World War II Themes Through 1968

In retrospect, eight themes stand out as characterizing the period from 1945 to 1968 and as forming the basis for changes since then.

Cautious Egalitarianism. Perhaps the most important theme was a cautious expansion of egalitarianism into higher education with the purpose of gradually bringing previously unserved groups into the mainstream of American life and socializing their members into the predominant culture. Opinion was mixed as to how much caution should be used in extending the egalitarian principle. The Commission on Financing Higher Education believed that only approximately 25 percent of high school graduates were qualified and could profit from normal postsecondary education (Millett, 1952, p. 48). James Bryant Conant was even more cautious, believing that egalitarian ideals would best be achieved through strengthening secondary schools and through creating two-year colleges, restricting enrollment into four-year colleges and universities to those individuals clearly destined for the major professions and scholarship (1953). But it was President Truman's Commission on Higher Education that established the generally accepted norm, by pointing out that "At least 49 percent of our population has the mental ability to complete fourteen years of schooling with a curriculum of general and vocational studies that should lead either to gainful employment or to further study at a more advanced level" (President's Commission on Higher Education, 1947, p. 41). To achieve that goal of enrolling half of high school graduates in college, several barriers should be removed, the most prominent being economic, geographic, religious, and racial. These barriers were judged serious but susceptible to being overcome by allowing processes already in operation to continue. For example, concerning the reduction of racial barriers, by 1950 there appeared reason for optimism: "The emotional conviction, as distinguished from the mere intellectual agreement, that segregation has no rational basis, is manifesting itself in the active stance taken by the church and other organized groups. The youth of the land is beginning to show itself relatively free from bias, a situation in which educators may take pride, since curricular planning seems to have been a significant factor in the change. The intermingling of young men in the armed services has done much to dispel strangeness and fear, which formed so large a part of prejudice (Kennedy, 1950, pp. 42–43).

While some modification of existing curricula was envisioned, to meet the needs of students from groups previously prevented from attending college (remedial or improvement centers became popular), in general it was anticipated that students would enter college to be educated and trained in traditional ways and for well-established purposes. Students were expected to pursue a strong program of general education as well as rigorous and realistic vocational or professional preparation. Although there was a uniform belief that market demands should not impose quota setting on institutions, the relationship between education and jobs was clearly recognized, as was the relationship between aptitude and professional education. It was assumed that counselors could channel students into productive and satisfying occupations and that they should routinely redirect students during preprofessional training if students lacked the necessary qualifications for their desired profession. It also was generally recognized that the professional disciplines required long,

intensive, and specialized education, with few or no shortcuts. And
it was understood that the social utility of education was the production of people needed to make a democratic society function:
"Higher education must inspire its graduates with high social aims
as well as endow them with specialized information and technical
skill" (President's Commission on Higher Education, 1947, p. 11).

Enrollment Expansion. A related theme stressed between
1947 and 1952 and again as 1960 approached was the collection of
ways to cope with large numbers of students. When World War II
ended, the financial assistance of GI Bill of Rights suddenly allowed
several million veterans to enroll in higher education programs of
various sorts. In addition to being numerous, these veterans reflected
distinctive characteristics. They had a background of military service
in war; they were considerably older than typical freshmen; and,
because of the financial subsidy of the GI Bill of Rights, their attendance was not as determined by the socioeconomic standing of
their families. Remarkably, these veterans were for the most part
accommodated in traditional institutions, which made modifications
in housing arrangements, class schedules, and some services, such as
counseling and guidance, yet which used traditional curricula and
traditional modes of teaching to deliver the primary educational
service. Other means could have been adopted to cope with large
numbers of veterans wishing to prepare themselves for postwar
careers. The military services themselves might have assumed a substantial educational mission. Federal funds might have been used to
stimulate extensive apprenticeship programs. Or universities might
have offered many, different, new kinds of short courses designed
to move veterans quickly into the labor market. Instead, existing institutions simply extended capacity and enrolled veterans into quite
well-established, orthodox degree programs and subjected them to
the same kinds of teaching and evaluation designed for younger student with no war experience. A few institutions, such as the University of Chicago and Michigan State University, did provide a system
of comprehensive examinations that would allow students to finish
college earlier. However, for the most part there was no systematic
modification of time requirements. The educational program conceived of as being appropriate for college students in the past was
judged appropriate for the veteran group, which adapted to the

system extraordinarily well. As a group, veterans were serious about their collegiate work, were highly motivated, viewed their college work as highly utilitarian, and typically surpassed other students in academic work. They did not participate as much in extracurricular activities, including student government, but they did exploit the curricular opportunities afforded them. And they were generally satisfied with the teaching they received and the programs in which they were enrolled (Frederiksen and Schrader, 1951).

The veteran enrollment rose and declined in a relatively short time. By 1952 decrease had begun, and by 1955 the veteran component had become a negligible factor. This decline in veteran enrollments produced overall reduced enrollment and financial problems in collegiate institutions. Thus, from roughly 1952 to 1958, colleges and universities faced economic depression and a stable or declining state comparable to that which they experienced in the early 1970s. However, institutions did not modify their practices significantly during that economically depressed time. Some faculty members were let go, and budgets were kept stable or even reduced, but there was no rush to find new clientele nor was there much apocalytpic talk about the potential demise of American higher education. While there were a few predictions that the enrollment decline would be of relatively short duration, there were also those who believed that because of a number of factors, such as saturation of the labor market, enrollments would continue to decline. Yet no unusual means were suggested to make up the budgetary deficits those enrollment drops implied, nor were institutions active in recruiting new students or offering new programs to attract them. Dean Rusk (1953), then president of the Rockefeller Foundation, after reviewing the entire financial situation of the early 1950s, expressed mild optimism that the needed additional funds would be secured without resorting to any new devices, with the few exceptions of increased alumni and corporate giving.

By 1954 it had become apparent that within six years higher education would start to experience dramatic enrollment increases as a result of the increased birth rates following World War II. Again the question arose as to what responses should be made to increased demand and which of a variety of alternatives should be adopted. A first response would obviously be to ration enrollments vigorously, perhaps accompanying such a decision with a strengthening of high school curricula. If the decision were to allow enrollments to rise, then the question arose as to whether to expand the capacity of existing institutions or to create new institutions. Since the anticipated enrollment would likely involve a more heterogeneous group of students, another question was whether to create radically new programs to fit new kinds of students or to continue existing programs for the most part. The solution turned out to be a blend of several suggestions. With respect to space a continuation of traditional patterns, existing institutions allowed to grow, and new institutions, particularly two-year junior colleges, were planned and formed—but always in traditional form. Rationing was used by some institutions whose prestige was such as to attract larger numbers of applicants than there were available spaces. But for most institutions expanding capacity seemed preferable and more consistent with their missions than limiting enrollments through rationing. In theory, the junior college was supposed to provide the distinctively new programs that new kinds of students might desire; however, in practice the newly created junior colleges typically stressed college-parallel work, and as a rule about 75 percent of all students who enrolled in junior colleges claimed to want entry into the transfer program that would allow them to proceed to a bachelors degree.

From the mid-1950s onward, educational technology having high educational potential, such as radio, films, and then television, had become available, and a few people suggested that one answer to burgeoning enrollments would be to teach large classes through the technology. There was some experimentation of that sort, but the mainstream of practice in colleges and universities remained substantially as it had been, the lecture being paramount, followed by discussion, laboratory work, and library work. Similarly, from time to time the idea of differential staffing was suggested, as well as the utilization of large numbers of retired professors to staff the classrooms needed for the millions of new students. But here again the decision was against radical changes. Instead, the decision was to allow a slight deterioration of the quality of faculty, by appointing more people without doctorates, but to make no appreciable change in staffing policy or patterns.

American higher education thus responded in traditional

ways throughout a period of rapidly expanding veteran enrollments, rapidly dropping veteran enrollment, and then rapidly increasing enrollments. Existing institutions expanded to capacity, first by using temporary structures and then, in the late 1950s, by creating new permanent facilities. New institutions were created in the latter period, but most followed traditional models, even in two-year junior colleges. Curricula, methods of teaching, class schedules, assignment of academic credit, and staffing patterns typically followed tradition, with only modest modifications.

Primacy of Liberal Arts. A third theme was the general belief in the values of studying the liberal arts and sciences, particularly as reinterpreted in programs of general education. It was generally assumed that there was a body of information, skills, values, and insights that all educated people should possess. These could be developed best through sequences of courses that would expose students to the broad domains of human knowledge and that would develop quite specific and well-accepted skills, such as critical or analytical thinking. Although the literature of the period reveals considerable difficulty in reaching agreement as to a specific definition of general education, examination of many different programs indicated a firm underlying consensus. General education should be required of most if not all students. It should expose students to the natural sciences, social sciences, humanities, and the several modes of communications. It should give the student the values, attitudes, knowledge, and skills that would equip him or her to live rightly and well in a free society. It was specifically designed to provide students insight into the cultural heritage, so that each individual could base his or her own life on that cultural substructure. Spokesmen for general education accepted American society as it was (always assuming improvement possible) and would help students understand and accept the purposes and character of the political, economic, and social institutions comprising the American society. Once again the Truman Commission caught the essence of the consensus regarding what education was all about: "General education is not sharply distinguished from liberal education; the two differ mainly in degree, not in kind. General education undertakes to redefine liberal education in terms of life's problems as men face them, to give it human orientation and social direction, to invest it with content that is directly relevant to the demands of contemporary society. General education is liberal education with its matter and method shifted from its original aristocratic intent to the service of democracy. General education seeks to extend to all men the benefits of an education that liberates" (President's Commission on Higher Education, 1947, p. 49).

General education was concerned with values and personal adjustment, but above all it was rational and intellectual. Faculties from nineteen institutions that participated in the Cooperative Study of Evaluation in General Education reached the conclusion that the essential element was critical, analytical, or reflective thinking. What general education was supposed to do was to train people to detect problems, sense assumptions, collect and evaluate evidence, and reach warrantable conclusions or assertions. Faculty members unquestioningly believed they had the right and responsibility to select what students would study and to develop exercises that would develop a clearly conceptualized mode of thinking. The possibility that college students might be turned loose to construct their own curriculum for the most part does not appear in the literature of general education. It is true that a few institutions, such as Bennington, Sarah Lawrence, and Stephens College, allowed for free election, but it was free election exercised under extraordinarily close supervision and guidance.

General education programs typically were prescriptive and for the most part sought to achieve some generally agreed-on objectives. A student was to develop a code of behavior based on generally accepted ethical principles. This would enable him to participate actively as an informed and responsible citizen. It would also provide a psychological base to enable the student to understand and deal with different peoples of the world. It was intended to develop the student's understanding of the physical environment and his ability to apply habits of scientific thought. General education was in important respects a verbal and mathematical form of education intended to teach the student to express clearly his own ideas and to understand the expression of ideas of others. Further, general education could help the individual attain a satisfactory emotional and social adjustment; to maintain and improve health; to understand and enjoy literature, art, music, and other cultural activities; to develop and enjoy a satisfying family life; and to choose a socially useful and personally satisfying vocation. All of this was to be done by cultivating the intellect. Furthermore general education clearly placed professors in a central role. "The effectiveness of any general education program will depend on the quality and attitudes of those who administer and teach it. Its success will be commensurate with the faculty members' recognition of the importance of such instruction to society and their willingness to assume initiative and responsibility in reorganizing instruction and rearranging the life of the institution to accomplish its objectives" (President's Commission on Higher Education, 1947, p. 60).

Research Support. Perhaps the most revolutionary theme of the immediate post-World War II period was the emergence of federally supported science and research as an essential element of American higher education. This was not an inevitable development. During the early part of the nineteenth century, American scientists in search of patrons typically did not view the nineteenth-century college as a particularly hospitable home. Even after the emergence of the utilitarian university, which accepted research and scholarship as a major mission, scientific research was underfunded and carried on by scientists in addition to quite heavy teaching responsibilities. Right up until the outbreak of World War II, with the exception of some medical and agricultural research, governmental sources of potential funding and the university-based scientific community regarded each other with deep suspicion. In 1938, for example, it was estimated that universities throughout the country were spending somewhere in the vicinity of $50 million a year on research, with only about $6 million provided by the federal government, mostly for research in agriculture. Even when the potentialities of nuclear energy for warfare had become apparent, the Carnegie Institution of Washington only reluctantly accepted $1,500 from the Naval Research Laboratory to facilitate research and stipulated that the funds be made available through a third, independent party so there could be no possibility of government control of research. Gradually, however, under the leadership of Albert Einstein, Karl Compton, Vannevar Bush, and James Conant, federal funds were provided to universities for war-related research and for the creation of separate research centers. The successful development of the atomic bomb, the proximity fuse, and radar established what research could produce and established a model for the post-World War II period for a continuing liaison between the federal government and university scientists. That relationship was symbolized in 1950 by the creation of the National Science Foundation and exemplified four years later by the investment on the part of the federal government of $121 million for basic research in universities or in research centers operated by universities. This amount, of course, was piddling, by subsequent standards, but in terms of prewar budgets it was enormous (Greenberg, 1967, p. 131). From that time on, federal contributions to university research ballooned, passing the $1 billion mark in 1949 and the $4.4 billion mark in 1957.

It is true that the bulk of federal and foundation research funds went to a limited number of universities, but its significance for all of American higher education far transcended those few campuses. Externally supported research as an essential mission of colleges and universities became the ideal. Its implications included reduced teaching loads as well as the emergence of graduate education as the most rapidly expanding segment of all higher education. Just how deeply imbedded the ideal of research and graduate education become is revealed by the comments of presidents of 156 developed and developing institutions interviewed in the late 1960s. The presidents expected that their faculty members would in the future spend 50 percent or more of their time on research and that their teaching loads would drop to typically one course. They assumed continued federal financing of research, but they also assumed that the states would begin massive categorical appropriations to support research without reference to the teaching activities of the university.

Professionalization of Faculty. A related theme, which also would be elaborated continuously through the 1960s and then seriously challenged, was the professionalization of college and university faculties. Gradually, during the late nineteenth and twentieth centuries, the Ph.D. had come to be regarded as essential preparation for college teaching, although only a minority of college professors actually held that degree, even well into the post-World War II period. In a few institutions, faculties claimed responsibility for their own membership and for the substance of the curriculum, and faculties did maintain a national organization, the American Association of University Professors, to help safeguard the ideal of academic freedom. Typically, however, colleges and universities were governed by their presidents, who were assisted by a few administrative associates. Teaching loads were high, and faculty remuneration was low. While publicized arbitrary actions regarding faculty on the part of administration were relatively few, this seems more due to the benignness of presidents and the reluctance of faculties to resist when actions were taken than to the strength of the professorial faculty as a professionalized entity.

During the 1950s, a new conception steadily emerged. Using the rhetoric of the past but making it operational, the advent of federal and some foundation support of research created an economic base for some professors outside of their institutions. The Ford Foundation symbolically recognized the need for higher professorial salaries by making a grant to accredited private liberal arts colleges to improve faculty salaries. This need was also symbolized in 1958 by the recommendation of President Eisenhower's White House Conference on Education Beyond High School that faculty salaries should be doubled in the succeeding decade. As administrators began to anticipate the enrollment increases that were to come, they began to attend more to the recruitment and retention of faculty members. The American Association of University Professors began to publicize faculty salaries by individual institutions, thus stimulating institutional competition with respect to increasing faculty salaries. All of this established a firmer economic base for a professionalized faculty.

As a result of these and other related events, the 1950s produced an ideal of a college or university faculty that was sought in most institutions, completely achieved in some, and given strength by growing organizations and agencies concerned with academic affairs. The faculty was assumed to be responsible for its own membership, the substance of the curriculum, the condition of student entry and exit, and the condition of student life. The individual professor enjoyed academic freedom, which allowed him to seek and teach the truth according to his own criteria, and his freedom to do so was protected by formal statements granting continuous appointment or tenure. The professor was expected to obtain a doctorate or the appropriate terminal degree, the training for which provided him a legitimatized esoteric knowledge to be used by him as a self-regulating professional. Regional and special accrediting agencies lent support to such a conception by regarding the number of doctorates as important in institutional quality and by concerning themselves with conditions of faculty autonomy. Organizations such as the then Association for Higher Education stressed, through committees and conferences, the rights and prerogatives of faculty members, and philanthropic foundations contributed funds for various sorts of activities designed to increase the professional quality of faculty members. This ideal, with its stress on quality, intellectuality, rationality, and training, is captured by J. Douglas Brown:

> In a liberal university in particular, the faculty as a corporate body must assume a heavy responsibility for the educational traditions and policies of the institution. In its corporate capacity, as a total faculty, it represents the unifying mechanism for bringing all knowledge, understanding, insights, and values to bear upon the manner in which succeeding generations of students and younger scholars are developed. Consisting of highly educated men and women, dedicated to an age-old profession, it must seek to uphold standards of truth, integrity, dedication, and service within itself and on the part of its institution and the disciplines it professes. The faculty of a university has some of the attributes of a medieval guild in its participation, in a large degree, in self-government, in the selection of candidates for membership, and in the determination of standards of performance. That teacher-scholars are *appointed* to membership and not *employed* on a staff is of real and not merely traditional significance. On appointment, the member joins the partnership or a complex system of partnerships. The designation of membership should therefore be definite and not casual, and the responsibilities of membership should be clear [Brown, 1969, pp. 22–23].

Internationalism. A different sort of theme, which emerged in the 1950s and which flowered during the 1960s, was a significant international concern on the part of colleges and universities. The indicators of this concern begin with the Point Four idea of 1949 and the federally sponsored educational exchange programs under the Fullbright and Smith-Mundt Acts. The philanthropic foundations became active in international education activities, and universities themselves undertook exchange programs of various sorts designed to make their own faculties and student bodies more internationally minded and to provide service for other nations. Thus, by the 1957–58 academic year, 184 American institutions had organized 382 different exchange programs (Widner, 1962). By 1960 there were almost 54,000 foreign students from 143 countries enrolled at almost 1,700 collegiate institutions in the United States. Almost 16,000 American students were attending foreign universities, and 2,200 American faculty members were teaching abroad. Thirty-six hundred members of foreign faculties were affiliated with 304 American colleges and universities (Widner, 1962, pp. 4–5).

Prior to and immediately following World War II, American collegiate institutions could have been characterized as being parochial and essentially concerned with American culture and that of northwest Europe. A distinguished president of Kenyon College remarked in the early 1950s that the proper business of collegiate institutions was with Western civilization and that the only elements of non-Western civilization that might be included in an American curriculum were those that tended to elaborate or corroborate essential principles of the Western tradition. Such a point of view, however, quickly lost favor during the 1950s as Americans began to experience at first hand the cultures of Asia, Latin America, and eventually Africa. Such exposure, as was true of so many other developments, was motivated by intellectual and utilitarian concerns. There was general awareness of the position of the United States in world leadership, as well as of the implication that such leadership could be exerted only through highly trained, sophisticated individuals. "Encouraging our young people to look back to their cultural and linguistic heritage from other lands or to choose early some other culture for study, we could prepare thousands of our best students to acquire an expert knowledge of one such culture and its language. If we started systematically now with the children in the elementary grades, it would take about ten years for this program to bring results. If this seems like a long time to wait, let us remember that it looks as if Americans, for decades to come, will be traveling, studying, and residing abroad in greater and greater numbers. They will indeed be our ambassadors, our representatives in many parts of the world. The very future of our country may well depend on how skillfully and truthfully these Americans interpret our civilization to other nationals and how intelligently they have been trained to report to us about other peoples' cultures and aspirations" (Girard, 1953, p. 117)'.

The point that differentiates this development from the point of view developed in the 1970s was the purpose of studying new regions and cultures. It was to prepare American leadership to aid other regions and to deepen appreciation for the Western tradition. This is in sharp contrast to the ethnic studies movement of the 1970s, which sought to emphasize a vital tradition for racial and ethnic groups that would be different from that of the West. Ethnic studies moved *against* a commonly shared body of allusion, idiom, and metaphor, rather than *toward* one.

Student Personnel Movement. Still another theme that was to be elaborated during the 1960s and then seriously called into question was the expansion of the professionalized student personnel movement and the psychological testing movement. Prior to World War II, the concept of a dean of students had emerged as an office concerned with student discipline and supervision of student activities. After World War II, however, as collegiate institutions assumed responsibilities for new functions, an entire new range of services coalesced into the student personnel unit of a typically three-part administrative structure for colleges and universities. Institutions began to construct residence halls, whereas previously they had relied on fraternities, sororities, and private rooming houses. Thus the supervision of housing became essential. To aid veterans in coping with the problems of making wise academic and vocational choices and to cope with the Bureau of Veterans Affairs, externally financed offices of counseling, testing, and guidance were created on college campuses, offices that then evolved into counseling centers supported by institutions themselves once the veteran population had left the campus. As it became apparent that selection of students for entrance into some colleges, graduate schools, and professional schools would be needed; as student counselors demanded more precise information about students' abilities, interests, and aptitudes in order to assist them; and as psychological research began to flourish in the United States, the need for sophisticated testing procedures became evident, and institutions had to make administrative provisions for such testing and the interpretation of test scores. The veteran enrollments brought to the campus many individuals not from college backgrounds, and these were followed by representatives of other groups previously excluded from higher education, thus producing a much more heterogeneous student body than had characterized collegiate institutions prior to World War II. Many of these students required special assistance to develop reading ability and improved study habits, assistance that came to be offered by a variety of student clinics. And the very heterogeneity of student bodies produced the need for new special services, such as veterans' advisory services, foreign student programs, and marriage counseling. All of these activities coalesced to the extent that by 1958 the American Council on Education could authenticate an extensive list of activities administered by the chief personnel officer: selection for admission, registration, and records; counseling; health service; housing and food service; student activities; financial aid; placement; discipline; special clinics; and special services. These activities were engaged in by individuals constantly seeking to improve their professional qualifications and professional status. Thus student personnel workers followed the paths toward professionalization that the professoriate followed during the same period. The new specialists developed a rationale to explain the need for their services and a doctrine to govern their behavior. It was claimed that faculty preoccupation with research and scholarship left in the concern for students as individuals a hiatus that student personnel people could fill. The larger and more heterogeneous enrollments produced needs that the academic faculties could not serve. During the post-World War II period, institutions adopted a greater range of educational objectives, many of which could not be achieved through traditional academic courses. And, as new and more sophisticated techniques for aiding people emerged from research, such as greater psychometric elegance and more clearly formulated counseling techniques, well-trained specialists had to be available to use those techniques. The doctorate of the student personnel movement is based on the premise that the human personality is a complex of various parts

that function as a whole. It posits that the intellect is the most
human of all humanity's characteristics and is the essence of striving,
growing, and living. However, temperament, character, physical
traits, and interests are other aspects of personality involved in intellectual progress, and these elements, to function effectively, require
the practice and experience gained from extracurricular programs
for their proper development and maturity, programs that require
direction by professionally qualified individuals (see Mueller, 1961).

The significance of this development, which contrasts sharply
with beliefs held in the 1970s, lies first in the attempt to help students—through housing, counseling, or health services—to optimize
their academic or intellectual development. Feeling and emotion were
not central concerns of collegiate institutions except to the extent that
understanding and controlling feeling helped the cognitive development of students. Secondly, these services were to be provided by
full-time professionals whose practice rested on an intellectual base.
Thus the movement was comparable to the professionalization of
faculty.

Probably the most significant subtheme of the student personnel movement was the rapid expansion of psychological and
mental testing during the 1950s. Before World War II, professionally
prepared tests were used for educational purposes for specialized and
limited populations. The College Entrance Examination Board
tested students' aptitude for entry into—for the most part—eastern
seaboard colleges and universities. The Educational Records
Bureau similarly tested for entry mainly into private preparatory
schools. The American Council on Education provided a psychological test and several tests of subject-matter knowledge that could
be used by some institutions or by a few states seeking better knowledge about the students they enrolled. And the Carnegie Foundation
for the Advancement of Teaching had since 1937 made available
the Graduate Record Examination to assist in the selection and
guidance of graduate students. After World War II, those programs
expanded rapidly, and new testing activities were undertaken, so
that by the end of the 1950s professionally developed tests represented a major and highly influential segment of American higher
education. In 1947 the Educational Testing Service was created and
assumed the testing responsibilities of the College Entrance Exam-

ination Board, the American Council on Education, the Cooperative Test Service, and the Carnegie Foundation for the Advancement of Teaching. Demand for its services expanded as more and more institutions began to use tests for admission and guidance purposes and as various agencies of states and the federal government began to use tests for job placement, job promotion, and vocational counseling. The Educational Testing Service simply symbolized the expectations of the testing movement. It would make admission judgments more rational. It would help students make educational and career choices. It would provide educators information they needed to help students. It would be a rational means to validate higher learning. It would allow institutions to try ideal mixes of student ability, aptitude, and talent, and it would provide a scientific means for auditing the outcome of an annually more expensive educational effort. In sum, the testing movement of the 1950s and 1960s represented the optimistic faith that social science could be applied directly and passively to human problems and could produce rational solutions.

Centrality of Higher Education

The last theme to emerge during the 1950s can be simply stated. By the end of the decade, it had come to be regarded, in the eyes of many of its leaders and spokesmen and in the eyes of a substantial portion of the society, as one of the, if not the, most pivotal social institutions. Its services were widely sought, and its faculty and administrators were in great demand to consult about the most vexing problems facing the society. President John Kennedy, in turning to Harvard for his closest presidential advisors in 1960, was simply expressing the culmination of a decade of aggrandizement for higher education in the United States.

Elaboration of Traditional Themes

Thus the stage was set for the expansion during the 1960s, and the directions for that growth were established. Education was judged to be a rational, intellectual, and professional enterprise serving quite specific needs of clients. The traditional college or university was viewed as an essentially sound structure that would accommodate increases and decreases in enrollment with no significant dysfunctioning. There seemed to be no particular reason to search for other solutions to the educational problems of society. Similarly, the traditional liberal arts professional and graduate curricula were judged as essentially valid, especially if a few minor modifications were made as; for example, tailoring the traditional liberal arts and sciences into programs of general education. There was an elitist concern for egalitarianism by which, over time, more and more groups could be exposed to orthodox higher education and thus be socialized into the mainstream of American society. And there was an optimistic faith in the soundness of the American educational enterprise, which fostered the belief that collegiate institutions could respond successfully to virtually any question or problem presented them by the larger society.

American higher education during the 1960s has been viewed as undergoing revolutionary changes. To be sure, there were some new elements and concepts that created a facade of enormous change. Federal involvement in finance certainly increased. New ways to prepare college administrators were attempted. Egalitarian rhetoric flourished, and pleas for academic reform gave the impression that things were happening. Scholarly and professional organizations increased in number, affluence, and programs, and the public seemed more aware and respectful of higher education and its potentialities. However, closer analysis of that period reveals few, if any, radical departures from the past. The major changes of the 1960s were quantitative ones. Enrollments doubled from 3,047,000 in 1957 to 6,758,000 in 1968. The number of institutions of higher education increased by almost a thousand, from approximately 1,500 toward the end of the 1950s to 2,374 in 1968. The numbers of institutions adding advanced degree programs to their offerings also steadily increased; for example, the number of institutions offering doctoral degrees increased from 175 in 1958 to almost 250 in 1968. And the system of higher education in the United States became more complex. In 1957 only ten states had some form of suprainstitutional coordination or control, while in 1968 only ten states did *not* have such a superstructure. The size and complexity of campus administrative structure also increased, typically moving from a president, dean, and small secretarial staff arrangement in the late 1950s to the president, four or five vice-presidents, and a large administrative specialist staff by the late 1960s. The cost of higher education also rose dramatically, from about .75 percent of the gross national product in 1958 to 2.5 percent of the gross national product by the late 1960s. The amount of externally supported research also increased in at least a few institutions, and the amount of federal support for basic research jumped from $335 million in 1958 to $2.1 billion in 1968. Although accurate comparative statistics are difficult to obtain, there is a strong basis for the inference that the heterogeneity of student bodies increased markedly during the period from 1958 to 1968 as the number of blacks and members of lower socioeconomic groups attended colleges in larger and larger numbers.

These changes produced other quantitative changes. The number and remuneration of faculty both advanced significantly. The amount of student financial aid increased, as did the amount of tuition charged by both publicly and privately controlled institutions. Libraries increased their holdings; scientific equipment, including computers, increased in number and cost; and physical plants were expanded more rapidly. However, with respect to the core and support activities of American higher education, the 1960s presented no significant variation from the 1950s. The themes of the 1950s were the predominant themes during the 1960s, elaborated and reaffirmed.

The period from the end of the 1950s throughout most of the 1960s was a time of statewide planning for higher education. Once educators, legislators, and the public had generally recognized the likely numerical and cost expansion of higher education during the 1960s, it became generally accepted that rational planning would be the route taken to ensure orderly development of needed institutions and programs. Planning was carried on variously in the different states—by state offices of education, select citizens' committees, outside consultants, or statewide coordinating bodies. However, virtually all plans were based on a limited set of assumptions and espoused a limited number of values. So similar were recommendations from state to state that a credible master plan could almost be drafted by first determining the size of several of these groups, the centers of population in the state, and the ranking of the state with respect to a number of economic and demographic factors. A plan could be produced by discussing those variables and applying accepted principles from the conventional educational wisdom.

Consider how typical provisions parallel the themes from the early 1950s. Gradual egalitarianism appeared to be a basic premise, with allusions made to the Morrill Acts of 1862 and 1890, the GI Bill of Rights, and the recommendations made by President Truman's Commission on Higher Education. There should be universal access to higher education, at least through the fourteenth grade, and this access could best be assured by increasing the numbers of junior or community colleges. These would be campus institutions located in reasonable proximity to centers of population and would offer transfer programs, general education, and some technical and vocational programs. The plans assume general understanding of the concept of general education, which would be academic and rooted in large measure in the tradition of Western civilization.

Meritocratic and elitist elements also were typically stressed. Plans assumed the need for more technologically sophisticated people, and institutions of higher education were presumed to be the best vehicles for developing necessary competencies. Plans did accept social stratification based on merit and hence typically envisioned systems of higher education that would assign differing roles to different kinds of institutions. Universities were to offer graduate training and professional programs in the professions of law, medicine, and scholarship. Below the university level, state colleges typically were to provide general education and preparation of people for such professions as teaching, business, and engineering. Below the state college level would come the junior or community colleges, which would have missions of offering low-cost, lower-division, and general education work and preparation in certain technical vocational fields. It was also assumed that a strong relationship existed between university research and general social and economic well-being. This relationship could best be fostered in the senior universities of the state.

Plans also typically expressed the need for some coordination of institutional effort, some provisions for adult and continuing education, and explicit attention to the recruitment and training of college teachers. There was no questioning of the beliefs that the collegiate campus was the primary instrument for that traditional curricula and that traditional modes of teaching were appropriate. Reviewing those plans reveals little in the way of anticipation of the developments that would begin by the late 1960s (see Mayhew, 1969).

Evolving partly out of experiences of state planning and partly out of the recent American tradition of creating national commissions to examine complex problems, there was created in the late 1960s a cluster of commissions or committees, both publicly and privately supported. The three most widely publicized were the Carnegie Commission on Higher Education, the Assembly on University Goals and Governance, and the Task Force on Higher Education that produced the two reports on higher education popularly known as the Newman Reports (named for the chairman, Frank Newman). There were some significant differences in the substance of the reports made by these three groups. The Newman Report was by far the most radical and perhaps the most prescient concerning at least some changes that were to be attempted in the future. It did propose the creation of quite new and different kinds of institutions, and it suggested that higher education back away from incremental financing based on traditional sources. The Assembly on University Goals and Governance was the most traditional of the three. It did urge greater access to higher education, and it did question continuing increases in credentialing based on academic degrees. However, it urged restoration of academically based general education offered on campuses by professors trained in the arts and sciences. It especially warned against institutions attempting too much in efforts to solve vexing social problems. It pointed out that the major contribution of higher education should be an intellectual one, which meant that institutions should reassert their traditional purposes.

It was the Carnegie Commission on Higher Education that received the most professional and public attention and that most faithfully reflected the immediate past. Through research and technical reports, interpretive essays, and major policy statements, the commission codified the conventional wisdom. It expressed a real but cautious egalitarianism and urged federal assistance to various minority group members to enable them to enter higher education. However, it also recognized the need for elite institutions to prepare leaders. It endorsed academic freedom within constraints to avoid license. It assumed an ordered quality of academic life governed by long-standing principles and values, and, while it did recognize the possibility of unionism, it clearly preferred governance of institutions through shared responsibility.

To accommodate the increased enrollments, many new institutions or branches of institutions were created during the 1960s. Their structure and practices dramatically revealed that adherence to tradition and the pervasive values regarding higher education that had characterized American higher education in the preceding decades. Generally there have been criticisms of existing practices, but few of the institutions created in the period 1958 to 1968 were based on a desire for a radical departure from previous practice. There were, to be sure, spontaneous appearances here and there of atypical kinds of institutions, such as the free universities, and cluster colleges were created that sought to alleviate the problems of enormous institutional size. But for the most part the logic used to justify new institutions between 1958 and 1968 and the rhetoric employed to describe them is not the logic nor rhetoric of extreme egalitarianism and extreme pluralism. A possible exception is the doctrine of the community junior college movement (and practice was highly orthodox even in junior colleges), which stressed multiple purposes and programs tailored for students whom four-year institutions did not service, such as adults and students with academic deficiencies. The prevailing tendency seems to have been to create new institutions modeled after older ones and to assume that students attending would adjust to those institutions just as earlier generations had adjusted.

Especially significant in revealing the prominence of traditional values and modes in higher education during the 1960s is the public junior or community college. The leaders of the junior college movement hailed it as a revolutionary idea. It was likened in significance to the creation of land-grant institutions during the nineteenth century and was considered to be the ideal educational manifestation of egalitarianism. The junior or community college was viewed as being community based—it would provide whatever range of educational services members of the community needed. It would take people where they were and, through many techniques, help them get to where they wanted to be, personally, educationally, or vocationally. These institutions were expected to pursue five or six major objectives, which were broad enough to assume virtually any kind of service people wished. Junior colleges were to offer transfer programs, general education, technical and vocational education, adult and continuing education, and counseling and guidance, and were to serve as a focus for community service and activities. They were to be specially designed to serve all segments of society and the full range of human talents, traits, and attributes.

But, as actually put into effect during the late 1950s and 1960s, the public junior or community college was much more faithful to traditional collegiate forms, values, and purposes. Junior college campuses were typically built as places to which people went to obtain educational services. Although the clientele was a commuting one, strenuous efforts were exerted to emulate the tone and range of activities characteristic of the residential college. And although the ideal of the junior college movement was to serve the full range of socioeconomic groups, junior colleges created during most of the 1960s were placed close to middle- and upper-middle-class population centers rather than in the central city. It was not until 1970, for example, that a public junior college was created in the metropolitan area of Minneapolis-St. Paul, although seven new junior colleges had been created in the outlying suburbs. Similarly, the first new campus of the Peralta Junior College District of Oakland, California, was not built in the densely populated minority-group center, but in the foothills, to serve the traditional college-attending population.

Junior colleges were also programmatically closer to the traditional college than to new kinds of activities. Typically some 75 percent of entering students matriculated in college transfer programs with a heavy emphasis on English, mathematics, science, and history. Those sorts of courses were valued most highly by the faculty members and were ones with which they were most familiar and comfortable. Even in junior colleges, which started out with a heavy technical-vocational thrust, once college transfer programs were initiated, with their emphasis on the liberal arts and sciences, the technical-vocational programs began steadily to lose enrollments and faculties to the more traditional curriculum. General education requirements during the 1960s typically followed the distribution mode of requiring students to take English and then to select courses in each of the three domains of the humanities, sciences, and social sciences. While the courses eligible for selection to meet general education requirements theoretically would exhibit a substantial range of appeal, in actuality they were academic, stressing words, numbers, and abstract concepts.

Nor was the egalitarian goal expressed by the phrase "the open-door college" realized. While admissions standards were typically relatively low, so that most high school graduates could matriculate, attrition was enormously high. In California, for example, during the 1960s, two thirds or more of entering freshmen each fall would not be enrolled the following fall. While the junior colleges stressed the college transfer program, in actuality only somewhere in the vicinity of 12 percent of entering freshmen ultimately received a bachelor's degree. The fact that the theoretical open door is really a revolving door also can be demonstrated in another way. California has perhaps the most elaborate and comprehensive system of public junior colleges in the country. It also has the highest proportion of high school graduates entering college. However, it drops to the bottom quartile with respect to proportions of college entrants completing four years of college, as well as the proportion of those completing the first and the second years of college. What seems to happen is that large numbers of students enroll, matriculate in college transfer courses, and then fail to cope with academic forces, thus becoming disillusioned and dropping out. Junior colleges have sometimes sought to modify these programs, but they typically do so by establishing tracks of courses in a given subject offered at various levels—students being assigned to levels on the basis of test performance.

Beginning in about 1957 and continuing on through the next decade, a great deal of research concerning college students and the impact of college on students was conducted. In 1957 Philip Jacob summarized existing studies and reached the conclusion that the curriculum had very little impact on the attitude, values, beliefs, or life-styles of college students. Several years later, Sanford and his associates (1961) presented an even larger synthesis of research having curricular implications, by pointing out the developmental needs of college students. From these and other studies and compilations of studies, as well as from theories of learning and of personality, experimentation and attempts to reform the undergraduate curriculum were stimulated. Throughout the period from 1958 to 1968, there were experiments with cluster colleges and team teaching; interdisciplinary, problem-centered courses; removal of some course requirements; modification or elimination of formal letter-grade assessment; including overseas experience in undergraduate education; uses of educational technology; and giving explicit curricular attention to moral and religious values. Mayhew and Ford (1971), as well as Dressel (1968) and Reynolds (1970), have summarized and interpreted the flood of recommendations, experiments, and theoretical exhortations for curricular change. If one were to judge by the descriptive and polemical literature of the period, one would infer that the undergraduate curriculum in institutions of higher education in the United States was in ferment. Efforts were made to involve feeling and affect in the curriculum, to cater to specific needs of minority groups and students now beginning to enter college in larger numbers, to modify the impersonality of the larger institutions, to relate learning to living, and to focus the curriculum on significant social and personal problems of youth.

All of this suggests a revolutionary departure from an early emphasis on verbal, quantitative and conceptual intellectuality. However, the actual instructional and curricular practices in the majority of collegiate institutions remain strikingly similar to earlier practices. Dressel and DeLisle (1969), after examining actual college catalogue requirements in 1957 and in 1967, reached the conclusion that there had been little significant curricular change. There appeared to be some modification and loosening of graduation requirements, on the grounds that the individual differences of a more varied and better prepared student body should be accommodated; however, the total percentage of requirements devoted to general education remained substantially as it had been. In theory, there should have been considerable modification of the nature of the undergraduate major by making it interdisciplinary or by the conscious use of cognate or related course requirements, and some efforts to do so were in fact found. However, the modal practice remained as it had been; that is, a major was defined as the accumulation of a specified number of credits offered by an academic department. Evidence also emerged that electives might be used to broaden student experience. However, institutions typically placed such constraints as prerequisites for majors on the availability of elective choices, so that the students really were not free to follow their own interests and inclinations. Catalogues contained provisions for students to obtain academic credit by examinations; however, such constraints again seriously limited actual utilization of that device. And there were honors programs, provisions for independent study, special undergraduate seminars, provisions for study abroad, and cooperative work-study opportunities. While the underlying rationale for those provisions is individualization of the curriculum and while individualization is the most pronounced trend during the period, nonetheless only a few institutions that claimed extensive use of such devices and procedures had reduced or eliminated traditional requirements to provide the flexibility essential for individualization. The study led the Dressel and DeLisle (1969, p. 75) to conclude that "Despite all of the talk about innovation, undergraduate curricular requirements, as a whole, have changed remarkably little in ten years. In many cases, the most that could be said of a particular institution was that its curriculum had been renovated—that is, requirements were restated in terms of new patterns of organization and course offerings and updated to recognize the rights of newer disciplines to a place in the sun."

Much the same could be said concerning curricula and instruction in graduate education in arts and sciences. There was considerable criticism of graduate education, and many recommendations for reform were suggested. Graduate degree programs, especially doctoral programs, were judged to be overly specialized and to require excessive periods of time, to be unrelated to college teaching responsibilities that would be the vocation of graduate students, to have excessively rigid sequences of examinations and hurdles, and to be too idiosyncratically related to interests and concerns of individual professors. However, with just a few exceptions, graduate education remained essentially as it had been throughout the 1950s.

The master's degree remained an ambiguous degree, sometimes viewed as a consolation prize, sometimes as a prelude to a doctorate, and sometimes as a mere extension of baccalaureate-level work. The doctorate continued to be a departmental degree, perhaps even more sharply focused now, because of the intensive research activity that took place during the 1960s. Little change could be detected regarding the average length of time required to earn a doctorate. There was, however, some modification in foreign language requirements, the trend being to shift responsibility for the requirement from the university to the department. There appeared a slight tendency to ensure some teaching experience on the part of students. It should be noted that considerably more change occurred in professional education than in undergraduate education or in graduate education in the arts and sciences. Greater provisions for electives, for clinical or field experience, for work to be taken outside of the professional school, and for the use of educational technology were sufficiently apparent as to constitute clear trends or tendencies. However, even in professional education schools were lodged in universities, programs were typically residential, admission requirements were imposed through testing, and degrees were obtained through accumulation of a specified number of academic credits.

Of the many salient elements of higher education in the United States, admissions policies and practices during the 1960s represent the most direct continuation of themes that had emerged in the decade before. Prior to World War II, although some institutions had scrutinized high school academic rank, had insisted on certain high school courses as prerequisites, and had used admissions tests, the admissions process was essentially self-selection, assuming the possession of a high school diploma. The public colleges and universities, with few exceptions, required only an academic high school diploma, and even the highly visible East Coast institutions, such as Harvard or Yale, accepted almost all the students who applied. After World War II and after the exodus from campus of the veteran students, that more or less open approach to admissions began to change, especially in the latter part of the 1950s, when heavy enrollment pressures could be anticipated. It was generally assumed that undergraduate programs required verbal and mathematical aptitude and that the best way to gauge that aptitude was to consider previous academic performance and performance on tests designed to measure aptitude. The period of 1958 until 1968 was characterized by steadily increasing selectivity (or hopes of such selectivity) on the part of four-year institutions, exercised by requiring high academic performance in high school and high aptitude test scores. As the volume of applications mounted, the prestigious private institutions increased selective requirements each year; less prestigious private institutions attempted to do so but at a somewhat lower rate; and senior public institutions eliminated the open-admissions policies that required only a high school diploma—some such institutions becoming almost as selective as the prestigious private institutions. Each year directors of admissions would report with pride that the average Scholastic Aptitude Test (SAT) scores of that year's freshman class were appreciably larger than the previous year and that the number graduating in the upper 10 percent of high school graduating classes had similarly increased. Occasionally someone would express concern for admissions policies that stressed exclusively verbal and quantitative aptitudes, but as long as application pressures continued those voices went unheeded. Even supposedly open-admissions public junior or community colleges were caught up in the academic selectivity euphoria. In states that allowed it, such as New York, junior colleges used high school grades and test scores for selective purposes, just as did the four-year institutions. In California there appeared to be tacit acceptance, at least on the part of junior college faculties, of the "cooling out" function so designated by Burton Clark (1961): Students were admitted to academic programs, but the majority either quickly dropped out or were urged to enter the less demanding technical-vocational programs. Willingham (1970) indicates the national situation as of approximately 1968: There were 530 institutions accepting all high school graduates, and 1,351 institutions were selective at one of various levels, ranging from accepting the top 75 percent of the high school graduating class to accepting only the top 10 percent of the high school graduating class.

Developing forms of administration and governance in higher education during the 1960s was for the most part gradual and consistent with earlier values. In the immediate post-World War II period, administration and governance were essentially quite similar to prewar conditions. The operating unit was a single institutional campus and a single board of trustees. Institutional decision making was centered in the president and a relatively few close associates. It was assumed that faculties would be generally responsible for the curriculum and other academic concerns and that they would be consulted, albeit somewhat informally, on major issues of institutional policy. The total faculty was considered to be the educational policy-discussing group, which would meet perhaps monthly or, in some institutions, three or four times during the academic year. When faculty constitutions existed, they were couched in rather broad and general language and assumed a considerable body of shared beliefs, values, and aspirations as a means of ensuring institutional functioning rather than being based on sets of detailed bylaws, handbooks, and statements of rights and responsibilities. While on some campuses an especially autocratic president occasionally took office, for the most part presidents would consult informally with faculty members and groups in whom the president had confidence, and this would typically suffice. Stanford University in the 1950s is a clear example. There was an academic council composed of the fully ranked faculty, which had overall responsibility for the curriculum and academic programs. There were two standing committees: the executive committee of the academic council and the advisory committee to the president. The academic council met once each quarter and rarely achieved much over a minimum quorum. The executive committee would meet from time to time with the president but was for the most part rather impotent. The advisory committee was a more powerful group, having the responsibility to pass on recommendations for appointments, promotions, and tenure. The president maintained a small staff, consisting of a provost, chief financial officer, and several assistants. His prevailing style of operation was to consult broadly with faculty members and the deans when an issue had to be decided, and for the most part he believed he could reflect the consensus of the faculty when he finally made decisions. There was a great deal of mutual trust on the part of the president and the faculty, and it was assumed that decisions would typically be made with the best interests of the entire institution in mind.

Beginning about 1958, several developments took place that suggested some modification in the prevailing style of administration and governance, the chief among which was the beginning of the intense expansion of higher education. As enrollments grew, with attendant increases in size of faculties, the informal modes of the past appeared inadequate. A faculty of 300, while large, might still be small enough to enable a good bit of informal consultation to take place and could reach consensus through informal means. But when that faculty suddenly consisted of 1,000, different approaches seemed necessary. An additional factor was the increased sense of professional status and professional prerogatives that had begun to develop in the postwar period and that had accelerated as the demand for college faculty outstripped the supply. Almost through the operation of the marketplace, faculty members were in a position to expect and demand a greater voice in the conduct of institutional affairs. There was thus a general recognition of the need for some changes, but at the same time there was a reluctance to depart substantially from the traditions of collegiality and shared values. What gradually emerged during the early 1960s was a conception of academic governance conducted through shared responsibility. Abstractly this concept was well described by the American Association for Higher Education (AAHE) Task Force Report entitled *Faculty Participation in Academic Governance* (1967). It argued (p. 2) that "The concept of 'shared authority' can best be implemented through the establishment of an internal organization, preferably an academic senate. An effective senate should meet the following requirements: The senate which has decision-making authority normally should include both faculty members and administrators. Faculty members should comprise a clear majority of the senate. The structure of the senate should take into account the structure of the institution in which it operates. This means that in states with comprehensive plans of higher education, the structure of the senate should be extended to multicampus units. Most 'aggregate' issues, affecting the faculty as a whole, should be decided by the senate. However, it is recognized that some issues, such as grading standards, should be primarily under faculty control, while other issues, such as the business management of the institution, should be primarily under the control of the administrators."

This general theory can be exemplified by continuing the Stanford example. By the early 1950s, President J. Wallace Sterling of Stanford became persuaded that a more formal structure was needed to accommodate increased size and increased quality of faculty. He came to believe that some form of academic senate would be appropriate but that it should be created in such a way as to preserve the spirit and trust of the past, which would enable a new president taking office after Sterling's retirement to inherit a sensitive instrument for faculty governance and yet retain the freedom to reach timely decisions. Sterling appointed a committee of senior professors, most of whom had been his close confidantes, and asked it to examine the problem of governance at Stanford and to recommend some structure consistent with traditions yet responsive to a rapidly changing future. Although the final decision came as student dissent had begun to escalate, a senate was created to serve as the instrument of the traditional academic council. The senate essentially took over the powers of the academic council, and only council members could be members of the senate. Thus the senate remained a faculty senate and provided a way for continued shared responsibility between the president and the faculty.

Some institutions were less successful in achieving a shared-responsibility model. Some had delayed change until forced to by the outbreaks of student dissent during the last part of the 1960s, but even in such institutions as Cornell, Columbia, or Harvard, which did come late to a revised structure, the purpose was to achieve shared responsibility that could preserve traditional values, goals, and relationships.

The second and related development in the organization of higher educational also had its inception in increased enrollments and costs. This was the development in the public sector of statewide systems of coordination. By the late 1950s, it had become clear that many new institutions would be needed and that the size of existing institutions would be increased markedly. In order to produce the needed expansion with some degree of rationality that would provide the services needed at not excessive costs and to avoid costly duplication of effort, some form of coordination seemed desirable. However, during the 1960s, as coordinating structures were created in the various states, a great deal of attention was given to preserving individual campus autonomy. The idealized structure would assign to coordinating agencies the responsibility to accumulate data, to conduct long-range planning, to approve locations of new campuses, and to recommend with respect to institutional budgets. Those who urged coordination as being essential were for the most part highly sensitive to the need to maintain considerable campus autonomy. Robert Berdahl (1971, p. 270) captures the beliefs held by advocates of coordination who were also conservative of campus traditions:

> The "appropriate machinery," I believe, will turn out to be some form of coordinating agency. . . . Perhaps it is not too negative to urge that the tensions and disagreements besetting the coordinating process are less evil than either a return to the political jungle, where only the strongest institutions prosper, or a move to direct state administration, which could reduce higher education to mediocrity and uniformity. Though politicians and the public may find it irritating to be told over and over that higher education is qualitatively a different kind of operation from other state activities, such happens to be the case. With roots that go back for hundreds of years, with a delicate interrationale that differs markedly from those of government and industry, our universities and colleges are geese that lay golden eggs, and to kill them by improper treatment would rob our society of enormous benefits. The state has every right to assure itself that the institutions within its jurisdiction are operating in the broad public interest, but it must be careful, in interpreting that interest, to recognize the special need of universities and colleges for a high degree of autonomy. . . . We must hope that the coordinating and planning agencies, which will have such vital roles to play, will always be characterized not only by their concern for the public interest but also by their genuine affection and respect for our institutions of higher education.

At first glance, patterns of financing higher education between 1958 and 1968 may appear substantively different from the previous decade. However, when viewed retrospectively such differences either disappear or become minimized. Although variations in financing higher education appear throughout the period in different states and regions and although some inconsistencies appear with respect to federal financial policy, some significant common elements nonetheless also appear. The most important commonality was the enormous increase in overall cost and expenditure for higher education. The cost increases can be indicated in any of several different ways. Higher education used less than 1 percent of the gross national product at the beginning of the period and approaching 3 percent at the end. Throughout the period, educational costs per credit hour consistently rose more rapidly than did the Consumer Price Index (an annual average rate of 3.5 percent to the rate of 1.6 percent for the Consumer Price Index). The reasons why costs increased are well known, can be quickly summarized, and are indicative of the academic and intellectual tone of the period. "The student body more than doubled. The output of high-cost Ph.D.'s tripled. The new student body required more remedial work and more student aid from institutional as well as external funds. New programs were added, for example, in ethnic studies and ecology. Computers were introduced on a large scale. The heavy capital investments also led to greatly increased costs for building maintenance. Many new research institutes and endeavors were added. And there were also some costs in terms of fast promotions and added amenities that resulted from twenty years of high demand for faculty members" (Carnegie Commission on Higher Education, 1972b, p. 2).

Such increased costs appeared tolerable to individuals, communities, states, and the federal government because of the widespread belief in the economic values of higher education—the level of education was typically assumed to be positively correlated with economic levels. Collegiate institutions produced the trained manpower needed for an expanding technology-based society. Research carried on in the universities was considered likely to have a relatively immediate payoff in solving many problems and to contribute directly to economic well-being. Individuals were presumed to gain because of the higher salary differentials associated with the possession of collegiate education and advanced degrees. Throughout this period, no significant voices were raised to counter the doctrine of human capital, which is exemplified by the observation that human capital, consisting of mainly education, accounts for a smaller part of the income in the less-developed countries than in the more-developed ones. To explain the large differences in per capita income between poor and rich countries, it is observed that the difference in human resources between the United States and less-developed countries accounts for more of the difference in per-capita income than any other group of factors combined and that the attribute of human resources that matters most appears to be education (Schultz, 1972).

In analyzing the financing of higher education that was characteristic of the 1960s, Bowen (1974) identifies ten developments that he labels as spectacular changes but that can also be interpreted as elaboration of earlier established themes. Two of these are related to financial support of college students: grants to students based on a systematic means test and the use of loans in financing students. These two appear to express a gradual or cautious sort of egalitarianism rather than a more extreme doctrinaire egalitarianism that appeared later, at least in the rhetoric concerning higher education. The amount of individual scholarship aid granted was typically not enough to be of significant assistance for students from quite low economic groups, and the use of loans certainly were made for additional reasons than solely extending higher education to lower-income groups and members of minority groups. The National Defense Education Act of 1958 provided both undergraduate and graduate student loans, but these seemed particularly designed to produce needed kinds of specialists. The Higher Education Act of 1965 in Title IV provided grants of $200 to $800 to needy, *qualified* students in the freshman year and $200 to $1,000 each succeeding year if the student remained in the upper half of his class. That same act made provisions for work-study programs and guaranteed loans, the latter apparently designed for students from middle- and upper-income families. Indicative of the sorts of student aid provided are estimates by Froomkin and Pfefermen (1969) of $948 million provided for undergraduate student aid during the academic year 1966–67. Half of that amount was in the form of loans and the other half in grants, part-time wages, and veterans' benefits. The educational opportunity grants, which were those most clearly egalitarian in purpose, amounted to only $58 million. The same year $441 million were provided for graduate students. This is not to say that the needs of the poor were not explicitly attended to. There were such programs as Upward Bound and Talent Search, both designed for young people from low-income families. But on balance the determining purpose seems to have been more meritocratic than egalitarian.

Throughout the period under consideration, the largest amount of federal contribution to higher education was earmarked for the categorical purposes of supporting research and graduate training. In the 1955–56 academic year, the federal government spent about $355 million on academic research and $1.3 billion a decade later. The bulk of those funds went to a limited number of institutions judged the most highly capable of carrying out the research the several federal programs envisioned. Thus the pattern of the 1960s directly continued the patterns of federal support for research during World War II and following 1950 and the creation of the National Science Foundation.

An essential ingredient of the financial profile during this period, which was consistent with the steady increase in the professionalization of the professoriate, was the pattern of steady and substantial increases in faculty salaries and decreases in the course load. Prior to 1958, the American professoriate had lost salary ground, in real dollars, as compared with 1939, a fact that was recognized by President Eisenhower's White House Conference, which called for doubling of professors' salaries within the next ten years. This policy was given force by the changed market condition, in which demand for college professors was greater than the available supply. And it was given symbolic recognition when the American Association for University Professors began its annual reporting by institutions of average faculty salaries by rank. The changed economic outlook for the professoriate and the generally improved conditions of work produced a number of outcomes that would affect profoundly the pattern of higher education in the 1970s. Coupled with some federally supported training programs, the improved economic conditions attracted steadily increasing numbers into graduate school, and in the latter part of the 1960s some predicted that by 1980 graduate schools would be producing between 60,000 and 70,000 doctorates a year. Without going into any consideration of possible changes in quality, we may note that the general reduction in teaching load—to one or two courses in research universities, to three and four courses in liberal arts colleges, and to four and five courses in junior and community colleges—contributed to the high rate of cost increase that characterized higher education in the 1960s.

An especially vexing element to interpret involves attitude

and practices with respect to tuition. There was considerable rhetoric calling for low or no tuition for lower-division work, and public junior or community colleges for the most part seemed to be achieving that goal. Almost 70 percent charged tuition and required fees of less than $400 (Carnegie Council on Policy Studies in Higher Education, 1975, p. 9). However, tuition in both public four-year institutions and private institutions continued to increase year by year—tuition for private institutions increasing at a much faster rate. This steady rise in tuition appears to have had an interesting impact on the burden of support for higher education borne by students themselves or their families. The per-capita income of families increased more rapidly than did tuition charges and thus set the stage for justifying even more rapidly increasing tuitions during the subsequent period.

The most stable element of finance, other than the steady cost increases, has been the steady increase in the portion of costs of higher education provided by the states. State support of higher education rose during the depression decade of the 1930s and fell during World War II. Thereafter, it rose quite steadily, including during the time of student unrest during the 1960s (Carnegie Foundation for the Advancement of Teaching, 1976, p. 29). And this is correlated with the steadily shifting enrollment patterns showing that in 1950 public and private institutions each enrolled about 50 percent of all students and that by 1968 the rate had shifted to approximately 65 percent public and 35 percent private.

Like the kinds of new institutions created during the 1960s, the attitudes and opinions concerning college teaching that prevailed during that period were highly consistent with the immediate past and divergent from the recommendations and experimentation of the 1970s. Throughout the 1960s, there was steady criticism of college teaching. The conflict between research and teaching served as the typical premise for criticism, which would then be followed by recommendation for improvement. Those recommendations are instructive and revealing of the times. Some critics say conflict between research and teaching should be reconciled by redressing imbalances rather than claiming fundamental incompatibility between research and teaching. Research and scholarship were seen as clearly essential for effective teaching because the collegiate curriculum was intellectual and conceptual and required a solid base of scholarship. Even the most acerbic critic of college teaching during the period, William Arrowsmith, who claimed that there was no necessary link between scholarship and education, still idealized the relationship. Thus he argued (1967, p. 60) that "The teacher is both the end and the sanction of the education he gives. This is why it is completely reasonable that a student should expect a classicist to live classically. The man who teaches Shakespeare or Homer runs the supreme risk. This is surely as it should be. Charisma in a teacher is not a mystery or nimbus of a personality, but radiant exemplification to which the student contributes a correspondingly radiant hunger for becoming. What is classic and past instructs us in our potential size, offers the greatest human scale against which to measure ourselves. The teacher, like his text, is thus the mediator between past and present, present and future, and he matters because there is no human mediator but him. He is the student's only evidence outside the text that a great humanity exists: upon his impersonation both his text and his student's human fate depend."

College education was judged to be intellectual and conceptual; hence college teaching should deal with intellect and concepts. Comprehension of intellectual and conceptual matters required specific intellectual abilities; hence quality of teaching relied in considerable measure on the quality of students. Allan Cartter wryly made this point when he suggested that a university wishing national acclaim for its undergraduate teaching should first develop outstanding graduate and professional schools whose reputation would then attract the kind of undergraduates who would personify outstanding undergraduate education. Essential preparation for college teaching was a firm grounding in an academic discipline, symbolized by the possession of the doctorate. Assuming that grounding, then there were things that professors also want to know, such as better ways of organizing lectures or of conducting discussions. Here and there could be heard criticism of the doctoral degree and its concentration on specialized knowledge and conceptualization as preparation for teaching. The argument was advanced that the master's degree was the appropriate preparation for teaching and that teaching was the primary professional activity of instructors. Much more prevalent within four-year institutions was the notion that what colleges wanted most from graduate schools in the way of college teachers were people with a good command of their discipline, a high professional competence, and scholarly aspirations. Wilbert McKeachie, professor of psychology at the University of Michigan, was probably the most astute observer and student of college and university teaching during his period, and his opinions probably reflect the enlightened opinions of the majority of the professoriate. He saw the college teacher as serving the roles of expert, authority, socializing agent, facilitator, ego ideal, and person. These roles require limited but definite skills, all of which reveal the essential nature of collegiate education. Thus the competent college teacher would have skills in scholarly preparation, class organization, planning structure and standards of excellence, clarifying rewards and demands of the field, sharpening student awareness of their interests and skills, demonstrating the ultimate worthwhile nature of or personal commitment to one's materials, and being self-revealing in ways that clarified one's beyond the task at hand (McKeachie, 1969).

TWO

The Nontraditional Movement

Nontraditional education, as described in the literature, is seen variously as ushering in a new educational age, as just updating traditional educational pragmatism, or as being educational fraud disguised as egalitarian romanticism. The phrase "nontraditional movement" is used deliberately, because since the late 1960s there has evolved a group of spokesmen, a doctrine, and a collection of practices reminiscent of the general education movement of the 1940s and 1950s. Whether the nontraditional movement will follow the trajectory of the general education movement—rapid rise, brief stabilization, and equally rapid decline—cannot be known. Given the nature of movements in education, the odds are it will. But it might last, and higher education would then become dramatically different from what it has been in the past.

Definition and Characteristics

Defining nontraditional education defies ingenuity, especially since many components of it are highly traditional when viewed historically. Independent study is no newcomer, nor is work experience. Early nineteenth-century physicians and lawyers typically were educated through apprentice training and independent study, and several centuries of British experience have legitimatized tutorials. Nonetheless, at least the parameters of the meaning of nontraditional learning must be understood. Gould and Cross (1972) are less than satisfying but still somewhat helpful in their early attempt to assign meaning to the concept. At the crudest level, definition is obtained by comparison. Traditional learning takes place in reasonably formal groups, each consisting of an instructor and a group of students. The prevailing mode of communication is, for the most part, unidirectional, with the instructor responsible for the direction of all activities. Students study assignments made by the instructor, and the principal educational resources are textbooks, libraries, and laboratories. Nontraditional learning stands in sharp contrast to that—and the more different from such practices, the more nontraditional. However, Gould proceeds further, he sees four interacting patterns as comprising the fabric of nontraditional education. The first of these involves the goal of assuring to each individual the amount and type of education needed to develop his or her potential as a person. The nontraditional doctrine is essentially democratic or egalitarian: All individuals, regardless of age, background, or previous educational attainment, should be provided an education that is peculiarly tailored to the individual's needs. That purpose leads directly to the second strand, which is flexibility in education. If education is to provide for extraordinarily heterogeneous groups, many of the rigidities inherent in traditional campus, large-group, tightly scheduled educational experiences must be broken. Teaching and learning should take place whenever it is convenient for students, instead of on an institutional timetable. Residential requirements and regularly scheduled meetings of classes may be antithetical to the needs of some people. The third pattern concerns the responsibility for instruction. Traditional education assigns primary responsibility to formal educational institutions. However, business, industry, labor, cultural groups, governmental and social agencies, the military, proprietary schools, and correspondence institutes also seem to possess educational potential, and nontraditional learning would entrust much developmental effort to those agencies. (It is this matter that proves to be most troublesome: Once the educational potential of such groups is posited, an almost meaningless definition of education follows. Physicians, lawyers, social workers, journalists, and architects all presumably modify behavior of their clients as they interact with them, and if education is grossly defined as modification of behavior then all those professions can be properly presumed to be part of the educational structure.)

The last pattern embraces individualized learning. This means both individualized opportunity, with each individual searching for the kind of education suitable and necessary for himself, as well as individualized work in pursuit of those personal goals. More traditional forms of education posited that professional educators would know what the majority of individuals needed and could provide it for them. The nontraditional doctrine rejects that assumption and says, in language reminiscent of the progressive education movement, that there should be as many different curricula as there are individuals seeking education (Gould and Cross, 1972).

Central to the nontraditional movement is a concern for new students. Historically, in the United States (as well as in other developed nations), formal higher education has assumed responsibility for a limited and reasonably well-defined segment of the population. Colleges and universities have offered their services to the relatively young (sixteen to mid or late twenties), to the relatively able (possessing the ability to use words, numbers, and abstract concept), to the relatively high achieving in academic matters, and to the relatively affluent (who can afford several years out of the work force to pursue uninterruptedly an educational program). Left out of any consistent exposure to formal higher education were older people, workers, the economically disadvantaged, the culturally different, the academically underachieving, and those whose talents lay in mechanical, artistic, kinesthetic, or relational directions, rather than toward verbal and numerical abstractions. The nontraditionalist argues that those individuals should be provided for, and to do so demands specially contrived educational activities. Cross rhapsodizes on this matter as she identifies four major dimensions that must be accommodated. The first of these is the fact of significant individual differences and the need for methodology to conform to each individual's style. The second dimension is that the majority of students are part-time, and education should therefore conform to individual schedules rather than impose a schedule on the individual. The third dimension is a bit more fuzzy and involves the relationship between individual learning styles and the tactics and strategies needed to accommodate those styles. A mosaic statement of this concern is the question: What methods work for which students? Her answer is that the mix must be varied and extensive. The last dimension concerns the goals of learning, the premise being that goals differ from one individual to the next, and thus individual goals should determine curricula and educational practice, rather than goals posited by the faculty and entombed in the catalogue (Cross, 1974).

Origins of Nontraditional Education

The roots of this amorphous nontraditional movement are many, complex, and tightly entwined. Further, it is difficult to gauge the proper valence of any of them. Probably much of the ferment underlying the nontraditional movement is related to the pleas for academic relevance during the late 1960s. This relationship is difficult to establish, because much student speech and writing between 1964 and 1970 really did not address essentially educational matters. Nonetheless, certain things happened that indicated elements of the nontraditional movement. Seminars dealing with contemporary social issues were created, both formally and informally (as in the case of the teach-ins). These seminars were intended to make academic materials relevant to real-life problems. Cooperative work-study programs and dropping out of school for a time became accepted and even popular, in a belief that, far from being hurtful, experience in the real world was of considerable educational potency. The free university concept caught hold for a few years, providing a structure in which anyone wishing to teach something could do so if there were those who wished to learn. Course offerings needed no judicial review nor quality control. Quality was assured if faculty and students were both interested and working at the same thing. Grading techniques were modified on the ground that arbitrarily assigning a value to students who did well at something assigned to him by a professor was coercive and stifled students' quests after their own essential interests. The pass-fail grading system was intended to facilitate greater curricular flexibility and to allow students to pursue their own interests and goals. Students came to be included in faculty academic councils, on the ground that they should have considerable to say about those things that affected them so intimately. And in some institutions admissions standards were modified, on the ground that traditional standards excluded many different kinds of people who might with profit pursue a formal educational program.

Probably of more direct influence on the nontraditional movement was a generalized spirit of educational reform that grew up during the 1960s in orthodox institutions, both in professional schools and in undergraduate colleges. From approximately 1910 through the 1950s, with the exception of the general education movement and a few other relatively minor modifications, the form and practice of American higher education remained the same. The prevailing modes of instruction were lectures and formal discussions enriched through textbook reading, use of laboratories, use of libraries, and an occasional field trip. The focus of education was on a single campus offering many different courses and programs that students pursued until they had acquired the requisite number of numerical units to qualify for a degree. Academic work was considered separate from other kinds of activities. The model and (very likely the ideal) student attended full-time for a given number of years, took five or six courses each quarter or semester, and was graded on the basis of performance in a limited number of academic activities. Then quite suddenly the validity of that style came under questioning here and there, and experiments to change things were undertaken. The range of these new efforts was rather substantial. However, what was undertaken can be for the most part classified under ten rubrics, many (if not most) of which subsequently become central in the nontraditional movement. There were temporal changes, which included trimesters, modules, and greater use of interim terms and summer sessions. There were serious attempts to break the monolithic quality of institutions by creating

new groups of students and faculty. These efforts included the creation of cluster colleges, of team teaching, and house plans or theme
houses, which attempted to bring living and learning together. One
of the more prevalent kinds of activity were the different attempts to
individualize instruction. These attempts paradoxically included
both highly structured programmed courses and completely unstructured situations in which students were to define their own
problems and solve them in their own way. Methods of grading,
evaluation, and assessment also began to change. Pass-fail systems,
academic credit assigned by examination, and elaborate systems for
judging competency were devised. The domain of experiment involved in many of the other categories of reform was that of educational technology. This included experiments with computer-based
instruction, closed-circuit television, automated and computerized
library systems, and multimedia classrooms. An entire cluster of
endeavors, which was widely discussed and praised, yet was actually
practiced on a more limited scale, was interdisciplinary work. Examples range from revised courses in general education to black studies,
to complex new professional programs, such as the master's program in biomedical engineering. On the ground that there should
be a closer relationship between academic work and real life, such
experimentation began to provide students with off-campus experi-
ience: simple foreign travel, cooperative work-study plans, or supervised internships. It was believed that individuals should set their
own goals and determine their own agendas but also that they
required help to do so. This produced a resurgent interest in
counseling and guidance, manifested, for example, in peer counseling, computer-based counseling, and relying much more on counseling than on the curriculum to devise curricular structure. College
professors historically have not paid too much attention to explicit
psychological or learning theory, yet during the 1960s, in at least
some places, discussions of pedagogical theory became at least
modestly respectable. Behavior modification, developmental psychology, and competency-based learning all reflected a renewed
interest in theory. The tenth and last category is represented by
attempts to create new institutions specifically designed to accomplish
new and somewhat atypical educational purposes. Thus there were
created universities without walls, external degree programs, and

free-standing professional schools. It is from this pool of experimentation and reform in higher education that the logic, rhetoric, and technology of the nontraditional movement is drawn.

A major root of the nontraditional movement, one that in a sense provides its basic rhetoric, is the vulnerability of any established educational practice to criticism and caricature. Cohen and March (1974) have described educational institutions as being organized anarchies. They are uncertain of goals, lack a technology for achieving goals, and have no effective ways for evaluating success or failure. Much of what takes place in formal higher education relies on faith that what is done is somehow good and worthwhile. As long as that faith is generally shared, prevailing practice continues without much difficulty. However, once that web of faith is torn, devastating criticisms of education are possible and plausible. Take, for example, the meaning of a college degree. Degrees historically represent successful performance in an assigned body of work consisting of materials defined by the faculty as being of importance. Closer examination of work taken, however, indicates the enormous variety of practices by different faculty members and in different institutions. In one institution, a bachelor's degree requires four years of prescribed work on the great books of the Western tradition. In another institution, a bachelor's degree requires approximately 120 semester hours of work selected almost at random by each student, the ability to swim fifty yards and pass the freshman English course being the only common elements. The bachelor's degree is conferred at one institution only to highly able students, yet the same degree is conferred at another institution to many individuals who are barely literate. When transcripts of bachelor's degree recipients are studied, any intellectual integrity of the meaning of a bachelor's degree disappears, except for the fact that the pattern of subjects taken clearly reflects whatever the student claims as his major. Further, when the relationship between degrees received and subsequent life success is studied, a case can be made that a bachelor's degree is in many respects a meaningless concept. This confusion regarding academic degrees, of course, allows the critic to proclaim the meaninglessness of degrees and credentials and to call for new patterns of experiences and activities that might be more significant.

And the critic is provided additional ammunition by the results of educational achievement studies. When the impact of college on students is examined, using reasonably sophisticated measuring devices, interesting facts emerge. College graduates as a total group do seem somewhat different from those individuals who do not go to college. They tend to be somewhat more liberal, somewhat more tolerant, and somewhat more open to new experience. Until recently, recipients of bachelor's degrees, as a total group, seemed to earn considerably more money over a lifetime than did individuals who did not go to college. However, the factors within formal educational institutions producing those changes cannot be identified. The curriculum does not seem to be particularly important, nor does the style of teaching. How individuals perform on standardized tests of general education taken at the end of four years of college seems to depend far more on abilities possessed at entrance than on the particular school attended or program followed. Performance in academic courses seems to predict quite well subsequent performance in academic courses but does not predict at all well subsequent life achievement, regardless of whether that be personal happiness, economic success, or professional recognition. These failures are all demonstrable, as is the continuing high attrition rate among individuals beginning a college career. Thus the critics can say there must be ways of educating people that might produce more desirable outcomes. They can argue further in defense of nontraditional approaches that even if no significant differences appear between the traditional and the nontraditional mode (which would likely be the case), if the nontraditional mode makes people happier and if it affects more different groups of people, then it is as valid as or more valid than traditional modes.

Illustrative of this phenomenon is the ease with which graduate education can be criticized. From the awarding of the first Ph.D.'s at Yale in the nineteenth century to the 1970s, there has been constant, consistent criticism of the Ph.D. It is an overly specialized degree that trains people to do research in a minute field—work that is ill-suited for their subsequent careers as teachers of undergraduate students. Pursuit of the degree requires excessive amounts of time, ranging from four or five years to as many as fourteen years. The quest for the Ph.D. is a precarious undertaking, and the large majority of those who begin programs never complete them. The program requires students to write theses that for the most part are preoccupied with trivia and that in no sense represent the ideal contribution to knowledge. The hurdles students must surmount in the form of preliminary examinations, oral examinations, and the like are unreliable measures that operate capriciously or that are meaningless rituals. And each of these criticisms can be illustrated with horrible examples, thus providing a brief to defend completely nontraditional approaches to graduate education. The brief makes such comparisons as the following. Since graduate students in established institutions rarely see their major professors, a program making use of adjunct or part-time professors would really be an improvement. Since theses generally are written by students working on their own, they could with equal propriety be written in a place far distant from the institution conferring the degree. Since the amount of time earning the degree bears no relationship to professional competence and subsequent career success, the length of time could be sharply shortened to as little as a single year with no danger of sacrificing quality. Since the Ph.D. program in established institutions does not equip the recipient to do the job he most likely will do, a program emphasizing a great deal of real teaching experience in place of a great deal of formal classwork would be preferable. Since the title *doctor* is primarily a credential required for certain kinds of jobs, the substance of the doctorate being immaterial, credentialing could be more quickly and easily awarded in shorter and less-expensive programs—this criticism is reinforced in such fields as education, in which there is no difference in career profiles between recipients of the Ph.D. and the Ed.D. degrees.

An especial vulnerability of traditional institutions and practice is the demonstrable fact that they have not provided for major segments of the population. Colleges and universities have catered to relatively young, relatively able, relatively high achieving, and relatively affluent. They have not provided for older students, minority-group students, or those who possess talents and interests different from those with which collegiate institutions are concerned. This allows the person of egalitarian sentiments to provide a rationale for the nontraditional simply with the argument that the evidence is irrefutable and that nontraditional techniques can extend education to categories of people previously excluded. Here a poignant example (from Gould and Cross, 1972, pp. 19–20) is frequently used:

> Sergeant X, a career military man, plans to retire after twenty years. When he does, he would like to have a college degree so that he can move from the army to a civilian job of some responsibility with no unnecessary delays. Now in his fifth year of service, he has time to study and attend classes, provided they are held in off-duty hours nearby. Realistically, however, he must expect to be on at least five different posts—two of them outside of the United States—before his retirement. Careful analysis of the educational prospects of Sergeant X makes it clear that the likelihood of his obtaining a college degree under the current system is slim indeed. In spite of the availability of correspondence courses offered by the armed forces, extension courses from many institutions, the College Level Examination Program (CLEP), and all the rest—in spite of these, Sergeant X will be faced with numerous serious obstacles in his quest for a college degree.
>
> He will find first of all that there is a great deal of curricular diversity from one institution to another, such that the major field course requirements at one institution will almost certainly be different from those at another. Furthermore, he will discover that there are no common quality standards across institutions. Academic achievement awarded six hours of credit at one institution—whether by performance on a CLEP exam, completion of courses on campus, or whatever—may earn him only three credits at another college and no credits at still another. Finally, of course, there is the problem of the residency requirement. Regardless of how much Sergeant X may know in his chosen major field, he will discover that unless he learns "one year's worth" of knowledge at one particular institution, that institution will not award him a degree with its name.

Another vulnerability is based on the fact that the system of higher education in the United States is large, complex, and bureaucratic and is governed by many rules, regulations, and procedures that seem frequently to make the system hopelessly rigid. In order to rectify earlier deficiencies, American institutions began to assign numerical value to college work and to use aggregates of those values to signify when a degree had been achieved. This one facet allows for the criticism that higher education is a "numbers game" and does not consider matters of essential quality. In order for an institution to maintain some control over the meaning of the degrees they award, institutions have tended to require that a minimum amount of time be spent enrolled in the institution and to place maximum limits on the amount of credit that can be transferred in to count for a degree. Further, because the nature of academic work changes rather quickly, institutions have also created regulations requiring that work transferred must have been completed within a specified time in the past, but these regulations appear to be inflexible and discriminatory toward certain kinds of people, as was seen in the case just cited. Inflexibility and discrimination are pejorative terms that are used effectively by those who would create nontraditional systems. Especially vulnerable to the attack are the means by which established institutions have sought to ensure some minimal level of quality on the part of programs offered to the public. In the United States, voluntary accreditation is a means by which institutions validate each other's efforts. Accreditation is a rather complex process that requires examination of an institution, its resources, and, to the extent possible, its educational outcomes. On the basis of such an examination, decisions are made to extend or deny accreditation. This is a time-consuming, bureaucratic, and expensive process, conducted by people who are clearly the products of their own experiences. To many, accreditation is a hopelessly rigid reactionary device used by established institutions to preserve the status quo. And, again, the piteous case is a potent weapon of attack. Keeton (1975, p. 35), after affirming that red tape is strangling reform in higher education, goes on to remark:

> The most readily perceived instruments for strangling reform are time and cost. The two are interrelated. In a growing number of states, an institution must possess accumulated assets that serve as a guarantee that it will not fall down on its obligations to students and to creditors. The purpose of the requirement is worthy. The method is an enormous constraint. I know of one institution, now closed, that had every prospect of becoming a high-quality institution and fulfilling a significant function. Its opening was delayed for over three years while it raised and spent money trying to accumulate the $500,000 required as a guarantee. The costs of both raising the money and trying to get state approval were enormous. If the institution had opened as soon as its plans and personnel were in good array, its operating income would

have enabled it to accumulate the guarantee or at the very least to meet its obligations to its students if it failed to continue. A possible solution to such problems would be a state or federally established guarantee pool available to innovating institutions that can provide evidence of good planning and a competent staff.

A last vulnerability to be cited, although there are many more, is the emotional defense that academics make of the traditional programs in liberal arts and sciences of established institutions and the ease with which those defenses can be attacked and demolished. Required schooling in a foreign language is defended on the grounds that knowledge of another language is the hallmark of an educated person; that through language can come insight into another civilization; that only reading works in their original language exposes their full significance; that knowledge of a foreign tongue enhances one's facility with one's native tongue; and that multilingualism is essential for life on a shrinking planet. The contrast between those goals and the typical student's two years of one language in high school and two years of another language in college, no use of either being subsequently made, allows the nontraditionalist to demand something more relevant than foreign language instruction. The precious, invidious comparison of a course on human sexuality with a solid course in history encourages cries that the traditional education really does not serve people's needs. The implicit argument that the nonutilitarian subjects of the arts and sciences are really the only subjects of true utility and that training for vocations should be someone else's responsibility opens the way for a charge of "ivory towerism" and provides a basis for new and nontraditional curricula. Elevating a subject's worth far above the needs of students to develop themselves personally also is a position vulnerable to attack. To illustrate the highly vulnerable position of distinguished apologists for the traditional arts and sciences, consider the following comments (quoted in O'Neil, 1975). First, from C. Van Woodward, historian from Yale, who says, "We have seen the curriculum trivialized and vulgarized and made relevant and these [trends] are part of the legacy of the late 1960s" (speech to International Council on the Future of the University Conference, Spring 1974). Or again, Charles Frankel (1974, p. 25), a philosophy professor from Columbia University, remarks, "Consider the following phenomena: grade inflation, the progressive elimination of foreign language requirements from the curricula, the steady dilution of even mild distribution requirements, the regularity with which curricular reforms turn out to involve simply less reading and writing, the living conditions in dormitories from which universities have almost entirely withdrawn their supervisory authority although they continue to pay the bills, [and] the double-talk about quotas that are not quotas, and apartheid that is not apartheid." Gordon A. Craig (1974, p. 144) a historian from Stanford University, remarks in a similar vein that "The insistence of the young, during the late 1960s, that the university establishment did not understand them and their world found an all-too-eager agreement on the part of faculty members who should have known better. Suddenly the cry of relevance filled the land; curricular requirements were heedlessly jettisoned because someone said that they prevented the investigation of the real problems that confronted our society. We entered the age of the Green Stamp University, in which the student receives the same number of stamps for a course on Bay Area population or human sexuality as he does for American history or the Greek philosophers, sticks them happily into his book, and gets a diploma when it is filled. Whether he has received an education in the course of all this is doubtful." And lastly Allan Bloom (1974, p. 64), a political scientist at the University of Toronto, looks at another element. "Connected with [the] new radical egalitarianism in the university were the abandonment of requirements, the demand for student participation in all functions of the university, the evaluation of professors by students, sex counseling, the renouncing of standards because they encourage discrimination and unhealthy competition, a continuing inflation of grades, concentration on teaching rather than on scholarship, open admissions, the introduction of new programs to fit every wish, and quotas in the admission of students and the hiring of faculty. It is questionable whether a university can pursue its proper end if it must be engaged in the fight against social inequality."

And then see how even without facts critics can assail such positions and through analogy destroy the position of the traditionalist and establish a base for the nontraditional.

Somewhat to our chagrin, we in education are discovering that Detroit is not the only establishment having trouble adjusting to the new needs of society. If you are tooled up for Cadillacs and your staff knows how to make quality Cadillacs, it is hard to believe that Volkswagens and Toyotas may really be superior models for the changing world. Colleges and faculty that won their prestige with an all-out push for academic excellence in the 1950s find it difficult indeed to tool up for new models. The position that is staunchly defended by most faculty members is that, while it is quite alright to admit a diversity of talent to colleges, academic standards must be preserved and no one should be graduated without meeting those standards. It is as though we put a Volkswagen on the assembly line, added a heavy motor, extended the hood, enlarged the trunk, put in expensive carpets and interiors, and insisted on the smooth ride of a heavy car—all in the interest of maintaining standards. A Volkswagen is not a cheaper, lighter Cadillac; it is a different car designed for different purposes. Similarly, college for the masses is not a low-standard version of college for the elite; it is a different kind of education with high standards true to its own purposes [Cross, 1974, pp. 87–88].

The nontraditional movement of the late 1960s and 1970s is rooted in two major strands in American life and in American education. The first of these is the underlying egalitarianism, the landmarks of which are quite clear, at least from the 1860s onward, with respect to higher education. This egalitarianism is exemplified in the Morrill Acts of 1862 and 1890, which provided for federal land grants to help support institutions catering to the agricultural and mechanical classes. The 1890 act also helped to extend educational benefits to black students in the South. It is again exemplified in the veterans' benefits provisions at the end of World War II and in the recommendations of the Truman Commission on Higher Education that over half of all high school graduates could profit from postsecondary education. It is clearly involved in the rapid expansion of the two-year public community junior colleges throughout the post-World War II period and in the National Education Association Educational Policies Commission report (1964) calling for universal higher education. Explicit in virtually all of the state plans for higher education developed during the 1960s and early 1970s is the public policy position of extending access to higher education until it has become universal. Much of the rhetoric of the nontraditionalists is of an egalitarian nature. Once again Cross is the most representative spokesperson, stating that "The new clientele of higher education is a more diverse group of students than any in the previous history of higher education. Open access to college must mean more than opening a broad funnel to admit diversity and then narrowing the neck so that only the preferred pass through. We need to expand the concept of academic excellence and to speak in broader terms of educational excellence. The most disturbing data that I had to deal with in my research on new students was that students who had not done well in school learned to think of themselves as below-average people. School is geared to the development of a narrow range of talent consisting of approximately one twelfth of the known human abilities; it is not surprising that students whose chief talents lie among the unexploited eleven twelfths have trouble demonstrating that they can make contributions to society" (Cross, 1974, pp. 88–89).

The parallels between the nontraditional movement and the progressive education movement of the early twentieth century are so distinct as to force at least the inference that the one is a direct continuation of the other. The progressive educationists believed that the conduct of the pupil should be self-governed, and the nontraditionalists believe that the interests and needs of the individual should determine the curriculum and mode of learning. Progressive education posited that interest should be satisfied and developed through direct and indirect contact with the world and its activities and the use of the experience thus gained. This position is clearly similar to the nontraditionalist belief that real-life activities should be part of a program and that academic credit should be given for real-life activities. Progressive education held that teachers should be guides, not task masters, and should spend most of their time teaching students how to use various sources of information, rather than conveying information and hearing recitations—a role not dissimilar from that envisioned for the professor in external degree programs. Progressive education held that school records should be much more comprehensive than simple marks and should convey information about a full range of characteristics and activities, the better to help in counseling students. It also stressed the physical and psychological

needs of students and noted that the school should cooperate closely
with the home and other institutions to facilitate human development. These concepts are not substantively different from the nontraditionalist view that the full profile of an individual's background
should be carefully evaluated so as to plan an educational program
appropriately and that the college or university properly should join
hands with other social institutions to provide students with the
richest possible array of educationally potent resources (Cremin,
1961).

An essential premise on which much of the nontraditional
movement, as well as the quest to serve new students, is based is the
presumed demand for educational activities on the part of large
numbers of the age group eighteen to sixty. It is to the service of
these presumed millions of people that the movement owes its reason for being. Some of the nontraditionalists argue the case deduc-
tively, from the premise that there are many and complex individual
and social needs for more education. By then converting that
presumed need to demand, a case is made for older institutions to
enter into new programs and for the creation of new institutions.
Others have used a kind of market research, one of which was a
survey conducted by the Commission on Non-Traditional Study.
Responses of a sample designed to reflect the 104 million people in
the eighteen to sixty age group suggested that there were approximately 79 million who wanted some kind of more or less formal educational experience. The data from the questionnaire, together with of
course, the judgments of the members of the commission, led to the
two major policy recommendations that in a sense undergird the
nontraditional movement and the concern for new students. Those
were "(1) full educational opportunity should be realistically available and feasible for all who may benefit from it, whatever their
condition of life [and] (2) basic, continuing, and recurrent education should be strengthened and made more available than at
present to adults of the United States" (Commission on Non-
Traditional Study, 1973, pp. 7, 21).

Academic degrees and credentials operate in a strangely two-
edged way to serve as an important strand in nontraditionalism.
First, the alleged unhealthy preoccupation of Americans with de-

grees and credentials has led to searches for educational experiences to be had for their own sake rather than for the sake of obtaining a credential or degree. What is visualized here is a nation of lifelong learners who continuously take courses and study things simply because it is a highly desirable kind of activity. But at the same time the demand on the part of many to obtain credentials and degrees contributes substantially to the practices of nontraditional programs; for example, the practices of shortening programs, awarding academic credit for life experience, and facilitating credential upgrading through more flexible kinds of scheduling. Present evidence suggests that the desire for credentials and degrees is the more productive of actual enrollments, while the presumed value of education without credit or degrees provides the idealistic rhetoric characterizing the nontraditional doctrines.

Reinforcing and legitimizing the nontraditional movement are the reports and pronouncements of the several national policy-making groups: the Carnegie Commission on Higher Education and its successor the Carnegie Council on Policy Studies in Higher Education; the Task Force on Higher Education, under the chairmanship of Frank Newman; the Assembly on University Goals and Governance; the Commission on Non-Traditional Study; and the Commission on Financing Post-Secondary Education. Of these, the Carnegie Commission eventually took a position in favor of at least some of the elements of nontraditional learning. It urged that greater provisions be made for older students through more flexible scheduling; it argued for the creation of alternative ways by which college-age youth could develop; it called for new and more flexible degree structures, such as the Associate of Arts Degree; it stressed the potential value of educational technology; and it identified new groups of students for whom specific and special curricular and instructional provisions should be made. Several of its major policy statements such as the one entitled *Less Time—More Options* (1971) are quoted extensively in literature describing nontraditional programs and institutions. Some new and nontraditional programs that have been judged as being of dubious educational quality by regional accrediting associations have rested their defense so firmly on Carnegie Commission statements that one association officially requested that the chairman of the commission publish a warning against exaggerating the significance of its policy statements suggesting modified procedures and practices.

The Task Force on Higher Education may prove to have been more influential in the nontraditional movement than the Carnegie Commission. Its first report was a stinging critique of many prevailing practices and urged radical new educational departures. It recommended the creation of quite new kinds of institutions, extensive use of off-campus and real-life experiences, as well as a reduction in the influence of formal accreditation, on the ground that formal accreditation retarded experimentation and prevented the establishment of new programs for new students.

The report of the Assembly of University Goals and Governance has not been particularly influential and its recommendations for the most part were so general as to provide no true guidance for curricular or instructional modifications. The Commission on Financing Post-Secondary Education also does not appear to have been influential with respect to the nontraditional movement, chiefly because the focus of its efforts involved financial policy rather than educational policy.

Clearly the intent of the Commission on Non-Traditional Study was to be the major shaping influence of the movement. Its publications, such as *Explorations in Non-Traditional Study* (Gould and Cross, 1972), *Planning Non-Traditional Programs* (Cross, Valley, and Associates, 1974), and *Diversity by Design* (Commission on Non-Traditional Study, 1973), have been widely quoted and have been used as a rationale for specific undertakings. Several of the members of the professional staff of the commission emerged as major spokesmen for nontraditional education and have carried the message throughout the country. As an additional legacy, the Educational Testing Service and the College Entrance Examination Board have institutionalized offices concerned with nontraditional study and nontraditional institutions, and it maintains a record of various undertakings. The ultimate test of this commission's influence will be whether or not nontraditional modes do become thoroughly established and assimilated into the mainstream of higher educational practice in the United States. The likelihood of this happening is somewhat conjectural, given the history of other deviations from educational orthodoxy. The general education movement was one of the longer-lived attempts, and its potency lasted essentially from the end of World War II to the beginning of the decade of the 1960s. The attempts during the 1950s to make specific provisions for the education of the gifted and to stress non-Western studies remained active concerns for only a few years before events overtook the attempts and they faded into obscurity. During the late 1960s, there seemed to be a major movement involving establishment of courses and programs designed for quite specific groups of people; thus black studies, Chicano studies, Native American studies and women's studies rose quickly into vogue, but by the mid-1970s the movement seems to have crested and explicit interest in such matters is on the decline.

Major Tenets of the Nontraditional Movement

The major tenets of the nontraditional movement may be quickly summarized. The fundamental belief is that there should be available educational experiences for all people at all stages during their lifetimes. There is especially a concern for the availability for educational programs for adults specifically arranged to conform to their working schedules, their other adult commitments, and their particular educational needs. When all of the practices and techniques recommended under the heading of nontraditional learning are examined, they seem to have greatest relevance for adult students who are either seeking degrees and credentials or who wish learning experiences for the sake of learning. Most of the newly created institutions stressing nontraditional education appear similarly to focus on the adult and part-time student. Not that a number of nontraditional methods are theoretically inappropriate for other kinds of students—credit by examination and packaged self-instruction courses are theoretically appropriate for traditional students or for other kinds of new students, such as the culturally disadvantaged or the individuals whose talents lie in fields other than the traditional academic concerns. But time and again, when actual practices are described they concern the adult and part-time learner. The central thesis of the argument of Ernest L. Boyer is contained in his statement (1975, p. 20) that "One approach would be to shorten or interrupt the sixteen prebaccalaureate years and lengthen the students' post-B.A. education. The notion that education is something one gets only before going to work must be replaced with the idea that education is a lifelong process, going on during, after, and in-between working days. If we can change the idea, our colleges will increasingly move from serving the calendar to serving people of all ages."

Patricia Cross's underlying premise is that "The largest group of citizens systematically excluded from education by the classical model of a college was composed of those who were unable to pursue formal education full-time. In 1972, the number of part-time students began to exceed the number of full-time students in institutions of higher education. Part-timers now constitute the majority of American college students, and the growth rate of part-time students in the 1970s has been more than three times that for full-time students. This means that the *majority* of students today have other responsibilities" (1974, p. 58).

Describing one of the more widely publicized nontraditional efforts, Jack Lindquist reveals the same attitude. "First, most contract learning students are older than the traditional age of eighteen to age twenty-two college students. At Empire State, 63 percent are married, 60 percent work full-time, and only 3 percent are unemployed. When asked why they enrolled at Empire State, students responded that the flexibility and independence were especially attractive. They could keep their jobs and often use those jobs as learning laboratories" (1975, p. 76).

Sylvia G. McCollum elaborates this concern in her description of educational programs for prisoners. She says "The underlying goal of all prison education efforts is to develop students in continuing their educations, both as a means of staying out of prison and of enriching their personal lives" (1975, p. 102). Howard R. Bowen and W. John Minter sums up the orientation of nontraditional education and its clientele: "By 1975, the campuses were serving vast numbers of commuters, including part-time and older students, and the concept of parental supervision had been swept away. In the process, without anyone intending it, the traditional idea about the campus as a closely knit community that influenced student character and outlook was largely abandoned. I estimate that not more than 30 percent of the total higher education enrollment today

consists of residential students in closely knit academic communities"
(1975, p. 155). And he foresees major increases in higher education
enrollments only if adequate provisions are made for adults and
part-time students.

A second major tenet is the belief in the academic validity of
life experiences and on-the-job learning. It is assumed that many of
the things people do and learn in noneducational contexts do bring
about the same kinds of changes in behavior and belief that traditional colleges seek to produce. Persons having manifested those
changes should be allowed to demonstrate them and to convert that
evidence into academic credit counting toward a degree or credential. There is also the related belief that many jobs can be so
organized as to bring about academically desirable changes and the
belief that on-the-job training should be an integral part of nontraditional programs. The values of clinical or practical experience is
not a particularly new concept: Practice teaching, internships in
medicine, and clinical work in social work education have long been
used. What is new is the range of nonacademic activities that are
considered to possess educational potency and the inclination to
award academic credit for those experiences.

A related tenet is the belief that many nonacademic institutions and materials have educational potency and should be exploited. There is also the belief that many people not involved in
academic pursuits have knowledge and experience to contribute to
an educational program and that these also should be exploited.
This has led to the view that public libraries, museums, research
installations, governmental and social agencies, and even businesses
and labor unions represent educational resources that should be
used in a program focused on a formal degree. It has also led to a
belief in the desirability of using large numbers of part-time faculty
on the ground that the insights from practice that such faculty trans-
mit to students more than compensate for any lack of continuous
availability of faculty to students, such as is assumed in traditional
modes of educational organization.

Traditional education has used a limited repertoire of techniques of evaluation and assessment. Written tests, oral examinations,
and an occasional judgment of student-produced products define the
parameters. These, in the eyes of the nontraditionalists, seem in-

sufficient to measure the outcomes of a work experience or a student-designed course of study; thus there is a steady plea in the literature of nontraditional learning for other, more valid means of appraisal. Indicative of the nontraditionalists' belief in new methods of evaluation but also indicative of the lack of precision in identifying those methods is the policy statement made by the Commission on Non-Traditional Study that "New devices and techniques should be perfected to measure the outcomes of many types of nontraditional study and to assess the educative effect of work experience and community service" (1973, p. 125), and the imprecision is revealed in discussion subsequent to that statement (1973, pp. 129–130):

Ways must be found for measuring the effect of work experience on the individual's accomplishment of the goals of his educational program. The ingenuity of the educational evaluator, of which Howe spoke, will perhaps devise new forms of tests which can measure varied learning outcomes with a precision not previously achieved. In doing so, however, the evaluator will have to turn away from the traditionalism of the school-college-university setting to examine other areas of experience, for in the world outside the school the assessment of the effect of experience on the individual has not only been studied deeply by theorists but also put into practice in systems which influence the lives of many adults. Assessing growth and merit is a central concern of public administration, the armed services, professional societies, business management, and universities themselves. Rating scales, rotating work systems, and examinations which admit individuals to the elite or specialized groups of professions are everywhere.

The Commission therefore suggests that some generalized testing agency such as the Educational Testing Service follow up this recommendation by analyzing the vast experience available outside the formal education system to discover ways of evaluating work or service that may be usefully applied to non-traditional study.

A somewhat idealistic tenet of the movement is that there should be more emphasis on learning for its own sake and less on credit and degrees. What seems to be intended here is that the entire society should become a learning society and that people should engage in educational activities throughout their lifetime. While this is the ideal, the practices of nontraditional forms of education nonetheless seem specifically designed to facilitate acquisition of credentials and degrees. The issue is well elaborated in the large survey conducted by the staff of the Commission on Non-Traditional Study (1973, p. 21) indicating that approximately two thirds of those surveyed wished to receive academic credit and that the two principal outcomes the majority wanted from learning programs were specific vocational skills and/or academic credit that could count toward a degree or a credential.

A last tenet to be discussed here, although other derivative points could be enumerated, is the belief that educational technology should serve as an important element of nontraditional learning. Open- and closed-circuit television, videotape cassettes, audiotape cassettes, and miniaturized equipment with which to simulate laboratory work are all counted as important resources. Walton speaks for the nontraditionalists when he argues that "When the needs and interests of the adult learner are put first and institutional interests are subordinated, it becomes unmistakably clear that telecommunications technologies have become essential components for the delivery of instruction. Without them it is impossible to deliver instruction to the adults who want and need it and the technologies beneficial in a diversity of styles of adult learning are now in being" (Cross, Valley, and Associates, 1974, p. 96).

Issues in the Nontraditional Movement

The nontraditional movement has generated a number of issues that are relevant and that must be resolved. The first of these is quite startling. The traditional concept of what is formal higher education stresses the use of words, numbers, and abstract symbols: Individuals are prepared to deal intellectually and conceptually with complex phenomena. This concept recognizes that other social institutions modify human behavior but does not consider these an essential part of formal education. Thus presumably an annual physical examination should bring about changes in the behavior of the patient. Surviving a lawsuit also modifies behavior, as does witnessing a particularly moving drama. However, simply aggregating the range of experiences that modify behavior, regardless of how intense, does not comprise a formal educational program. Higher education seeks to modify behavior through use of a varied but still limited range of techniques and processes, such as reading books, writing papers, discussing complex ideas, conducting laboratory exercises, and undergoing specific but limited evaluations. The nontraditional mode seems to expand the concept of formal education and indeed to equate solving a problem of interpersonal relationships on a job with developing conceptual skills through manipulation of words, numbers, or other abstractions. Once the earlier or limited conception of formal education is abrogated, the serious problem intrudes of how to set the outward limits of what can be considered valid education, and that problem has not been solved. The point can be made by asking where, along a specific continuum, appropriateness for the formal educational program ends. Consider banking: Which of this range of activities is appropriate for academic credit? Reading a novel about bankers? Viewing a television show about banking? Taking a field trip to visit a bank? Working in a bank under the supervision of bankers? Working in a bank under the supervision of an educator? Working in a bank and taking a course on banking offered by the bank? Working in a bank and taking a course on banking offered by a junior college? Working in a bank and taking a related seminar concerned with bank work? Taking courses about business and finance? Taking courses deliberately planned to lead to a degree in business and finance. To answer, "It depends on the situation" begs the question, and to say "All of them" extends the concept of education to a meaningless abstraction.

The second issue is much more prosaic and has to do with the cost of nontraditional programs, especially those designed for adults and for the economically disadvantaged. If the costs are to be borne substantially by the individual, many of the new students will be excluded, because they can neither afford the fees nor the time off from work. If the cost is to be borne by an agency of government, then the issue of what is legitimate and not legitimate expenditure of public funds intrudes, particularly if adults wish to take a range of courses, from a short course on how to flycast to highly professionalized courses on new interpretations of constitutional law. If it is argued that some kinds of activities are legitimately the concern of an agency of government, while others are not, then the problem of delineation intrudes seriously. Consider the following range of subjects that might be offered by a public junior college and supported by state appropriations, and determine whether there is a position along the continuum beyond which expenditure of state funds would be inappropriate: strip-tease dancing, belly dancing, ballroom dancing, folk dancing, choreography, understanding the relationship between dance and the theater, understanding the history of the dance, the dance in motion pictures, staging a musical comedy, and taking courses leading to an associate degree in fine arts with a major in the dance. Of course, one answer with respect to cost is that sharing between the individual and a governmental agency would be appropriate. Nevertheless, the same problems of clarification are involved here.

A particularly troublesome economic matter, which for the most part has not been faced, is the cost of nontraditional techniques. A major mission of the nontraditional movement is to serve new students—many of whom are not particularly economically advantaged. It seems to be assumed that nontraditional modes are less costly than are traditional ones. Yet this assumption has not been validated. Indeed, experience from traditional education suggests an opposite conclusion—that most of the techniques, *adequately put into effect,* are terribly expensive. Clinical or field experience with adequate supervision is expensive, as medical education has shown and as legal education is discovering. Independent study, appropriately guided, becomes tutorial—again the most labor intensive and hence expensive kind of education. Reliable and valid measuring instruments are also expensive to create, especially if they are to obtain evidence of unusual and deeply embedded attributes. It could well be that well-developed nontraditional programs would prove too costly for anyone to afford.

The third issue is the problem of quality control to ensure that nontraditional experiences do have educational value. In the absence of any generally acceptable and economical measures of changed behavior, this issue poses serious problems. If academic credit is to be awarded for life experiences, how can those experiences be gauged and converted into academic values? If an adjunct professor located far distant from a home campus—hence without the daily scrutiny of his behavior by his students, colleagues, and superiors—how can the validity of what he does be measured? When a student decides to help a local school board work out a program of sex education as a practicum experience, what criteria are to be used to judge the educational outcomes for the student? When a student and advisor jointly develop a contract for activities that will lead to a degree, how can the validity of that program be compared to the validity of a program worked out by an entire faculty to be taken by all students?

A somewhat different issue, which does not appear significantly in the literature on nontraditional education involves the cost of using noninstitutional resources as an essential part of the educational program of a student paying tuition to that institution. A public library is supported with public funds and intended to be of service to the community; yet should that service be extended in massive proportions to students who are really transients in the community? Or consider a specific example of a state university library that has specialized holdings for its own students; then assume the creation of a new and nontraditional private university in the same town that does not have its own library but that enrolls large numbers of students in a given program and that assumes those students will be privileged to use the library holdings of the state university. If various field visits to business and industry come to be considered as essential elements of a nontraditional program, to what extent should the business and industry be expected to subsidize those field visits as contributed service? To what extent should there be actual payment for the time of individuals who must make the field visit a success? A related and particularly difficult question involves the use of part-time faculty, particularly those fully employed in another institution. Several of the more widely publicized external degree programs, such as the Union for Experimenting Colleges Graduate School or Nova University, appoint adjunct professors in various parts of the country who are already fully employed in colleges and universities. Typically the adjunct professor will be paid a fee for his services—but should there also be a fee payable to his own university, on the ground that were he not serving as an adjunct professor he could make a more substantial contribution to his own institution? Now it is true that many universities allow for individual consulting on the part of faculty members, typically at rates of one day a week, but in at least some situations adjunct professors are spending much more time than that and some situations are in actual competition with programs of their own institutions. Furthermore, additional teaching may not help professional growth the way consultation would. This raises serious questions of equity and ethics.

Of special significance is the issue as to whether (assuming they have validity for the nontraditional) nontraditional practices can be woven into the activities of existing institutions or whether, for fullest value, new institutions are needed. Although a substantial number of existing institutions offer some nontraditional activities, they seem frequently to be regarded as somewhat peripheral. The fullest expression of the nontraditional mode in its several dimensions is to be found in the new institutions, either public or private. Assuming that the 2,600 existing institutions will continue to provide the norm for the delivery of higher education in the United States, the fact that the nontraditional plays such a modest role raises questions as to the longevity of nontraditional studies as defined in the early 1970s. If nontraditional education is most effectively offered by new kinds of institutions and if traditional institutions continue generally in traditional ways, then a competitive scenario is produced. The outcomes of such competition involves a financial matter. The more complete and more radical embracing of the nontraditional has taken place more frequently in privately supported institutions than in public. There are, of course, such notable examples as Evergreen State College, Sangamon State, and Empire State, but the Novas and Laurences, which comprise the bulk of the fully committed nontraditional institutions, almost without exception, are seriously underfinanced and must earn the bulk of their operating expenses through tuitions. To further complicate the matter, these nontraditional institutions seemingly have enrolled a high proportion of students who are receiving veterans' benefits. When the program of veterans' benefits ends, as it will shortly, the matter of financial liability becomes serious indeed.

Two other issues can be briefly stated. The first of these is the problem of accreditation by regional accrediting associations that have developed their instruments and expertise dealing with traditional forms of education. The question, bluntly put, is whether they can devise ways of accrediting that will on the one hand encourage innovation but at the same time maintain traditional standards of excellence. The second, a little discussed issue, involves the likely perseverance of students working toward degrees who must conduct much of the work independently, away from the supportive presence of other students and the pervasive values of a residential campus. Sustained independent study without support is a lonely activity, especially if the individual has a job and other adult responsibilities. A good bit of the rhetoric of the nontraditional views learning as a pleasurable undertaking, the learning being its own reward. This may be contrary to reality, and some devices may be needed to help the independent student keep up his morale long enough to complete the degree or credential requirements.

THREE

New Institutions —Extending the Nontraditional

Between 1968 and 1975, approximately 500 new collegiate institutions came into existence in the United States, a fifth of which were privately controlled and financed. What makes this phenomenon so startling is that beginning at approximately the same time expansion of enrollments began to slow and well-established private institutions began to encounter such financial difficulty as to produce concern over the survival of private institutions of higher education. In order to understand the phenomenon, which in a sense is a manifestation of the nontraditional, and to compare these new institutions with those created at other times and predict their longevity, an examination of the forces giving rise to their creation is appropriate.

The largest number of these new institutions are publicly supported two-year community colleges or technical institutes. Most of these were planned during the expansion of higher education during the late 1960s as the states sought to implement a public policy of ensuring universal access to higher education. The momentum of this policy continued into the 1970s as groups such as the Carnegie Commission on Higher Education variously proposed the creation of between 150 to 275 new two-year institutions. Very likely, if enrollment trends of the mid-1970s continue, such numbers will not be achieved, but the mood of expansionism that generated such estimates did contribute to the actual construction of campuses in the late 1960s and early 1970s, even when the future need for them appeared doubtful.

Forces Producing Them

A powerful force—at least, powerful in the sense of creating an appealing rhetoric and a logic for public policy—was the sudden egalitarian concern for new students that is so central in nontraditional education. Such reformers as Samuel Gould, K. Patricia Cross, and Harold Hodgkinson argued in Rousseau-like terms that existing institutions served—probably badly—only one segment of the population and had ignored the needs of millions of others. They argued that the traditional students in American higher education had been so socialized through their family backgrounds to seek meritocratic advance that they could profit from existing programs almost in spite of the ineffectiveness of those programs. Other students—the older, less able, less successful and less financially secure—lacked the socially developed internal ability to cope with academic work and the motivation to persist in activities that appeared meaningless to them to the point of receiving a credential or a degree. These new students required a different kind of education, which very likely could not be offered in traditional colleges and universities. Hence new institutions or new branches of existing institutions should be created that could offer radically different sequences for learning.

If the validity of Cross's argument is granted, then logic leads inevitably to quite new institutions, programs, and methods of teaching. Thus there should be institutions that cater to those who cannot get to a collegiate campus. There should be programs scheduled so that full-time working people can take advantage of them. There should be courses that stress traits and skills other than the traditional cognitive ones of developing facility in the use of words and numbers. Cross argues that in the world of work alone there are three major functions—working with data, working with people, and working with things. Formal education should assume responsibility for developing in each student excellence with respect to one function and competence with respect to the other two. The choice of the function would rest with the student, and the obligation to devise ways of developing excellence would rest with the institution (Cross, 1974). This rationale is clearly evident in the charters of Metro State College in Minnesota and of Empire State College in New York, in the attempt on the part of the California Joint Legislative Committee on Higher Education to create a fourth public segment of higher education to serve new clienteles, and in the creation of Sangamon State College in Illinois.

The idea that new students require new kinds of institutions is clearly reflected in the creation of colleges for minority-group members in the private sector as well as in the public. Malcolm-King Harlem College Extension is a private institution operated by part-time personnel for members of the black community in Harlem. Its curriculum appears fairly standard, but the support services made available are specifically designed for economically disadvantaged adults who must attend college at night. Nairobi College in East Palo Alto, California, is also designed for the black community but is considerably different from traditional institutions. Its intent is to provide two years of academic training and a whole life-time of psychological reeducation for black citizens of the community. Located near Davis, California, Universidad Deganawidah Quetzalcoatl (DQU) serves American Indians and Chicanos by offering typical community college courses, such as mathematics and history, as well as courses and instruction tailored to specific interests and problems of Native Americans or Chicanos. The prevailing goal at DQU is to meet each student where he is and to help him where he wants to go. A somewhat similar but better-financed institution is the Navajo Community College, organized in 1969 in Many Farms, Arizona. It is seeking to provide higher education to a community in which the average family income is $1,500 per year, one third of adults neither read or speak English, and the average adult over twenty-five years old has spent less than five years in formal school. The purpose of the institution is to prepare people from that community to hold good jobs and to live both among the Navajo population and in the dominant society.

There are other minority groups for whom seemingly new kinds of institutions are needed but concerning which institutions cannot be so explicit. One such group, which is growing in numbers, is the children of middle- and upper-middle-class families, frequently members of professional and intellectual communities, who have found traditional schooling somewhat repugnant and who need a freer sort of atmosphere in order to find their own identities. Their parents are sophisticated enough at least to intuit these needs and can afford to provide their children four or five years of college experience involving no particular vocational orientation as they pursue self-generated educational activities, with the nurture and support of sympathetic faculty members. In institutions serving these students, great stress is placed on experiential learning, individual questing for problems and solutions, and psychologically varied experiences and activities. Although institutions organized along these lines cannot state explicitly that they are havens for the upper-class counterculture, examination of their student bodies suggests that that is indeed what they are. The New College of California, located first in Sausalito, California, and later in San Francisco, is such an institution. It offers a humanistic sort of curriculum and operates with a high degree of participatory democracy. The prevailing style of teaching consists of only slightly structured discussions aimed at helping students discover who they are. Fairhaven College, a part of Western Washington State College, is another example, as is also Evergreen State College in Olympia, Washington. These are both public institutions, which must publicly embrace a broader mission but which actually attract the same sort of student who attends New College of California. Fairhaven College presents as representative one student's description of her education. The first year she took a more or less traditional series of courses as she sought to define herself, through her studies, as being separate from those around her.

The second year consisted entirely of off-campus work, travel, and study. In summer I organized a political collective in Seattle; in fall I lived in a Mexican orphanage and organized and taught a village kindergarten; in winter I traveled widely over Mexico; and in spring I returned to the states for a series of off-campus independent research and writing projects. The second year marked the turning point of my education, and a leaping-off point in my life. Every aspect of this year and the work and study in which I was immersed concerned social relationships and, except for spring quarter, involved working with other persons. . . . The third year of my concentration provided a combination of on- and off-campus study and work. The first quarter I took courses which continued my previous lines of interest in literature and the social sciences. Then, after leaving school, both because of a lack of funds and because I wanted to pursue several independent research and writing projects, I returned to Mexico to resolve some unanswered questions both subjective and academic. Upon my return I was hired by Fairhaven College to design and implement a work-study program which I called Vocations for Social Change. I also taught classes in Spanish and Mexican Society and Culture, continued several long-term independent study projects, organized and participated in feminist groups, and worked on editing a nonfiction magazine for Fairhaven [Fairhaven College, mimeograph, n.d.].

Although this student alludes to some financial problems, a possible inference is that such an educational program would likely be viewed as an ill-afforded luxury by other than reasonably affluent and tolerant families.

There are powerful individual and institutional economic factors involved in the creation of new institutions. These are reflected in several different sorts of developments. The first is the phenomenon of existing institutions creating new branches, centers, or satellites, each designed for a specific clientele. The underlying rationale is to improve the economic viability of the parent institution through diversification. Of course, the rhetoric used is that of meeting needs and providing service, but the basic model is that of a business questing for new markets. Examples, both public and

private, abound. LaVerne College, in southern California, is a
church-related undergraduate liberal arts college that began to lose
enrollments in the late 1960s in the sharply competitive environment
of California, in which public higher education dominates. In order
to offset potential deficits, a new president created, on military
bases, centers offering degree programs suitable for military personnel; created other centers in public school districts to facilitate upgrading of teachers and administrators; created, in cooperation with
the University of Northern Colorado, centers that offered doctoral
work in educational administration for people who were fully
employed; and contracted with a proprietary organization to offer
programs for teachers throughout the country. In addition, it created
an evening law school. The result of such activities, which also included an external degree program operated on the home campus,
produced a home campus of approximately 800 students, with a
total enrollment of a size varying from 10,000 to 20,000 students.
The home campus continued to operate at a deficit, which was offset
by income generated by the satellite activities.

Antioch College, in Yellow Springs, Ohio, has also created
centers and branch campuses throughout the country, with the
avowed goal that each campus or branch must become financially
self-supporting, but with an implied goal that the campuses ultimately
should contribute to the economic viability of the entire system.
Public institutions also have sought new clientele to be served with
new structures out of economic necessity. The San Mateo Community College District operates three campuses, on two of which enrollments had stabilized, a situation that affected the receipt of funds
from the state of California. One campus then became aggressive in
developing new programs that could be offered in off-campus locations, such as in the headquarters of a corporation. The enrollments
from those branches were able to offset the declines elsewhere in the
district and to allow the institution to continue staffing and operations at desirable levels. The Pennsylvania State University, long
active in colonization, has created centers for in-service training of
teachers throughout Pennsylvania. These are staffed by part-time
people from the locality in which the centers are located and contribute to the enrollment levels on which state appropriations are
made to the state-affiliated home institution.

Individual or corporate profit are also involved in producing new institutions. The latter is fairly familiar in the form of proprietary or profit-making vocational schools. These institutions enroll upwards of 3,000,000 students each year. They offer specialized programs in cosmetology, technology, and business and create new programs as new vocational needs are identified or as new clientele are discovered. These proprietary schools are for the most part not individually owned and operated establishments but are owned by well-known corporations such as Bell & Howell, Controlled Data, Minneapolis Honeywell, and IT & T.

Less well understood is the possibility for private gain through operating not-for-profit educational institutions designed for a specific and typically new clientele. It is, of course, impossible to determine with any precision the number of new institutions created for such a purpose, for some practices would come close to being criminal and many would be ethically questionable. However, enough examples have been examined to support the belief that quest for individual gain is important in the creation of at least a few institutions. Consider three reasonably documented procedures. One is locating a not-for-profit educational institution on land acquired at low cost from the federal government adjacent to undeveloped land owned by an institution's chief executive officer and members of the board of trustees. Assuming the success of the institution, a substantial capital gain could be realized. The second procedure involves the purchase of a facility potentially adaptable to an educational program. A facility is purchased by an individual of considerable personal wealth at a relatively low cost and with a relatively small down payment. Then a not-for-profit institution is created, with a friendly board of trustees, and the property is donated for the institution, but a sharply increased assessed valuation is made by a sympathetic real estate firm. The educational program is put into effect with tuitions coming from students receiving veterans' entitlement, equal opportunity grants, or other external but assured sources. The educational program is conducted by inadequately remunerated part-time faculty and administered by a modest secretarial and administrative staff lodged in the facility, which primarily is used as an admissions headquarters. Students are charged tuitions in the vicinity of $3,000, while the actual cost for instruction remains at approximately $300 to $400 per year. Within the first year of operation, this institution earns a surplus of over $500,000 and projects still larger surpluses in the several years in the future. The individual gain for the creator of this new institution comes first through the tax write-offs, from the gift of the property, and, secondly, in the form of perquisites such as a president's residence or automobile purchased by the institution from its surplus funds. The third procedure is similar. This involves creating a special-purpose institution as, for example, the awarding of Ph.D. and Ed.D. degrees. Students are attracted to the program because they can earn a degree in a relatively short period of time—in this case in five weeks one summer, two weeks the following summer, and a completed thesis done part-time during the intervening academic year. The institution occupies rental quarters adjacent to a facilty to feed and house students during the two summer sessions. A small administrative and clerical staff takes care of admissions, registration, record keeping, and a casual, small library. Instruction in the summer is carried on by part-time faculty paid almost token salaries and by adjunct professors living near students who agree to direct the thesis in return for a stipend of between $300 and $500 each. Students are charged $3,000 tuition, which, for 250 students, generates income of $750,000. Of this, $250,000 is expended for operating the institution and in payment for instruction. The remainder is available to be expended for perquisites for those who organize and manage the institution.

A related but somewhat different force is the changing market for college graduates. This is most clearly revealed when the number of Ph.D.'s produced began to exceed available job opportunities. This caused many potential Ph.D. candidates to reconsider career opportunities and to decide that law represented a distinct possibility. Since established law schools were reluctant to increase the size of entering classes, a real economic demand for law schools began to operate in the early 1970s. Between 1968 and 1973, over forty new law schools came into existence, each stressing a rhetoric of distinctiveness, but each owing its conception to the fact that there was a willing clientele ready to pay tuitions to gain the degree that they felt would help them achieve upward social mobility. Some of these law schools appear to be serious efforts to create a new kind of legal education. The Antioch School of Law in Washington, D.C., offers a program carefully blending academic legal education with actual experience in the practice of law from the freshman year on. Others, however, are located in rented quarters, possess only the rudiments of a law library and make exclusive use of practicing attorneys, who serve as a part-time law faculty. Since the evidence of a genuine marketplace need for large numbers of new lawyers is far from persuasive, the best interpretation is that these new law schools have been created because large numbers of individuals want a law degree and are willing to pay for it.

Several other forces can be quickly summarized and exemplified. New institutions, especially proprietary institutions, come into existence rather quickly when a new technical specialty is demanded by the marketplace. Thus, when electronic data processing assumed considerable magnitude, this development was followed almost immediately by the creation of several hundred proprietary schools preparing people for work in data processing. When the nature of data processing shifted—for example, from keypunch to tape—the schools disappeared as quickly as they had been created. A few institutions have been created because of political pressures in the community in which the new institution is located or political pressure from an existing institution wishing to expand. Metro State College in St. Paul, Minnesota, was created as a distinctive kind of external program and degree institution for many reasons, including the fact that the state college system in Minnesota did not have a presence in the Twin Cities and its leadership believed that such a presence was necessary. An objective assessment of Minnesota revealed that the state had sufficient higher education capacity to take care of potential needs. Legislative authorization for Metro State, which did not include the development of the full campus, was a compromise that represented considerably less financial outlay than the state college system had wanted, yet that did give the state college its desired presence in the most populous region of the state. Some new institutions have been created as branches as one device for coping with excessive size. Other new institutions have been created, at least in part, through foundation support or activities. Hampshire College, in Amherst, Massachusetts, it will be recalled,

was originally planned by representatives from four other institutions, in response to a grant made by the Ford Foundation. And
some institutions are created simply because of professional dissatis-
factions on the part of their founders with prevailing forms of instruction. The Wright Institute in Berkeley was created by Nevitt
Sanford, who believed in the importance of personality and counseling and clinical psychology but who was persuaded that behaviorism
so dominated existing departments of psychology that there was no
hope for the kind of psychology with which he was concerned.
Creating his own institution seemed the best answer.

Difficult to establish, yet nonetheless plausible as an interpretation for proliferation, is the influence of federal funding for
various kinds of students at a time when traditional private institutions run annual deficits and fear for their own survival. The
creation of a new private university with 80 percent of its total
enrollment receiving veterans' benefits strongly suggests that such an
institution would not have come into existence had a federal program not been operating. Such an institution as International University in Southern California states quite worthy purposes: to
provide several kinds of vocational programs for people who are
working full-time. Since the institution does not possess an endowment and must generate all income from tuition and since a large
proportion of its students are receiving veterans' benefits, the conclusion is certainly warranted that it would not exist without the
federal program, and one cannot be sanguine as to its institutional
longevity, once veterans' programs terminate and if other federal
programs, such as equal opportunity grants are curtailed.

New Institutions of the 1950s and 1960s

The first great period of expansion of the number of institutions of higher education in recent times extended roughly from
1958 to 1968. That expansion seems to have resulted from somewhat
different factors and forces, and those factors and forces operated
differently in different institutions or types of institutions. The broad
pressures are well known and can be quickly enumerated. There was
the post-World War II population increase, which created a large
cohort of potential college students in the 1960s. Then there was the

factor of rising expectations on the part of segments of the population that had never before contemplated college attendance. These, of course, were sparked by the continuous period of relative affluence during the two and a half postwar decades. The rationale for institutions of higher education to provide for these increased numbers was developed by several national commissions and by the adoption of state studies of higher education of the public posture that at least 50 percent of high school graduates could profit from collegiate education and that the states had the responsibility to ensure them adequate opportunity. Formal education in graduate and professional studies was additionally stimulated by federal policy of support of research—hence the need to prepare research workers for the increasing complexities of professional practice and the need for larger pools of highly trained individuals—and by the generally accepted belief that the college industry was the most rapidly growing sector in the American economy and would continue to grow almost exponentially into the foreseeable future.

Obviously some new institutions were created as a result of similar forces operating in the 1960s. Two state universities were created with the expectation that they would become comprehensive research-oriented institutions. Because of the easy availability of federal funds and largely because of political factors, some new institutions were located in specific localities, and the junior college expansion of the late 1950s and 1960s represented a straight extension of developments extending back as far as the early 1920s. But other factors were either not operating, not recognized, or at least not discussed. Within American higher education generally, there have historically been criticisms of existing practices, but few of the institutions created in the period 1958 to 1968 were based on a desire for a radical departure from previous practice. There were, to be sure, spontaneous appearances here and there of atypical kinds of institutions, such as the free universities, and there were created cluster colleges, which sought to alleviate the problems of enormous institutional ties. But for the most part the logic used to justify new institutions and the rhetoric employed to describe them is not the logic nor rhetoric of extreme egalitarianism and extreme pluralism, with the exception of the doctrine of the community junior college movement (and even in junior colleges practice was highly orthodox), which stressed multiple purposes and programs tailored for students whom four-year institutions did not service, such as adults and students with academic deficiencies. The prevailing attitude seems to have been to create new institutions modeled after older ones and to assume that students attending would adjust to those institutions just as earlier generations had adjusted.

These points can be illustrated with several typical examples from the earlier period. The University of South Florida at Tampa, Florida, was planned as a part of a state plan for higher education and was located where it was because the Tampa Bay region represented the most rapidly industrializing area in the state. The institution was to be a comprehensive university offering arts and sciences and a number of professional fields, with the expectation that at some time in the future it would enter graduate education. The institution was moderately selective, using test scores and high school rank as a basis for admission, and stressed the ideals of academic excellence. It is true that the University of South Florida emphasized teaching, but the kind of faculty recruited, the general education program adopted, the reward system adopted, and the kinds of services provided for students all conformed to the norm of the multipurpose university—an emphasis on academic excellence and an assumption that the primary mission was to help students understand and use cognitive skills.

Somewhat closer to the new institutional model of the 1970s is the creation of New College at Hofstra, a private institution on Long Island, New York. This was to be an specially designed college in which good average students could obtain the equivalent of two years of academic work by pursuing an accelerated, intensified, extended one-year course. This was to be accomplished through an intense year-long core course, together with relevant electives. However, students entering New College were expected to devote a full forty hours a week to academic work, even though one full day per week was freed so that students could remain home and do other things.

Michigan State University-Oakland was created as a branch of Michigan State University and was intended to serve students in the Oakland-Detroit area. When the institution was originally planned, it was seen as being somewhat different from the parent institution but not radically so. Its programs were intended to be academic, and its professional fields were designed to prepare people for immediate job entry. No particular provisions were made for minority-group members, older students, or part-time students. What actually was created was an even more traditional institution than had been envisioned by its planners. The original faculty were recruited from East Coast Ivy League-types of institutions, and its members were lead to believe that Michigan State University-Oakland was to be intellectually the most commanding place, with very high standards in preparation for entry into graduate work. The students, however, typically did not come from college backgrounds, and they viewed attending college as a means of entering desirable vocations. The conflict between these two points of view produced some difficulties during the first several years of the institution's life. Eventually those difficulties were resolved, and the institution became a reasonably typical, moderately selective state university, having multiple purposes and serving its modestly pluralistic student body through different vocational programs, all of which stressed traditional academic values.

Orthodoxy also prevailed in the private sector during the earlier period of expansion. Florida Presbyterian College opened in 1960 and was presented to the nation as a highly selective and demanding liberal arts college that would gain its distinctiveness from the way in which academic knowledge was integrated, not from presenting new kinds of knowledge and new experiences. At the same time, New College at Sarasota was planned and developed by the Board of Higher Education of the Congregational Church. It was to be selective and academically rigorous and was intended to be for the southern region what such other Congregationalist-created institutions as Harvard College had become for other regions of the country. It was to be a residential campus, with a curriculum that was somewhat interdisciplinary and a faculty that would be required to possess the highest of academic credentials. Also in Florida was the Florida Atlantic University, which was intended to be different, but not with respect to purpose. It sought the traditional goals of training in the liberal arts and sciences and in professional fields, but would stress the use of educational media and technology. It was also to be different in that it would be an upper-division university and would rely on nearby junior colleges to be responsible for the lower-division education of students who would attend.

Illustrative of the intent and plan for the more radical of the new institutions created between 1958 and 1968 are the Raymond College of the University of the Pacific and Grand Valley State College in Allendale, Michigan.

The Raymond College opened in 1963 in a new series of dormitories, classroom buildings, faculty offices, and lounge facilities on the edge of the parent campus. It is staffed with a relatively young faculty and offers a rigorous liberal arts curriculum to a small student body. When all four classes are in residence, it will enroll 250 students, whose principal educational activities will be contained within this campus. The Covell College is a similar unit but features inter-American studies. Both its faculty and student body will be composed of North and South Americans, and instruction will be in both English and Spanish. The emphasis in both these colleges is on close faculty and student relations and considerable use of tutorials, discussion, and independent study. Perhaps the single most critical problem to be resolved is whether the cost per student credit hour in this highly individualized education can be kept reasonably consistent with the costs in the rest of the institution.

Grand Valley State College, in Allendale, Michigan, is a state-supported institution that owes its creation to the diligent efforts of Grand Rapids citizens who saw the values of a state college and who were willing to make contributions of land and money to assist in starting it. The college, which opened in the fall of 1963, plans to be relatively small. It will operate year round and thus will be able to function with a modest physical plant. All students at Grand Valley take a core of foundation studies in general education, including courses in the humanities, social sciences, natural sciences, mathematics, and languages. Specialization begins in the second year, and all students are required to take some general education for each of the four years. A major innovation of the college is the heavy reliance on tutorial education, with each student meeting at least once each week with his tutor. The cost of this is partly offset through equally heavy reliance on large lectures and television and considerable independent study. The library has many of the attributes of a learning resources center and provides carrels wired to central reserves of tapes and records. The institution is chiefly a liberal arts college, although teacher preparation receives major emphasis [Mayhew, 1965, pp. 16–17].

With the exception of publicly supported two-year community colleges, of which those created in the period 1958–1968 are quite similar to those created subsequently, institutions of higher education created in the two periods are remarkably dissimilar. During the period up to 1968, new institutions even in the private sector possessed or set about obtaining an adequate financial base. Legislators provided adequately—if sometimes not handsomely—for the new institutions or branches produced, and private institutions sought, through benefaction, operating and building funds and the beginnings of an endowment. While some of those plans eventually aborted (for example, New College in Florida), there was never any expectation that private institutions could operate on tuition alone.* Secondly, the institutions organized between 1958 and 1968 were all planned to occupy a definite campus with buildings designed or modified for educational purposes, and most assumed that at least a portion of the anticipated enrollments would be residential students. Even an institution such as the one then named Chicago Teachers College North, which was designed for commuting students, tried to approximate residential conditions by developing curricular organizations that would cause students to stay on campus. Similarly, when the University of South Florida opened, an asymmetrical class-scheduling scheme was originally adopted, with two primary purposes. The first was to ensure high and uniform space utilization, and the second was to contrive a schedule that would keep most faculty and students on campus for a significant portion of the academic day and week. It was believed that the interaction between faculty and students on campus possessed enormous educational value. Thirdly, while the earlier new institutions attempted some innovation (general education, use of media,

* A notable exception to the general refusal to allow institutions to operate on the basis of tuition alone was the reorganized Parsons College in Fairfield, Iowa, and the satellite campuses its president created. President Millard Roberts argued that private institutions, if properly managed, could operate primarily on tuition and that they could even produce profits that could be used for eleemosynary purposes.

interdisciplinary courses, independent study, cooperative work-study, and accent on teaching), there is no indication that faculty members would surrender to students the design of the curriculum and of the several educational programs. If general education courses were required, it was because the faculty decided those were what new students needed, and, if the educational technology were to be used, it was because planners believed they knew how to organize instructional programs. Fourthly, the new colleges of the earlier period all assumed that specific intellectual abilities were required for a student to do academic work, and all, in one way or another, tried to erect admissions standards based on the traditional evidence of prior academic achievement and measured academic aptitude. Even Parsons College—which, toward the end of its period of expansion, tended to accept virtually anyone who applied—employed the language of selectivity and claimed to seek a tripartite division of its student body: underachievers, medium achievers, and high achievers. Further, the rhetoric used to describe the institution was the traditional rhetoric of valuing the liberal arts and sciences and stressing academic rigor. If an institution offered cooperative work-study programs, there was no serious debate in favor of granting academic credit for work experience. The work experience was of value itself, as a motivator for further academic work and as a source of student income.

New Institutions of the 1970s

The new institutions of the late 1960s and early 1970s contrast with those of the earlier period in almost every regard. While new public institutions, such as Evergreen State College or Sangamon, rest on a reasonably stable appropriation base, the typical new private institution does not. The latter have been created on the assumption that there was a paying clientele if suitable programs could be developed and if the tuition income were sufficient to keep the institutions going until reserves could be built up from operating surplus, contracts and eventually from private benefaction. Secondly, although some new colleges occupy space created or adapted to serve as the campus (for example, DQU, a former military installation and Navajo Community College, a $15,000,000 new campus), the prevailing style is to occupy limited physical space and to transport programs to where students are. Thus, as will be seen, the graduate programs for Nova University are actually offered anywhere in the country where there are enough students to make it feasible financially. Laurence University (Florida, California, and Washington, D.C.) occupied modest office space and conducted the essentials of its program away from the local campus, and even institutions with a clearly defined base campus stressed an off-campus theme. Illustrative is a description of Portland Community College, which does have a specially designed and constructed campus: "When a dozen women expressed a wish to study French before visiting France, the college set up a course for them in a private home. It rented swimming pools to provide kayak training for 250. At forty sites, including hospitals, homes and jails, it tutored illiterates. To reach the bean and berry pickers, large trailers converted into mobile classrooms visit migrant workers' camps. There they teach basic English, show workers how to fill out a drivers' license application form, and provide other simple but essential bits of information" (Hall and Associates, 1974, p. 187).

Some new publicly supported institutions claim to be moderately selective, as is consistent with state policy, but a careful review of enrollments suggests that such selectivity is more apparent than real. Other public institutions make no pretense of being selective, and, among the new private institutions, especially those catering to minority groups, academic selectivity is rejected as a valid concept. Curricula and instruction typically conform to no perceivable intellectual rationale (although the influence of John Dewey is sometimes strong) but rather seek to conform to student needs as students themselves perceive them. Thus at Evergreen State College students may work on an individual project for a year, work with a small group of students on a project for a year, or work as part of a larger group (in the vicinity of a 100 to 120) with a team of faculty members on a rather complex large-group project. At Fairhaven College, professors list, on the bulletin board, courses they believe will be interesting, and students sign up for the ones they wish. After the class meets, the purposes of the course may change quite radically. Great stress is placed on some variant of a contract, developed by a student and a faculty member, stating what kinds of activities the student will undertake in return for a specified amount of academic credit. There is a Jove-like quality to the claims of the new institutions that whatever students need the institution will provide, either through its own resources or through brokering the contract for the needed services to some reasonably qualified individual or organization.

An analysis of the period from 1958 to 1968 and a contemporary analysis of more recent creations reveal many of the essential differences between the two periods. Mayhew, writing in 1965, after remarking on the need for fast-growing states to create new systems of public higher education, noted that

Some regions, notably the southeast, have sought to upgrade the educational level of their people in order to attract the industry and commerce necessary to ensure a reasonable economic growth. As industry has come to these areas and as they have shifted from a rural to an urban character, the need for new facilities of higher learning became all the more pronounced. New industries have demanded highly skilled workers and technologists, and these individuals in turn have demanded more and better medical, dental, and other professional services; better teachers and schools for their children; and new outlets for their cultural and intellectual interests. Since existing facilities were inadequate and unable to meet these needs, new institutions of higher learning were sorely in demand.

Intellectual forces have, of course, also been of major influence. Thoughtful men and women have been deeply disturbed by the relative impotence of many collegiate institutions. Changing a college or university that had existed without change for a century or more was difficult, if not impossible; the only real hope for improving higher education lay in starting new institutions. The feasibility of creating new institutions and experimental ventures in higher education had been enhanced by developments in the use of new methods, theories, and technology for teaching and learning; it was given impetus by public dissatisfaction with education when Russian technology surged forward in the mid-1950s; and it became a realistic possibility as major philanthropic foundations began to put risk capital into educational innovation.

In addition, several other forces have been operative. Some religious denominations, having seen a number of their institutions evolve into secular schools, sought to resume their role in higher education by establishing new colleges and universities. In some states, new schools were created to give expression to an educational philosophy rooted in a political system of values. In California, for example, the creation of many junior colleges, state colleges, and branches of the state university, is partly the result of the belief of state political leaders that all young people should have an institution of higher education close to their home. Similarly, some new institutions, which were really branches of a mother institution, have been created because of the belief that the values of higher education were being lost through the sheer size and complexity of the original campus. New campuses, or new configurations of older campuses, seemed a way of capturing the essence of the small college campus without losing the power and efficiency of a large organization. And sometimes simple historical accident has been involved, such as when a physical plant suddenly became available.

Without doubt the self-interests of men and of regions have also been involved. Although town and gown have coexisted with considerable tension, a college campus is still an economic asset, and chambers of commerce and businessmen have exerted significant pressure for the establishment of collegiate enterprises. Further, creating a new institution is a powerful ego-stimulus, and thus must be counted as one of the creative forces. And there is in the American character a missionary vein. Creating new institutions is one more way of carrying a particular message of salvation to those who need it [Mayhew, 1965, pp. 3–4].

Note the change in tone and language between that and the remarks of Hall, who premised them on an affirmation of a continuing surge of egalitarianism: "By the end of the 1960s . . . pressure for additional reform was mounting steadily. From almost every direction came recommendations for reform—from individuals, public and private commissions, governmental studies, and reports of higher education associations. It was the era of commissions . . . and their findings included some alarming statistics about the failure of the system to engage and hold its students. According to Newman's report on higher education . . . 'only about one third of those who enter college each year will ever complete a four-year course of study.' The dropout rate for the 'new student' was even more alarming. For example, Martin Mayer, writing in the February 1972 issue of *Commentary* magazine about the open admissions program in New York City, reported that 'Half of those who did enter left during the first two years.' Clearly, if the postsecondary education community is going to carry the egalitarian commitment beyond its doorstep, it must provide a more rewarding educational experience for the new students" (Hall and Associates, 1974, p. xiii–xiv).

Hall also notes that the new colleges can play an important role in providing effective education for new students. "These colleges are willing to stake their future on meeting the needs of a very specialized student clientele. This can be a risky venture, particularly when the college focuses on the 'high-risk' student. However, it opens the opportunity to test new solutions that, if found successful, may be implemented in other settings. In this way, these colleges can be seen as not only important in their own right, but as laboratories for the discovery and examination of the needs of new students and as testing grounds for examination of long-standing assumptions about education" (p. xiv).

Significance of Differences

It is premature to attempt any definitive interpretation of the significance of the differences between institutions created in two different but contiguous times. Yet certain strands do appear that might be advanced as hypotheses. The first of these would take the rhetoric describing or calling for new institutions in the 1970s at face value and would argue that they represent needed efforts at reform. The argument is made that, although the goal of universal access to higher education was approached during the 1960s, that goal was not realized, especially given markedly high attrition rates in some types of institutions and given the fact that existing institutions did not serve important segments of the population. It is also argued that earlier institutions stressed academic values that seemed irrelevant to many people and divorced from their real-life concerns. It is contended that the traditional modes of instruction of lecturing, reading, writing, and discussion were insufficiently potent to produce the educational changes people expected. And it was alleged that the formal structure of typically residential education discriminated against older people, people required to work full-time, and people who had been forced to discontinue their education. The new colleges were intended to correct those abuses.

It is also possible to conceive of the new institutions as representing the inexorable evolution of egalitarian tendencies long present in American society. That egalitarianism was presumably reflected in the Northwest Ordinance reserving public lands for schools, the Morrill Acts of 1862 and 1890 allocating public lands for the support of agricultural and mechanical education, the creation and expansion of community colleges seeking to serve many different segments of the population, and the quest throughout the 1960s to ensure the realization of the doctrine of universal access to higher education. While each of those events accommodated new groups, they still fell short of the ideal, so new institutions frequently designed for new kinds of students appeared as the next logical step. Just as the land-grant colleges served the previously excluded agricultural and industrial classes, so the new colleges served the previously excluded blue-collar working class, economically disadvantaged minorities, and the aging.

At least some of the new institutions appear to have been products of the revolution of colonial peoples in the United States and abroad that began to take place at the end of World War II. In previous colonial areas in Africa and Southeast Asia, an important early step, after the establishment of political independence from the colonial powers, was the modification of educational institutions to be more supportive of a new national or racial consciousness. Collegiate institutions established by colonial powers were modeled after institutions in those countries and frequently offered courses and programs inappropriate for needs of the indigenous people in the colonies. Eric Ashby, commenting on African institutions in the postcolonial period, points out that "There is a desire to see the incorporation into the undergraduate course of material about the indigenous cultures of tropical Africa: its traditional political systems, with their subtle checks and balances; its passionate identification with the soil through religion, customary law, the cultivation of crops, and the care of animals; its philosophies and codes of behavior; its languages; its folklore and music and dance" (Ashby, 1964, p. 60). And he illustrates his point with a policy statement for the university college at Accra, which stated "We must in the development of our university bear in mind that once it had been planted in African soil it must take root amidst African traditions and culture" (p. 61).

Within the United States, that same colonial revolution was taking place as first the blacks and subsequently Native Americans, Chicanos, and Puerto Ricans obtained a measure of political and civil freedom and then sought to develop institutions that could enhance ethnic and racial consciousness. Just as African universities did not reject completely some elements of the Western intellectual tradition, particularly those linked to technological development, so new American colleges designed for minority groups have tried to keep what was essential from the dominant culture but at the same time have tried to stress materials that heighten pride and consciousness of the minority condition and minority history. Thus Nairobi College offers some courses stressing basic intellectual skills but many courses and experiences stressing black nationalism. Similarly DQU and Navajo Community College stress both elements.

In a somewhat more speculative vein, we may consider the possible strand of American antiintellectualism in the creation of many of the newer institutions. Without entering into an extended discussion of intellectualism and intellectuals, we can note certain elements usually found in both. The intellectual makes rigorous use of words and numbers as tools to consider phenomena around him. He is inclined to value contemplation and sophisticated dialectic as he refines his ideas about life. He is inclined to see the necessity for logical and disciplined progression from the simpler to the more complex, and he is inclined to believe that his own ideas should become beacon lights that the rest of the society can follow. He is inclined to believe in the value of elites and considers himself to be one of the most valuable elites. Hofstadter, distinguishing between intellect (which in American society has quite frequently been unpopular) and intelligence (which is rarely criticized), points out the salient characteristics of intellect and thus of the intellectual. "Intellect . . . is the critical, creative, and contemplative side of mind. Whereas intelligence seeks to grasp, manipulate, reorder, adjust, intellect examines, ponders, wonders, theorizes, criticizes, imagines. Intelligence will seize the immediate meaning in a situation and evaluate it. Intellect evaluates evaluations, and looks for the meaning of situations as a whole. Intelligence can be praised as a quality in animals; intellect, being a unique manifestation of human dignity, is both praised and assailed as a quality in men" (Hofstadter, 1966, p. 25).

The orientation and programs of many of the institutions created since 1968 can be interpreted as rejecting intellectualism and intellectuals. Stress is placed on individual learning and on the teacher's role as manager rather than as a stimulator and purveyor of ideas and information. Courses are organized around psychological needs of students rather than following a disciplinary logic. Great value is assigned to experience, even experience quite remote from formal education. Academic work is viewed as a part-time activity, undertaken at the end of the day, with stress placed on achieved competence rather than on broad understanding. Many of the new institutions rely on part-time faculty members, who interact with students only occasionally and whose everyday work role may more typically be that of a practitioner rather than a theoretician.

Such a comparison should not be judged invidious. Intellectuals and intellectualism can be precious, arrogant, intolerant, and almost religious with respect to the intellectual calling. However, the comparison shows that new institutions—presenting a pattern of credit-for-experience, setting one's own day-to-day goals, working on a carefully scheduled sequence of materials and demonstrating mastery of small segments of them, providing infrequent contact with mentors, and basing large parts of an educational program upon quite applied experiences—are different from the prevailing traditions of intellectualism in Western society.

Even more speculative is the suggestion that American higher education, indeed all of American education, can be considered a declining industry. Certainly throughout the remainder of the twentieth century and into twenty-first century, enrollments at all levels are likely to stabilize and then decline in numbers, compared with the earlier 1950s and 1960s. Whether or not American higher education is in reality a declining industry, it is so perceived by many of its leaders and participants. And this perception affects most, if not all, of the developments since 1968, such as interdisciplinary programs to attract students, use of technology to save money, and steady tuition increases. Doubtless this perception is produced by the sudden shift from rapid expansion of clients and resources during the 1960s, when many believed growth could go on forever, to a period of economic depression and a projected loss of public regard and potential clients. Granted the generally shared perception of a declining industry, both individual units (institutions) and the total industry have begun to behave in predictable ways. Generally, when industries begin to decline, they begin to do and experience specific acts and conditions. Leadership begins to age and to lose the joy that comes from expansion. More potential workers are available for the declining number of positions, and the surplus workers hunt for, or try to create positions that are close to or resemble the mainline positions now closed to them. Industrial institutions and all institutions collectively begin frenzied activities to invent new products and to find new clients or to reattract clients who ceased to seek service. As the decline deepens, there comes a widespread distrust of the previously prevailing ideology, accompanied by a search for new beliefs that might recapture the magic of the earlier happier times. Older myths are called into question, frequently on the ground that they failed because they had grown too remote from eternal verities. (See March, 1974.)

Now let us consider the two periods of new institution building. During the late 1950s and most of the 1960s, there was a general sharing of major myths and values. The traditional arts and sciences, or the general education mutation and the traditional professional fields, were regarded as the primary responsibility of institutions, which was discharged in well-understood ways. Growth and improvement of equality were the twin ideals, and leaders could take pride each year that they had moved their institution closer to that ideal. The occasional atypical institution caused no particular concern, because it operated outside the pale of respectability and was in no sense a serious competition. Nor were innovations or practices of those institutions copied, for they were judged unsuitable for the pacesetters of the industry. Institutions that did seek to be different and still respectable had to prove, by using the measurements of orthodoxy, that their graduates were as good as those graduating from orthodox institutions. In general students were satisfied with the services received, partly because the programs led to goals that they valued. Those preparing to enter the industry itself found no reason to question a system that ensured they would receive what they wanted. All in all, it was a happy time.

But then came the indication of decline. Whether the student revolt from 1964 to 1970 should be judged as one such indication is open to question. Quite likely it was a different phenomenon—a historical accident, although many of the episodes suggested language and activities that would be elaborated when decline did set in. But certainly reductions in federal fellowship programs, oversupply of degree holders, loss of public regard, and stabilizing of enrollments all indicated that a new era had been born.

With the new depression in higher education, individual institutions undertook a number of changes that were comparable to the activities of many of the new institutions, thus in aggregate presenting a clear and consistent pattern of behavior in the presence of decline.

Established institutions began short minicourses, of an applied and frequently avocational nature, in order to increase full-time equivalent credit for appropriation purposes. A distinguished private university began to contract with neighboring corporations for in-service training programs and began to encourage part-time older students to return. Another major public university relaxed residence requirements for graduate degrees for teachers, and another established graduate centers in many parts of the country that required in total only eighteen weeks of residence work on the home campus to receive a doctoral degree. Moderately selective private institutions, which had raised entrance requirements during the 1960s, began to lower them, to the point of accepting almost anyone who applied and who had a high school diploma.

At the same time, frequently dissatisfied with their roles in orthodox institutions or unable to find permanent appointments in them, individuals began to create new institutions and to compete, by using similar devices. This is a difficult point to prove, for individuals do not willingly reveal such motivations in themselves, but there are many examples, ranging from an administrator who, after years as a president, found himself in an administrative cul-de-sac, to another person whose recent academic career had included appointments of less than two years at each of five different institutions, each one in succession making use of more and more competitive devices.

The techniques used to become or remain viable included shortening of time required to earn a degree; granting of academic credit for life experience; making use of considerable, relatively unsupervised independent study; taking programs to the students, rather than requiring them to come to a campus; using large numbers of adjunct professors paid a flat, per-capita fee; heavy advertising in mass media of various sorts; and contracting with for-profit institutions to award degrees to their students in return for a proportion of tuition paid. Now each of these techniques can be viewed as a genuine educational innovation of considerable validity for certain kinds of students. But they can also be viewed in economic terms as being activities initiated by declining industries to prevent financial disaster.

Many of the new institutions, especially the private ones, but certainly not excluding the public community colleges and technical institutes, claim as a reason for being the desire to serve segments of the population previously excluded from formal higher education. Thus institutions appeal to children of blue-collar workers, racial and ethnic minority groups, workers who do not have time to attend a full residential program, women wishing to return to school on a part-time basis, dropouts who have earlier experienced persistent academic failure, children growing up in impoverished regions of the country, and people whose talents do not include verbal and quantitative proficiency. Programs could be geared to each of these groups. As we have seen, such modifications of programs can be viewed as a reflections of genuine egalitarianism, as examples of valid needs for educational reform, as links to an underlying anti-intellectualism in American society, as expressions of search for ethnic and racial nationalism on the part of Americans previously occupying a colonial status, or as competitive techniques undertaken by institutions in an industry facing a declining social and economic posture. But they also can, with at least some slight propriety, be viewed as ways of extending the symbols of middle- and upper-middle-class social position to individuals from other segments of the population while still safeguarding the hegemony of the middle and upper-middle classes over positions of preferment and influence. It is possible to interpret the radical rise of public community colleges during the 1960s as performing a similar function. Children from low socioeconomic backgrounds and from ethnic and racial minorities were to be accommodated in public two-year colleges, while children of more affluent backgrounds who possessed requisite verbal and quantitative skills would proceed through four-year institutions and into positions of preferment. It is possible to conceive of many of the recently created institutions as serving essentially the same role. People can achieve degrees and certificates from them, but it is possible to speculate that these credentials will not lead to desired upward social mobility. Given, for example, a potential slight oversupply of practicing lawyers, one can theorize that those who do succeed professionally in the practice of law probably have graduated from established law schools—and the higher the prestige of the school, the greater the positional and economic success of the lawyer. Those who attend the more recently created law schools will, of course, have the satisfaction of having a law degree, but whether or not they will practice law or will engage in legally related activities and whether they will succeed positionally and economically is open to question. There is always the danger, in suggesting such an hypothesis, of also suggesting conspiracy. Evidence does not exist supporting a clear conspiracy of middle- and upper-middle-class people, but evidence does suggest that the educational and employment system in the United States is related to class. Even Panos and Astin, after establishing the lack of relationship between judged quality of an institution and measured achievement of graduates, still reached the conclusion that the specific school attended was related to subsequent positional and economic achievement.

Examples of the New

Two examples illustrate dramatically the changes taking place during the 1970s. Both Nova University and Fairhaven College were planned during the 1960s, according to the then prevailing values. When these proved unproductive, both institutions shifted and tried to conform to the newer ethos.

The elements found in many of the new institutions may be combined in different situations with radically different results. Exactly the same ingredients blended in one way produces a travesty almost bordering on fraud, but in another, a respectable institution.

Nova University. Since the 1960s, Nova University has

gained regional accreditation, some degree of financial security, a loyal alumni, and the support of reasonably distinguished educators throughout the country. It is also a place far different from the design for its original creation.

It was originally to have been the South's counterpart to a Rockefeller University, with perhaps some elements of the Princeton-based Center for Advanced Study. It was to be a well-endowed graduate university in which distinguished scientists and a few students would work on the frontiers of knowledge. Those few students would go on to become the Nobel Prize winners of the next generation and in the process bring long-deserved but mostly denied intellectual glory to the South.

The steps toward this goal seemed easy to take in 1964, when research had become a major doctrine for the university as a secular church. Federal contributions seemed destined to mount exponentially, and private benefaction was helping a few institutions make leaps toward greatness. First a few scholars in the biological and physical sciences would be recruited, together with their grants and advanced students. They would be housed in new facilities located on the site of a former air base, which would become an educational and scientific park—jointly shared by public and private institutions. A mighty fund drive would then be mounted to tap the growing and quite ostentatious wealth of southeast Florida. It was assumed that people of the region would treasure what would become a national intellectual resource and would willingly donate the funds that would endow an elite to work on the problems and questions that interested them. But there was pragmatic reasoning as well. Florida was rapidly industrializing, and the ideas and processes discovered at Nova would fuel the intellectual life of the technology. As funds accumulated, buildings would be constructed to house the laboratories required for sophisticated scientific investigation.

Those dreams were shortlived. Good, but not great scientists were attracted. Federal funds became more difficult to obtain. Local wealth saw scant reason to donate large amounts of money to be used for the few programs, which were educating even fewer advanced students. To keep going, the emphasis shifted more and more to the applied sciences in a few areas for which sustaining contract funding was available; for example, physical oceanography, science education, the production of germ-free animals for sale to laboratories, and some forms of behavior modification. These activities revealed life in the institution, but the annual budget revealed serious deterioration—so serious that by 1970 there was a deficit of $1.2 million and no prospects of a recoup. Clearly a time for decisions had come.

A new president was appointed—one who had earlier come to Nova to create a science education program to educate those who would later appreciate and support the Nova scientific and technological center. A search was undertaken to find new services that the university could offer and for which people would pay money. And an angel appeared, in the form of the president of the (solvent) New York Institute of Technology, which had been brokering a variety of on- and off-campus undergraduate educational services in and around Long Island and the greater New York area. New York Institute of Technology had wanted to expand and link up with a graduate program. Florida seemed ripe, and Nova had a few buildings and a charter to offer graduate work, so an affiliation was arranged. Nova would receive $1.2 million to relieve its budget strain and the funds that would pay for New York Institute of Technology rent in Nova's buildings for twenty years ahead. The president of New York Institute of Technology became chancellor and the president of Nova became vice-chancellor of New York Institute of Technology—a union of the two institutions. Each of the institutions would specialize—New York Institute of Technology in undergraduate education and Nova in graduate programs. New York Institute of Technology people would join Nova's board of trustees.

Financial affairs, calmed for the moment, allowed the quest for a new mission for Nova, which it found in the suddenly popular arena of nontraditional programs designed for people unable or unwilling to pursue degree or credential work in orthodox institutions. Nontraditional programs—as, for that matter, traditional educational programs—must either be subsidized by the state, an endowment, or private benefaction, or else the cost must be paid by those receiving services. Nova was private, had no endowment, and had scant appeal to potential benefactors. Hence it had to find a clientele that could be served at a reasonable cost and that could see enough potential value to be willing to pay that cost. Professional educators seemed to fit the need. Their salaries are based on credentials; the higher the credentials, the higher the salaries. Professionals work in areas that are changing, hence they need to modernize knowledge and skills. They value education and degrees. And their incomes, after the gains of the 1960s, are high enough to allow tuition payment, especially when viewed as an investment.

Two types of educators seemed especially well suited. Junior or community college teachers and administrators typically hold master's degrees. Yet they work in colleges and take pride in that fact. Colleges and universities, however, also require or value the doctoral degree as the appropriate evidence of qualification. Of course, the majority of college faculty members do not hold the doctorate, but it is always recognized as desirable. But junior college people, like other working folk, cannot afford to take the three or four years away from work to pursue an orthodox graduate program. Indeed, many had not completed a doctorate earlier because of their financial need to work. And there was a large pool of potential clients. During the 1960s, junior and community colleges were the most rapidly growing sector in American higher education. A well-developed and publicized program that appealed to junior college educators could have an almost inexhaustible market.

The second group was composed of elementary and secondary school administrators. Their salaries and positions were also related to the amount of advanced training they had received. They also valued education and degrees. In addition, as education has become more complex, they had been told or had sensed the need for administrators to cultivate new skills of management and decision making. If they could develop those skills while remaining on the job, they could be interested in enrolling in a degree program.

To cultivate these two groups, a concept of off-campus, degree-oriented education was developed that met many objections raised to other nontraditional efforts. Two programs were created—one for junior college educators and one for elementary and secondary school educators. To enter either program, applicants had to have earned a master's degree and be fully employed in a relevant institution or service. Thus initial placement was not a program goal. Rather, the goal was career advancement and promotion.

The degree to be offered was the Ed.D. degree, conceived of as a practical degree designed to improve job skills. The foremost American advanced degree is the Ph.D., and, while it reflects varying levels of quality, it is theoretically a research degree, and candidates for it are expected to make original contributions to knowledge. Not only were school administrators and junior college faculty members not interested in making original contributions to knowledge but a doctoral degree-granting institution that did not offer the Ph.D. degree also was not vulnerable to charges from traditional institutions that an off-campus program was cheapening the Ph.D. degree. It should be noted that Nova has and does offer residential Ph.D. programs in the sciences.

Clearly the educational program had to be taken to where potential students were, and equally clearly students had to be located in many parts of the country if an adequate enrollment were to be developed and maintained. Southeast Florida, although possessed of a large educational industry, could not provide the needed volume. But an educational program could not be taken to a single student or to quite small groups of students. The cost of sending instructors, of supervision, and of providing materials required that reasonably large groups be serviced as a unit. This led to the concept of clusters or centers located in many different locations. A group of thirty to fifty people in one general location could be brought together for group instruction or for counseling and guidance, and someone living in the region could provide some continuing supervision and could attend to organizational details.

Now, instructional costs in colleges and universities are high and are growing higher, for several reasons. Faculty members are expected to do many other things besides teach, and their salaries are expected to reflect that requirement. Full-time faculty members require expensive staff benefits and increasingly are placed on permanent tenure. An institution that has a high proportion of its faculty on tenure but that finds the demand for its programs eroding finds itself in a precarious financial situation. A private institution lacking endowment and charging tuitions that will attract students simply cannot afford to maintain a full-time, high-quality staff. It has several options: (1) employ a low-cost, low-quality faculty; (2) employ only a few faculty members and expect that students will be responsible for much of their own education (not unlike other self-service industries); or (3) employ part-time faculty members and pay them only for those specific instructional services covered by tuition. Nova opted for a combination of part-time faculty recruited for the most part from established and orthodox institutions and for placing considerable reliance on individual work on the part of the students. Since the primary employer of the part-time faculty takes care of fringe benefits, retirement, and the like, Nova is able to pay part-time faculty members respectable retainers and fees and still generate surplus funds—always assuming, of course, that numbers of students is large enough.

Formal graduate education requires books, clinical settings, and laboratories. These are typically found on a campus and can be used by residential students. However, an off-campus program cannot have those facilities, hence it must contrive some other arrangements. Once again, several alternatives are open. Students may be expected to use libraries of other nearby institutions. They may be expected to buy all of the books they need, or the institution can provide small amounts of materials for individuals and for the various groups. Nova has solved the problem by supplying some materials as part of the services for which tuition is paid. It also urges students to use libraries located near them, and it asks students to purchase some things themselves. The need for clinical settings is met by asking students to undertake practica and activities in the institution in which they are employed.

By the fall of 1975, Nova University had changed substantially from the original conception, although elements of that conception remained and caused some financial difficulties. Its physical plant is located on a 200-acre main campus and consists of six multipurpose buildings. One building houses the university school; another houses life sciences, law, a print shop, and offices for several other programs; another is the central administrative building; and still another is a complex of three buildings devoted to student apartments. A building off the main campus is the center for the oceanographic program. The remaining structure consists of recreational facilities (swimming and tennis). Assuming that programs evolve as planned, the only other building planned for the immediate future will be a home for the law school.

The principal programs reveal much about what Nova has become. Reflecting something of the original intent are three centers that stress graduate programs for a limited number of doctoral and master's candidates. These are the Behavioral Science Center, Life Science Center, and the Oceanographic Center. The emphasis of the Behavioral Science Center is on human development, child-centered education, and international planning. The various programs offered are reasonably orthodox, taught for the most part by full-time faculty, and at the doctoral level consist of full-time residential students. Master's programs may be either for full- or part-time students and are designed to produce people needed in various professions in southeast Florida. Support for this center comes from tuition, university funds, and contract research such as studies of the design features of swimming pools (made for the U.S. Consumer Products Safety Commission).

The Life Sciences Center is supported by two major contract research or service activities, the first of which is the breeding of germ-free laboratory animals and the second of which is research on tumor immunology. Teaching is limited to a few doctoral students, but there is hope that master's programs can eventually be created and that the entire center will have a major focus that will integrate a number of disparate programs and activities.

The Oceanographic Center also relies on grants and contract funding (largely from National Science Foundation and the Office of Naval Research) and concentrates on physical oceanography, particularly related to the Gulf Stream and waters around Florida. It usually maintains four to six residential Ph.D. candidates. Although the center does not plan extensive expansion, some growth in graduate enrollment is hoped for.

The relative significance of these centers in the total educational effort of Nova University is revealed by the distribution of enrollment in the fall of academic year 1975–76. There were somewhat in excess of 4,000 enrollments, of which 3,400 were enrolled in off-campus graduate programs, in a new law school, as elementary and secondary school students in the university school, and as weekend students enrolled in programs offered by the New York Institute of Technology. The remaining 600 or so were scattered between residential and part-time master's program students in such things as criminal justice and business administration and the three centers in the small doctoral programs.

That same balance is evident in the income side of the budget. The off-campus graduate programs generate the largest income and yield surpluses that help support the rest of the university. The university school generates enough income to support itself, with some occasional surplus. The law school, once the initial expenditure for a law library and rennovated space is paid for, will generate its own support and return a proportion of its income to the university itself. The on-campus graduate programs are underwritten by the university and, through contract research and the other programs, are variously self-supporting or are operated at slight deficits.

In more traditional private institutions, tuition, endowment, gifts, overhead charged on contracts, and profits from services produce the income on which the institution operates; the tuition from lower-division undergraduate students produces a surplus of income used to underwrite upper-division and graduate programs. Nova operates on funds derived from tuition, overhead on contracts, modest philanthropy, and even more modest income from services; the tuition from the off-campus doctoral programs (and eventually the law school) underwrites the other parts of the educational program and the central administration of the university.

Although Nova was created in the mid-1960s, it qualified for inclusion in this book because the essential parts of its program (defined as supporting the institution) were created in the 1970s. These essential components can partially reveal how nontraditional programs operate.

The first of these components was the last created and may be quickly described. Nova created a law school in 1974 as a daytime law school organized in traditional ways to produce practicing lawyers. It is one among forty or fifty new law schools created in the 1970s to serve the increased numbers of potential students who saw the law as one of the few professional areas in which demand for graduates exceeded supply. Since established law schools were able to fill all available spaces, new schools had to be created if the demand were to be satisfied.

The Nova Law School was created to serve Florida, which

had only four other law schools, and was intended to establish itself as a traditional law school before it considered any kinds of nontraditional programs. And it developed according to plan. A full-time faculty was recruited, space was ensured in an existing building remodeled to accommodate legal education, and a library was established. The first and second classes were easily filled with good, average candidates, and the program was put into operation. As of 1975 no class had been graduated, and no graduates had taken the bar examination. However, early observation by the American Bar Association, which awarded professional approval in August of 1975, predicted that the school would quickly become a solid, reputable one. Whether it will develop specific excellence in some fields is a question the future must answer.

The group of off-campus doctoral programs provide the life blood for Nova and give the institution a distinctiveness as a nontraditional but valid educational institution. There are three such programs, quite similar in broad outline and approach but differing from each other in detail. All are off-campus programs, serving groups of students in many parts of the country, with an adjunct faculty, carefully organized sets of materials, and carefully structured clinical or scholarly projects. All insist that accepted applicants have a job relevant to the program and have at least a master's degree. All are designed so that students can continue to work and to make use of their work situation as an essential part of their academic program. All are coordinated by a full-time administration and staff, who recruit students, maintain quality control, maintain records, and certify individuals who have completed degree requirements.

The first prototypic program was designed to upgrade elementary and secondary school administrators. Students are organized into thirty-two clusters located in different parts of the country. Each cluster has a coordinator who attends to scheduling and logistical matters and practicum supervisors who oversee the several projects each student must complete before graduation. The face-to-face instruction is done by national lecturers who, over a three-year period of time, will spend an evening and a day with each of the thirty-two clusters and who prepare or assign text material and grade students' achievement on assigned exercises or examinations. Each national lecturer is presumably a specialist in one field, such as evaluation or decision science, and is responsible for seeing that students master the essentials of that specialization. Students are expected to prepare to undertake both minor and major projects related to their jobs and, once approval of a proposal is given, to complete the project and write a solid report about it. These reports are graded by full-time staff located on the home campus. When reports have finally been accepted, that fact is recorded on the students' record, and the document is entered into the university collection. As a means of giving students a national outlook regarding educational problems, each is required to attend two eight-day summer institutes, held in Florida, that present local leaders as well as national figures concerned with educational administration. The entire program requires three years of completely prescribed activities, and no allowance is given for academic credit gained elsewhere. Early experience indicates that about 50 percent of those who start as a student in a cluster drop out before receiving a degree. Of those who do complete the requirements, most value the program highly and believe the program fills their needs exactly. The only degree awarded is the Ed.D. degree.

The second program to be put into operation is one organized for people working in junior or community colleges. Admissions requirements are comparable to the program in educational administration, that is, a job and a master's degree. Each student in the thirty to thirty-five clusters operating at the same time is assigned to an advisory committee consisting of some local individual possessing an earned doctorate and a member of the central staff located in Florida. Each cluster is assigned a local coordinator who supervises logistical and organizational arrangements. Then there is a cadre of lecturers who meet with each cluster and who are responsible for text materials and for evaluating the students' written performance. Students are all required to complete six projects during the program, one concerned with each of the substantive divisions of the curriculum, and to prepare full, written reports, which are graded both by the local committee member and a member of the central staff. Students in this program are also required to attend a summer institute staffed in part by the senior lecturers and in part by distinguished junior or community college educators.

The most recently created program is one in public administration, and in some respects it is the most traditional of the three. As is true of the others, clusters of approximately thirty people are matriculated into the program, which consists of a twenty-seven-month sequence of activities. Each month the cluster begins a new unit of work, which is introduced by an outside expert called the *preceptor*. He assigns the readings and the unit outline and distributes the books, which are furnished by Nova as part of the tuition fee. Thereafter the students meet in the smaller groups called *subclusters*, which discuss the assigned materials and work. The preceptor, in addition, is required to evaluate student completion of assignments and to assign definite grades, as well as to make evaluative comments that are made available to students. The public administration program requires something more akin to an orthodox thesis, called a *job-related analytical report*. This focuses on some reasonably complex issue and requires the student to apply traditional tools of analysis applied in preparing (in other institutions this report would be called an *applied dissertation*, requiring the student to conceptualize an applied problem and to bring relevant theory and evidence to bear on its solution). As in more orthodox programs, oral examinations are held on the substance of the entire program and the project report.

Such brief descriptions of what are really quite complex curricular arrangements do not do justice to the undertaking. Perhaps greater understanding may be obtained by presenting some impressionist judgments of the essential elements of the program.

The central staff members for each of the three programs are experienced in the relevant activities and have enough staff support to keep track of students, to make judgments of their work, and to coordinate the activities of the various off-campus faculty who must make the program work. The senior off-campus adjunct professors are for the most part reasonably well known; hold appointments in strong, relevant, academic departments, and apparently take their jobs quite seriously. Their associates are typically local practitioners who are available and whose positions make supervision of graduate students in an applied situation quite appropriate. The resource people on the programs of summer institutes appear to be better known, as a rule, than one would expect to find in other sorts of summer workshops.

Admission of students, while deviating somewhat from orthodox use of text scores, academic records, and the like, nonetheless has a defensible rationale. It is assumed that possession of a master's degree and a full-time professional position is indicative of the candidate's ability to do the sort of work the programs require. For the most part, the leaders of the three programs are satisfied with their approach, although they do wish they could predict dropouts, for the 50 percent attrition rate bothers them somewhat.

Once students have been admitted, the record keeping seems remarkably effective, considering that new clusters are added at any time during the year and that hence there are people graduating at any time of the year. The individuals responsible for processing student work not only maintain records but also as individuals manifest a remarkable memory of the status of individual students. Should any of the programs grow much larger, of course, there is the possibility that the system might break down. But the records for the approximately 700 students in each program are about as good as those found in traditional institutions and considerably better than found in some.

The level of course outlines and text materials is reasonably appropriate, although the extensive bibliographies used in some doctoral programs are either edited collections, specially written materials, or assigned materials available from commercial publishers. They seem likely to present the conventional wisdom about a number of matters but not a comprehensive view of a total literature for a field. The documents provided by the programs are well printed or reproduced and are in such form as to be quite useful for students. Examination of the materials provides the distinct impression that they will provide users with a limited but workable knowledge of a subject, which may be quite appropriate for administrators but which would be inadequate for an aspiring scholar.

The quality of teaching of the adjunct professors is no easier to judge in a nontraditional program than it is in a traditional one. Central staff contends it can judge from spontaneous correspondence of students whether adjunct professors are functioning effectively. However, this might be doubted, just as one might doubt that an on-campus dean can have any clear insight as to the teaching effectiveness of his faculty members.

The formal reports of student projects appear adequate for the purposes they serve. A few seem clearly of dissertation quality, and a great many appear to be effective reports or working papers. A substantial number are accepted by two ERIC Clearinghouses, and some have been judged to be of direct practical significance for the institution in which the work was done.

Apparently graduation requirements are clearly stated, and students are forced to complete them in a reasonable time or drop out of the program. There is systematic evaluation of written work, and students are given copies of assessments to help their further improvement.

Nova University was granted the standard ten-year accreditation by the Southern Association in the fall of 1975, which in effect validates some of the preceding judgments. It is, however, still too early to determine what the long-term future for Nova University is likely to be. Much depends on the resolution of some problems and critical issues.

The proposed budget for the academic year 1975–76 is balanced, although there is still an accumulated operating deficit and a cash flow problem that has forced some vendors to threaten to curtail service. Debt on parts of the physical plant (apartments) can be retired out of revenues. But debt on the purely academic or administrative facilities is being relieved out of operating funds derived chiefly from tuition. This is always a dangerous practice but is especially so here, since Nova has no reserves and no endowment and since a modest lowering of enrollments could put the entire institution into a precarious financial situation.

The viability of the small doctoral programs in the social and natural sciences is another problem. They represent something of Nova's original plan, but they also represent a drain on the rest of the institution. Further, what external funding there is for the work on those areas is contract research, hence is subject to the uncertainties of federal and private research policy. An additional matter is the few students in each area generally work in isolation from each other. This certainly departs from the ideal of graduate education in a university setting, which allows interaction between people in many different and unrelated fields.

The off-campus doctoral programs seem to have uncovered a

market of people who want an advanced degree and are willing to pay a tuition for the training offered. But there is probably an upper limit to the amount of tuition charged, and tuition must continue to rise if the kinds of services provided are to be continued. There was some evidence that a small increase in tuition in 1975 did result in a smaller applicant pool. An unfortunate choice may thus present itself: As costs of services, including travel, continue to increase, the choice could well be to increase tuition and possibly to decrease enrollments, or to maintain level tuition and to reduce quality of service.

A many-faceted issue is the use of adjunct professors in the central teaching roles. Can a professor employed full-time in one institution have the time or energy to teach large numbers of other students, prepare text materials, counsel with students, and grade their work? In the educational administration program, for example, the minimum load for an adjunct professor requires spending a full day with each of thirty-two clusters over a three-year period, grading rather extensive papers, selecting and supervising other adjunct faculty, and editing or writing text materials and course outlines. Another question is the use of adjunct professors in a program that could be in direct competition to the department in which the adjunct professor holds a regular appointment; for example, a professor in junior college administration may serve as adjunct professor in the Nova program that caters to junior college administrators. Is there a serious conflict of interest here? Or still another question—it is assumed that an essential of graduate education is the constant interaction between mentor and student: Can this be attained in one or two days of seminar work over a three-year period?

A related issue lies at the heart of much of nontraditional education. Traditional images of higher education assign to it a tranquil quality that allows for leisurely exploration of complex ideas and the opportunity to examine related matters as they arise. This is quite different from the Nova off-campus programs, which are, on the surface, quite precise and mechanistic. A decision is made as to which knowledge is of most worth, and then this is presented in the most efficient way possible. A specific number of lessons is devoted to one subject; then the student moves on to the next.

It could probably be demonstrated that such an approach is just as effective as is the more traditional and potentially deeper kind of graduate education for average students. But should the failure to achieve an ideal be justification for programs that do no worse?

To the extent that the off-campus programs at Nova University can be judged reasonably effective—and they can—they are so because of close attention to several critical details.

1. There is a sufficiently large and expert administrative staff to attend to the substantial organizational, logistical, and quality control problems. Nontraditional programs begin to attract suspicion when those matters are left undone or are accomplished in shady ways.
2. Adjunct professors are selected because of their relevant knowledge and reputation and not because of geographic proximity to a group of students. It is very easy for an institution to cut down on travel expenses and to settle for a mentor of less quality just because of proximity.
3. The institution makes serious effort to evaluate its program and has created devices to use evaluation evidence as a basis for program modification. With Ford Foundation support, Nova is making an elaborate study of its students and graduates, not only as a means of improving the Nova program but also as a means of helping other institutions attempting similar efforts.
4. Nova has refrained from trying to offer the Ph.D., thus making its relations with sister institutions and with regional accreditation considerably easier.

Fairhaven College. Like Nova University, Fairhaven College resembles only slightly the design according to which it was created. It was organized to be a cluster college of Western Washington State College and was approved in 1967, at a time when the cluster or experimental college movement was peaking. Michigan State University, the University of Michigan, the University of the Pacific, and the University of California had all created widely-publicized residential colleges within colleges. The Fairhaven design was for a campus adjacent to the main campus, which would consist of twelve 50-person residence halls to accommodate no more than 600 students. It was to be the first of an eventual galaxy of cluster colleges through which Western Washington could grow but still ensure an intensely personal kind of education. The curriculum was to be largely prescribed and intellectually demanding. It would focus on certain great periods of civilization and would especially stress the great books of the Western intellectual tradition. It would also be highly selective, attracting the more intellectually able students who applied to Western Washington State College.

But events made those plans obsolete. The late 1960s saw a decline in student desire to live in campus residence halls; instead they preferred to find off-campus housing, free of university restraints. By 1970 the anticipated continued admissions pressures had disappeared, and institutions began to court students to entice them to enroll. And students found the prescribed liberal arts curriculum singularly unattractive. Thus Fairhaven had to change if it was to fill its residence halls and receive its share of state appropriations, which were based on a formula of linking level of support to enrollment. If students wanted diverse living styles, the various residence units could be modified to provide them. If students wanted greater freedom of curricular choice, that could be authorized. And if students wanted greater relevance of academic work to the real world, that also was possible.

What has evolved is a patchwork sort of curriculum, its parts being related through a common concern for great individual latitude to do whatever was most congenial to their interests and moods. The educational credo is a direct continuation of the collegiate expression of the progressive education movement, which stressed that there should be a different curriculum for each student. The college exists in uneasy tension with its parent university but is orthodox enough that it can be tolerated, even with its disdain for formal structures and with its students' counterculture life-styles.

Fairhaven grants its own degrees but insists that all graduates present at least fifty semester hours of credit taken at another institution—typically Western Washington State College or one of the public junior colleges. This satisfies the parent institution as to some degree of academic quality and provides enrollments for Western Washington courses. The chief Fairhaven curriculum is a requirement of at least fifty semester hours in a concentration—which can be met through formal courses, independent study, work, or travel. A mix of these comprises the typical program. The specifics of the program for any given student are worked out with a chief adviser and an advising committee. At the end of the program, evaluation as to accomplishment is made by the same individuals, and anecdotal evidence is made available by faculty members who have had the student in classes.

The actual courses taught by the twenty members of Fairhaven faculty represent a mixture of fairly orthodox courses and the quite atypical offerings. Thus the courses offered in the fall of 1974 included "Introduction to Social Structures" on the one hand and "The Body: Awareness Through Movement" on the other. During the winter term, students could elect to take a seminar in social history or a course called "T'ai Chi (Long Form)," which introduces Chinese exercises to relax the body. The curriculum can be augmented or changed when professors list a new course on the bulletin boards and invite interested students to register for it.

Since each program is designed for an individual student, it is difficult to generalize, but the flavor of the concentration can be inferred through considering several examples. One student concentrated on international ethnic relations and took eight courses in history, as well as considerable independent study. He then spent a year off-campus studying the white treatment of the Nisqually Indians, a full summer doing manuscript research, followed by a year attempting to write a narrative based on his field and documents research. A second student spent the first year taking regular courses. During the second year, she organized a political collective in Seattle and then lived for a time in a Mexican orphanage. Her third year was divided between on-campus academic work and visits to Mexico. Her fourth year will also likely be a mixture of on-campus work and travel and reflection.

The other elements of the Fairhaven system are at once outgrowths of the concentration system and a means of perpetuating it. Two residence halls have been converted into cooperative houses, which enable students to reduce expenses and provide the loci for various sorts of work experience that can be fitted into a program plan. For example, serving as purchaser for a cooperative would provide a service and also be part of a formal academic program.

A second unit is a small organic farm, located on campus, which provides food and income and life experiences relevant to the curriculum. A third unit is a Center for Urban Studies, located in Seattle, which provides a variety of services for people in Seattle; for example, students may work in a Free Medical Clinic or in the Emergency Center for Seattle Public Schools. It also enables students to study and reflect on urban problems and to gain academic credit for doing so.

Students have also initiated a program called Vocations for Social Change as a clearinghouse for job and travel opportunities. This helps students explore career possibilities, provides a job placement service, and is an opportunity for students to serve as counselors and tutors.

Three other units complete the institutional profile. The first accepts junior college graduates in technical fields, allows them to organize a concentration, and graduates them with a bachelor's degree. The difference between this and the traditional mode is that the concentration is intended to be the liberalizing portion of the curriculum; specialized vocational work is done first, in a junior college. This mode cares for a group of students who in the past have been overlooked by four-year institutions because the junior college technical programs did not meet first- and second-year requirements for relevant university professional fields.

Then there is the Bridges project. A residence hall has been converted into small apartments rented to older citizens, who can then audit courses or take them for credit. The economic motive, of course, is utilization of previously unused space. The service motive is to assist senior citizens, and the educational motive is to help older and younger campus residents to understand each other better. This activity has attracted more than fifty individuals and, according to testimony, has achieved all three of the chief objectives set for it.

A program to interest women in the expressive arts, begun in 1975, is still too new to tell whether it will work. This can be either a degree-credit or noncredit activity. It is based on the idea that women as culture bearers are interested in the arts and would like to develop or strengthen competency in some one or several of these.

The following list indicates these and other nonclassroom learning opportunities. It is included to indicate the scope and diversity of the activities of the college.

Fairhaven Interdisciplinary
   Concentration
Travel-Study Program
Outback Program
Photography Program
Woodworking Program
Jewelry Program
Middle-Age Program
College-Wide Festivals and Fairs
Theatre Program
Dance Program
Governance Procedures
Outdoor Recreational Program
Book Reading Program for
   Faculty
Nooksack Tutoring Program
Educational Conferences
Art Dorm
New Students' Retreats

Vocations for Social Change
Program of Study at
   Other Universities
Student-led Courses
Textile Program
Pottery Program
Child-Care Center
Bridge Project
Co-op Dorm
Film Series
New Student Curricular
   Program
Seattle Urban Center
Team-taught Courses
Student Music Groups
Student Publications (News and
   Literary)
Language Dorm
Special Graduation Ceremonies
Community Pot Luck Dinners

The faculty of Fairhaven is a relatively young one; about half its members possess an earned doctorate. Members differ from each other with respect to educational philosophy, life-style, and the like, but most seem quite content in an ambiguous, flexible, educational program. Students, according to testimony of the registrar, rank slightly higher than the median Western Washington State College students on measures of academic aptitude. However, they differ substantially with respect to life-style and educational needs. They opted for Fairhaven because they disliked structure and program rigidity and preferred to set their own goals and educational programs.

The discussion thus far presents an image of a quite nontraditional program, and the general appearance of the campus, students, faculty, and a description of learning opportunities supports that image. However, below the surface Fairhaven is considerably more conventional. The majority of students take an orthodox major rather than the interdisciplinary concentration. Most of the course work for those majors is done on the main Western Washington campus. A survey of 136 recent graduates underscores this point: Forty-eight were employed, with seventeen of those teaching; Forty-one were in graduate or professional schools; Twelve were traveling; Twenty-five were seeking jobs; and for ten no information was available.

The college receives its atmosphere of distinctiveness from the various pieces of literature, which use considerable hyperbole to describe the learning environment, and from the dedication of those who make use of the newer learning situations of the nontraditional approach. Indicative of this atmosphere is the following discussion of the Fairhaven plan, as presented in the "Plan of Fairhaven College," prepared during the academic year 1974–75.

By design, in compliance with our charter, the curricular core of Fairhaven continues to remain in a state of flux, a curriculum-process: The spirit of educational adventure pervades not only our formal requirements and the courses supporting them but also the entire atmosphere of the institution. At the philosophical and functional center of the operation of this curriculum lies the close formal and informal contact between students and faculty.

Although the faculty-student ratio at Fairhaven is not higher than that for the institution as a whole, our faculty spend far greater amounts of their time in contact with their students . . . in classes, informally, and in a wide range of learning and enrichment activities outlined below. Such contact is, we feel, a good in itself, a positive attempt to combat collegiate depersonalization by offering the faculty as accessible learning-role models for our students. Close contact between students and faculty was, of course, central to the conception of Fairhaven outlined in our founding document.

But, equally important, this close and continuing contact between students and their faculty is the essential enabling condition of Fairhaven's curriculum-process, for it forms the flexible, *meaningful* link which can serve to unite all of the student's educational experiences into a relatively coherent whole. Close interaction between students and faculty becomes the means by which the diverse inputs of classwork as well as the rich ambience of special programs and alternative learning styles can be intelligently integrated, individually for each student.

Such interaction typically begins with a new student's arrival on campus. Since 1971 all new Fairhaven students have been invited to a two-day retreat to meet informally with the faculty and staff, some returning students, and with each other, to discuss plans and dreams, gain firsthand information about courses and the professors teaching them, and become generally oriented to Fairhaven and the way it operates. Informal discussion about areas of interest lead naturally into ideas for courses; students are introduced to faculty persons and returning students who share their personal and academic interests. New students meet for the first time with their faculty advisors and, after a day's chance to get acquainted, register directly with the faculty persons teaching the courses they want. Thus, bureaucratic means to advise students, channel them into appropriate courses, and get them registered are largely superseded by more relaxed and meaningful personal interaction.

The retreat thus sets a style of student-faculty relations which will continue as long as the student is at the college, and frequently for a long time after: Many of our graduates periodically return to visit, to ask advice, even to offer classes. Contact is not only close, it is continuous, for it typically is not confined to a single class, nor to the classroom at all, but extends into long impromptu discussions, committee work, social events, theater, and so on: Students and faculty work together in almost all the programs. . . . And as such interaction is not confined in type or place, so it is extended in time. Students can be *known* at Fairhaven; they can have an identity in the community, and often faculty and staff persons are heard to comment on a particular student's progress as of a mutual friend.

Because staff persons share this on-going, close relationship with faculty and students, a good deal of administrative flexibility is possible, and bureaucratic impersonality is minimized. Upon admission, students just out of high school are sometimes encouraged to take a year off from school to work, travel, and broaden themselves, prior to entering Fairhaven. Students for whom study has staled or students who discover opportunities for enrichment outside of school are encouraged to take a leave of absence, in consultation with their advisor, for any length of time, with assured readmission. Far from viewing such leaves of absence as problems, Fairhaven sees moderate use of leaves as healthy; returning students inevitably are more interested and interesting.

At the core of faculty-student contact at Fairhaven is, of course, the learning process itself, centered on classes and the curriculum. The curriculum of Fairhaven has undergone virtually continuous change since the beginnings of the college. Initially the humanities, the arts, and the social and natural sciences were organized around major historical periods in Western civilization. Student and faculty interest in a wider range of special topics then fostered the development of courses within the . . . area requirements, at first supplementing and then replacing the original rigid historical treatment. From a series of required courses, the curriculum has now moved to a new "project approach" to general education requirements. . . . This flexibility has permitted maximum opportunity for faculty to pursue those areas where their own intellectual interest and enthusiasm was greatest at the time. No longer required to teach repetitively a fixed set of material, the faculty member became free to serve as a model explorer of the frontiers of his or her own areas of knowledge and to convey the natural excitement of this exploration directly to the student. In addition, the project approach to general education enables students to work more closely with individual faculty persons in constructing and evaluating a coherently interrelated series of learning experiences.

Beside offering courses developed directly by faculty both singly and in team-teaching situations in response to their own intellectual needs and those of the students, Fairhaven provides the opportunity for student- and staff-led seminars under the guidance and tutelage of a faculty member. Some of the most exciting learning at the college occurs in the various formats where advanced students and staff people learn the skills of organizing and directing the intellectual activities of an interested group of student investigators. The results of these programs overwhelmingly support the old adage that "the best way to learn is to teach." Administrative flexibility again permits such interest groups to develop and grow as they arise: A class, seminar, or group independent study may begin and end for reasons of involvement and interest rather than as a slave to the calendar. Credit is awarded in proportion to effort and achievement rather than for blocks of time expended.

Fairhaven faculty have tried a variety of formats for the education of students in groups, classes innovative both in technique and content. Occasionally a large-lecture format is chosen by someone skilled and comfortable in this medium. More often a small class size permits a combination of lecture with discussion and an approach to the personalized style of learning which ideally characterizes the college.

Small classes permit the instructor to tailor the material presented to the individual needs, abilities, and backgrounds of the students and to have immediate feedback from them. This important feedback needs constant attention from all parties to maintain its effectiveness. In place of grades, each student receives a written evaluation from the faculty, stressing both strong and weak points of the student's performance and potential. These evaluations, along with the student's evaluation of his or her own performance and the value of the class itself, become part of the permanent record, the student's portfolio, filed with the Fairhaven registrar.

The small class size encourages participation by students in the active intellectual work of the group. To varying degrees students select independent research work apart from central readings shared by the class; thus each can come to feel the excitement and intellectual responsibility of being the local "expert" in some area of concern. Independent study within and outside the class format is one of the primary educational values stressed at Fairhaven. It was recognized early in the history of the college that only through emphasis on such techniques of self-motivation could students be properly prepared to continue their education throughout life.

Classes of this sort demand that students take an active part in their education; in classes, as in independent study at Fairhaven, students are encouraged to be self-directed learners. Many, coming from more passive learning situations, find this difficult. For this reason, various new student programs have been developed, aimed at developing confidence in the kind of skills needed for study at Fairhaven. Through close work with one or more faculty persons, and with a small support group of fellow new students, students work to enunciate personal educational goals and ask the questions and find the answers necessary to pursue those goals. They work on how to gain access to knowledge through research techniques, efficient use of the library, reading and note-taking skills, and they learn how better to communicate knowledge through teaching techniques, informal and analytical writing. Such skills are especially useful when a student elects to pursue a piece of independent study.

Basic to Fairhaven is the realization that learning is not and cannot be confined to the classroom. For this reason, Fairhaven makes provision to counsel, evaluate, and certify as creditable learning experiences a wide range of activities under the independent study program. Through close consultation with one or more faculty members, a student will draw up a plan of study, listing objectives, questions, and

anticipated resources, and will develop a reasonable process for evaluation. The range of learning activities coordinated through the ISP
[Independent Study Program] Programs is quite broad. Students may
do a piece of intensive research or creative activity on campus; they
may offer classes themselves; they may, through the Vocations for
Social Change office, engage in work experience with various agencies
in a myriad of different contexts; they may study at other institutions,
take on apprenticeships, travel, and study in other lands. What is
stressed is that the student make coherent sense out of his or her
learning experience and be able to communicate in some meaningful
way what was learned.

The need for the students themselves to pull their learning together into a meaningful whole is also the basis for Fairhaven's general
education program. Rather than base general education requirements
on credit hours accrued in general areas, Fairhaven asks that students
demonstrate competency in each of three areas—sciences, social science,
and humanities—through a project initiated in consultation with two
faculty members in that field and presented for evaluation to them
when completed. A fourth project, in the area of the student's choice,
and presumably in the area of the student's greatest interest, completes
the general education requirements at Fairhaven.

By the time of his or her last general education project, the
students generally have some firm idea of what field or area of inquiry
most meaningfully focuses their interests. Fairhaven students either
pursue majors in the College or Arts and Sciences or other cluster
colleges; or, if they find that their interests are not covered, in majors
officially offered; or, if their inquiries cross disciplinary lines, they
construct, in consultation with three faculty members, an interdisciplinary concentration of their own. Increasing numbers of Fairhaven
students have elected to undertake the difficult process of constructing
their own concentration, aided as they are by a new student program,
in refining the process of exploring their own interests, developing
educational goals and techniques for reaching those goals, and making
coherent sense out of their learning experiences.

A discussion of several other problems or elements of the program may augment this description of Fairhaven. Students new to
cooperative residence halls require considerable time before they
fully understand and can participate in group decision making. For
example, how to provide for a few vegetarians living in a co-op

house proved to be especially difficult for young students to decide. The lack of structure does require a great deal of faculty advising, which uses time that might have been devoted to research and scholarship. But since the faculty considers itself to be a teaching faculty, this is not a particularly vexing issue. Much more troublesome is the formal group evaluation of each student that is supposed to take place but that for the most part does not. Thus evaluation of students devolves on the student's adviser, and those judgments are for the most part not monitored. A similar lack of a monitoring mechanism is found with respect to the amount of academic credit that should be awarded for life experiences. This is the responsibility of the registrar—who uses no generally accepted criteria, however, for making those judgments. Since the essence of the Fairhaven program is flexibility, which does place unusual demands on people, there is constant temptation to make the procedures and processes more formal, thus easing the time demands made on faculty and students.

Conclusion

These two institutions almost epitomize the major changes of the 1970s. The mythology of academic purity and elite, meritocratic purpose gave way in each to the applied, the affective, and the egalitarian. The primacy of the campus yielded to the growing significance of off-campus activities. Reliance on a resident faculty was replaced with widespread use of adjunct professors and educational use of nonacademic people and agencies. The notion that education is gregarious and facilitated by interaction through discussion, while not rejected, was modified to accommodate a great deal of individual solitary effort. And both the public and the private examples underscored the importance of tuition or FTE appropriations by discarding hopes that external support could allow small groups of faculty and students to pursue their own esoteric interests. The ivory tower clearly yielded to the marketplace. The future of each may well rest on how firm is the market each has selected to serve.

FOUR

♀♀♀♀♀♀♀♀♀♀♀♀♀♀♀♀

Curriculum
and Instruction

By far the most characteristic developments during the 1970s were the new kinds of institutions and the nontraditional movement. But there were other educational developments that should be noted and assessed.

Curricular Developments of the 1950s and 1960s

During the expansionist period of the 1960s, a variety of curricular and instructional innovations were attempted, mostly linked intellectually to the ethos of the 1940s, 1950s, and 1960s. These efforts have been summarized many times by many different writers, and so no extensive elaboration is necessary here, except to suggest intellectual lineage. Changes in academic calendars originally became popular in the early 1960s as an economic technique. The University of Pittsburgh first adopted the trimester system to increase space utilization. The states of Florida and California attempted to modify calendars in all public institutions, for a similar reason. Other reasons for calendar modification subsequently were advanced, as in the case of a modular curriculum at Colorado College, which allowed for intensive concentration on a single course, followed by a brief but needed respite. There were various attempts to eliminate the "lame duck" period that the traditional semester system produced, and there were various adaptations of some sort of an interim term that would allow off-campus work. But the experiments of the 1960s typically assumed some kind of symmetry of academic calendars and reasonable progression of students through them.

The second significant curricular innovation of the 1960s consisted of a number of new ways to group students into subunits of existing institutions. These efforts included the creation of a house plan at Stephens College, cluster colleges at the University of the Pacific, the University of California at Santa Cruz and Michigan State University, and various attempts at team teaching. Those which achieved most attention specifically involved considerable curricular prescription and used the smaller grouping device as a means of intensifying intellectual development. In the Stephens house plan, students were required to take four prescribed courses and were allowed several electives. Illustrative of the movement was Raymond College of the University of the Pacific, which opened in 1963. It was staffed with a relatively young faculty and offered a rigorous, generally prescribed, liberal arts curriculum to the small student body. By the early 1970s, Raymond College had completely shifted emphasis and allowed an almost unlimited choice of courses, predicated on the belief that students viewed education primarily as a means of self-realization and personal growth rather than as a means of achieving professional or occupational preparation.

A third major development, which in some ways may be related to the national fright over Sputnik, was a reconsideration of general education requirements, which involved replacing some of the interdisciplinary courses, such as in the humanities, with a distribution arrangement that allowed requirements to be satisfied through election of one of several disciplinary courses. Overall, as

Dressel and DeLisle (1969) have shown, there was no significant decrease in the amount of required work between 1957 and 1967, but there was a movement toward greater use of departmental disciplinary courses for general education purposes, rather than interdisciplinary courses taught, at least in some institutions, by a special faculty. McGrath and Meeth (1965, p. 32) summarize the development during the period well: "The most common of the earlier arrangements to provide a general education was to have a group of required survey courses, which included a great range of information drawn from many specialized disciplines. A few years' experience with this kind of curricular structure, however, revealed serious defects. The most frequent criticism was that faculties attempted to include too much subject matter from the various constituent disciplines, which resulted in superficiality and excessive fragmentation. It was contended that even though students may acquire a considerable array of knowledge, they have been so concerned with the acquisition of facts that they fail to penetrate any subject in sufficient depth to understand its major generalizations or to master its intellectual methodological processes."

A fourth significant development was the embracing, on the part of a growing number of colleges and universities, of the cooperative work-study curricular arrangement. While cooperative work-study is a separate movement and began in 1906, it really began to flourish only in the 1960s, during which period it was given legislative recognition through funds made available by the Higher Education Act of 1965. Cooperative work-study related theory to practice and provided a systematic way by which students could help subsidize their own education. What was envisioned was a regular interchange of students between academic work done on campus and work experience in settings carefully selected by students and their advisers that would be most closely related to the academic part of the program. Cooperative work-study programs did not reduce the time spent in college; rather, it spread college work in a systematic way over a longer period of time, but in a carefully planned way. Academic credit typically was not awarded for the work experience, credit being tied to the academic portion of the program. Thus there was no equating of life experience with academic experience.

Another innovative effort, which started strong at the end of the 1950s but which became relatively insignificant by the end of the 1960s, were honors programs or programs for the gifted. The most illustrative example was created earlier, in 1922, namely the honors program at Swarthmore. However, following the Russian launching of Sputnik, honors programs became popular and spread rather quickly. Typically these programs were highly academic and stressed much deeper penetration into a given discipline than did regular programs. They were intended for the intellectually gifted and were elitist and meritocratic in spirit.

The late 1950s and the 1960s saw an increased interest in the use of educational technology. However, widespread experimentation involved a relatively few techniques and purposes. In a few institutions, there were substantial attempts made to offer large enrollment courses through closed-circuit television. Effectiveness was judged on the basis of test performance. Several attempts were made to offer academic sorts of courses over open-circuit television and a few institutions, such as the Chicago junior college system, offered such courses for academic credit. Secondly, there was a great deal of interest in language laboratories, which sought to combine traditional drill techniques with individual practice made possible through the use of audiotape systems. And colleges began to use computers to offer tightly programmed courses to students, based, in the early 1960s, on the concept of small incremental learnings with reinforcement provided by instant feedback. The changes in attitude toward and use of the technology that came about by the end of the 1960s will be elaborated further in Chapter Five.

Mayhew and Ford (1971) listed a number of transcendent issues involving the nature of the undergraduate curriculum: culture versus utility, general versus specific, elective versus prescribed, elitist versus egalitarian, subject centered versus student centered, disciplinary centered versus problem centered, oriented toward Western civilization versus oriented toward a world setting, and science dominated versus humanities dominated. The principal curricular developments of the 1960s tended to move in consistent directions. There was little retreat from prescription, although the nature of requirements shifted somewhat. There was a movement away from the broad and general toward the specific, although the specifics

were seen to possess great cultural values. Although there were such
egalitarian tendencies during the 1960s as the significant increase
in the number of junior colleges, the actual curricular innovations
seemed more elitist than egalitarian, as exemplified by honors programs, prescribed academic programs in cluster colleges, and more
discipline-oriented courses to be taken in satisfying general education requirements. It should be kept in mind that the 1960s saw the
flowering of graduate education as the highest expression of American higher education. Long-existing doctorate-granting institutions
enlarged their programs, developing institutions moved inexorably
toward creating graduate programs, and even liberal arts created
master's programs—among other reasons, to satisfy the demands of
faculty members who saw offering graduate work as most fitting
their intensively trained capabilities. Undergraduate curricula were
designed to prepare students to enter graduate and professional
schools, and so even in the curricular reform of the period the intellectual ideals epitomized by graduate education were clearly
perceptible.

Forces for Change

Significantly different curricular and instructional developments in traditional institutions began at almost the same time as did
the creation of radically new kinds of institutions and the development of highly nontraditional approaches to teaching and learning,
and the same or similar forces were involved in all three. All three
were influenced by egalitarian sentiments, the impact of criticism of
higher education, and the changed economic condition of higher
education from 1968 onward.

But there were other factors, which applied more specifically
to curricular and instructional changes in traditional institutions that
took place during the 1970s. Among those the significance of the student protest of the late 1960s is most difficult to gauge. That protest
did, at least by implication, call for greater curricular relevance;
lessened impersonality of faculty, administration, and institutional
behavior toward students; greater curricular flexibility; greater freedom of individual student choice; greater student voice in planning
their own education; greater curricular and instructional concern

with social, economic, moral, and ethical values—and some specific changes seem directly related to those criticisms and demands. The Experimental College at Berkeley probably would not have been approved and undertaken had there not been the pronounced student unrest that produced serious discussion of the nature of undergraduate education. Student participation in academic governance throughout the country also seems to have been derived from the complaints that protesting students made. It was out of a milieu of student dissatisfaction that students at Brown University prepared a document on needed reforms in higher education. That document, published in 1968, was the impetus for faculty action toward the formulation of the new undergraduate curriculum described by a faculty spokesman as "the most flexible and progressive undergraduate curriculum in any American university" (Heiss, 1973, p. 60). The new program assumed that the student held responsibility for his own intellectual and personal growth and for framing the design of his own education. On that premise an entire new curricular and counseling structure was created and introduced in 1969.

It will be recalled that a student-created set of recommendations were reviewed and acted on, first by a faculty committee and then by the full faculty. Freedom of election was the governing principle. Within that framework, there were to be many different "modes of thought" courses proposed by individual faculty members. Freshmen would spend much of the first year in one or more of these courses, which would focus on methods, concepts, and values, starting from a disciplinary base but transcending it. Each course would focus on a significant problem (which would change from year to year) as an organizing framework. The disciplinary major was replaced by concentrations, each created by the student and his adviser. Beyond the freshman year would be university courses, which would be on a high level but for the most part interdisciplinary. Students could earn as much credit as they wished through independent study. As for evaluation, students could opt for letter grades or pass/no-credit for most courses, but had to accept the pass/no-credit in the "modes of thought" courses. Close student-adviser relationships would provide structure for the curriculum.

To some extent the individuals responsible for some of the more widely publicized curricular innovations during the 1970s were aware of the literature of student protest, which probably affected their thinking and ultimately the nature of the programs they organized. Thus the president of Evergreen State College sought to make relevance and democracy key elements in a radically new undergraduate program. The chancellor of the University of Wisconsin at Green Bay had long reflected on the meaning of student dissatisfaction, and when he was given the mandate to create an innovative institution he tried to express those concerns in curricular form. The fact that he had been given a mandate by the president of the University of Wisconsin system to create an innovative institution may have been related to student protest. Certainly the first attempt to operate a new curriculum at the State University of New York College at Old Westbury reflected the deep awareness on the part of the first president of egalitarianism and of the complaints of students.

However, since the content of student protest from 1964 to 1970 rarely spoke to curricular issues and since even during the height of the student dissent students typically expressed reasonable satisfaction with their education, it seems likely that factors other than the student protest were more significant in stimulating reforms or changes that were attempted.

It is much easier to trace the relationship between, on the one hand, the struggles on the part of minority groups, especially blacks, for entry into the mainstream of American life and, on the other hand, significant curricular changes attempted during the late 1960s and 1970s. Following the 1954 Supreme Court decisions outlawing segregated education, institutions gradually accepted more blacks, and some predominantly white institutions actively recruited black students. However, little was attempted to provide special curricular or instructional services for these students. It was typically assumed that black students would become assimilated into the predominantly white student bodies and that the responsibility for coping with the educational program rested with the black students. Even the activities of the civil rights efforts during most of the 1960s seemed to have little effect on curriculum content, direction, or modes of teaching. It was only after the assassination of Martin Luther King, Jr., that predominantly white institutions suddenly began to make major efforts to increase black enrollments. As they did so and as the number of black students increased on those campuses, the stage was set for criticism of curricular and social divisions and for demands that substantial modification be made. The creation of black student unions stemmed directly from the increase in numbers of blacks on campus, and these in turn produced pressures for black studies, black residence halls, and increased financial aids for black students. The model established by blacks eventually came to be adopted by Chicanos, Native Americans, and ultimately, in a paradoxical sort of way, by women.

Some of the curricular and instructional development during the 1970s was directly related to developments of the 1950s and 1960s, either as reactions against or as elaboration of earlier developments. Between 1958 and 1968, faculties reemphasized disciplinary studies and deemphasized interdisciplinary general education courses, which were considered superficial. However, by the early 1970s some faculty members and groups, in discussing the nature of undergraduate education, realized that the values they sought were captured by statements of objectives for general education programs that had been created during the 1950s. The active experimentation with interdisciplinary courses and interdisciplinary programs seems to reflect in part a reaction to the specialization and departmentalism of the 1960s and represents an effort to recapture the general education mode. Also, by the end of the 1960s, considerable modifications had been made in grading systems, as institutions eliminated failing grades or went to a pass/fail system of assessment. Whether or not the two developments were causally related, as those modifications of grading spread there came a detectable inflation of grades throughout the country that, not unexpectedly, produced some consternation in the minds of academic purists. By the last half of the 1970s, institutions had begun to return to letter grades and to find ways of deflating grade-point averages.

But some of the innovative efforts of the 1960s typically produced desirable outcomes and so became models for emulation during the following decade. The two developments that seemed to generate the most favorable assessment were (1) new groupings of students into cluster colleges, colleges within colleges, or team teaching and (2) the inclusion of clinical or field experience in the formal curricula of all students. Throughout the 1970s, institutions, especially large ones, continued to seek smaller groupings of students and faculty, and in so doing they used as models the cluster college or house plan developed a decade earlier. The cooperative work-study programs and the inclusion of foreign travel as essential parts of some curricula during the 1960s suggested still other ways of providing for real-life experience carefully linked to formal academic work. Thus, in the 1970s traditional institutions contrived new ways of providing students with field or clinical experiences, and the new, nontraditional institutions allowed real-life experiences to comprise, in some situations, most of the requirements for various degrees.

In some institutions, notably the prestigious research-oriented institutions, faculty members were delocalized. The availability of contract and research funds and the opportunity for faculty members to function on a national or international stage produced a phenomenon in which faculty members' loyalties were transferred from their own institutions to other disciplinary and funding agencies that conferred political and economic status. This was a time when research, scholarship, and consulting appeared to epitomize academic success, and faculty members could engage in them without particular concern for the institution in which they for the moment held appointments. Now, the campuses on which faculty was really delocalized were relatively few, numbering probably less than one hundred, but the practice on those campuses appeared as the ideal, and the ethos of research and delocalized faculty pervaded all of higher education, except perhaps for the public community colleges and the most invisible of liberal arts colleges. However, beginning in approximately 1968, conditions changed profoundly, reducing many of the off-campuses bases of professorial, economic, and political power. Federal graduate fellowship programs were reduced; funds available for research stabilized; and foundations that previously had supported higher education as a major preoccupation began to enter into other domains of service. Almost simultaneously, younger faculty members and faculty members in tenured positions (with perhaps fifteen years to go before retirement) began to see their professional future more in terms of institutional activities than national or international activities. Thus in the 1970s came a gradual relocalization of the faculty, which produced a number of interesting changes. The use of evaluation of teaching and academic good citizenship as essential elements for promotion for tenure purposes became prevalent, whereas just a few years earlier such matters would have scarcely been considered at all. Tenured professors in academic departments, seeing that research outlets for their creative energies had become restricted, turned their attention to creating new kinds of programs for undergraduate students. One must not overemphasize this relocalization phenomenon. It appeared on only a few campuses, but the pace set by leading institutions is contagious, and the idea of a long-term (possibly even a lifetime) appointment on a single campus once again became accepted and even idealized. The rationale probably went something like this: "Since I am not likely to accept another appointment and will be at this institution for the rest of my career, perhaps I should spend more time on institutional and instructional concerns rather than being hyperactive in national or international educational affairs."

An important ingredient in some of the curricular and instructional development activities of the 1970s—although just how important it is difficult to gauge—is the existence of a cadre of professional individuals whose major concern is with bringing about educational changes and reforms. During the 1960s, several subspecialties began to appear on college and university campuses. The first of these involved professors of higher education who were professionally concerned with outlining a new field of study, preparing suddenly needed administrators, and seeking to improve instruction and other educational activities in higher education. Courses on the college curriculum and on the improvement of instruction began to appear, designed first for graduate students, then for faculty members at nearby but less prestigious institutions, and, here and there, for the improvement of instruction on the part of junior faculty at the higher education professor's own institution. This was related to the creation of centers for the improvement of instruction, first on a handful of campuses, such as the University of Michigan or Michigan State University, and then spreading to other campuses. The organizations that provided some institutional and some external support had missions of improving undergraduate education.

It is impossible to judge the long-term influence of these two subspecialties. However, their members did begin to publish, did organize conferences, seminars, and workshops, and did stimulate discussion about educational problems and issues. Out of those activities and discussions did come some of the more modal curricular changes in at least a few institutions. The dynamics can be quickly indicated in several examples. One of the more prevalent curricular efforts of the 1970s was interdisciplinary courses or cluster of courses. On the campus of the Oklahoma State University was created a Center for the Contriving of Educational Innovation, under the leadership of a former provost who had previously been a dean of engineering. Looking for new professional activities, he created the center and undertook programs to upgrade faculty teaching and thinking about curriculum. In both the college of arts and sciences and the college of engineering, major new interdisciplinary programs came into existence, stimulated in large measure by the center. The second example is a personal one. The author is a professor of higher education who has written and spoken a great deal about curricular matters. While his impact on his own campus is virtually nonexistent, he has been in constant demand on other campuses to help faculties learn about new curricular developments and to help faculties create new programs.

Although some of the major foundations had begun to work in areas other than higher education, a few foundations certainly had an impact on some of the more characteristic curricular developments of the 1970s. The Carnegie Foundation clearly stimulated interest in experimentation with a new doctoral degree—Doctor of Arts. The EXXON Education Foundation is equally involved in experimentation with computer-based college instruction and the application of systems analysis to curricular instruction. The Danforth Foundation has been associated with the upgrading of college faculty members, particularly in the liberal arts colleges. The federal Fund for the Improvement of Postsecondary Education has stimulated ways of extending higher education to new groups of students, and in a few states legislatures have appropriated funds to be used to improve undergraduate education.

The changing market for college graduates must stand as one of the more potent forces affecting educational thinking during the 1970s. When oversupplies of prospective teachers at all levels began to appear, students began to look for other vocational possibilities.

This produced immediate program reaction within institutions and the creation of new institutions. When prospective doctoral students saw the oversupply of college teachers being produced, they shifted their applications to medical and law schools. When students ceased applying for teacher preparation programs, liberal arts and state colleges began to create new vocational programs in such presumably popular fields as business and fields related to health and law.

New Directions for the 1970s—and Beyond?

Related to, affected by, or derived from such factors and forces are a number of curricular and instructional developments that have gained prominence during the 1970s. In presenting these, no attempt will be made to be comprehensive nor to establish a taxonomy of all curricular and instructional innovation changes and reforms. Nor will explicit attention be paid to the already treated matters of new instructions and nontraditional learnings. Rather, the most salient and characteristic curricular developments of the 1970s will be examined and allowed to stand in contrast to earlier developments. It should also be pointed out that while the focus here is on traditional types of institutions, many of these developments will be found in new kinds of institutions and as bases for nontraditional study.

New Vocationalism. Cheit (1975a) reports that the most notable trend among college students of the 1970s is a new focus on practicality or, as it has become known, the *new vocationalism.* The enrollment decisions of students during the 1970s clearly show that professional and occupational study is what they want. The first signs of the new vocationalism were apparent in law schools as they experienced enormous pressures in the early 1970s. By 1975, the phenomenon of growth was apparent in most other professional and job-related courses of study. It also appears that the growth of interest in the professions and job-related studies is a general phenomenon and not one limited to any particular group of students (Cheit, 1975a).

Institutions of all levels have begun to respond to student demand through active experimentation with and creation of new vocational programs. As they have done so, serious unresolved issues have emerged. There is no agreement, for example, as to the precise balance between the general, liberal, and vocational parts of a program. There is no good rule of thumb on how to balance broadly theoretical and definitely applied courses within the occupational area, and there is generally little agreement on whether collegiate programs should aim at preparing students for immediate job entry or for long-term career growth. Despite those complexities, however, there has been a great deal of curricular activity in the professional and vocational fields. Such experimentation, of course, differs somewhat vocation to vocation but in aggregate presents a rather consistent pattern.

The period of the late 1960s and the early 1970s may eventually come to be regarded as the period of intensive course experimentation, with an emphasis on instruction. Thus individualized instruction is being tried, as are ways to inject more reality into academic course work, to produce interdisciplinary activities, and to rearrange group time and space for more effective educational achievement. There are experiments designed to produce a better match between practice teacher and mentor teacher, using a computer to compare and match traits. There are also experiments in teacher preparation for more fully utilizing university professors, college professors, and teachers and administrators from cooperating public schools. Many of the new courses are designed to force students into more problem-solving activity, whether the field be business, engineering, or nursing. An example is a freshman-year course in engineering, taken by all students regardless of their specializations, that forces them to grapple with a real-life design problem. The effort to inject more realism into courses takes many different forms. An increasingly popular one is the development of game simulations based on a computer program that allow students to experience vicariously the range of problems and emotions produced by real-life stituations.

Within each of a number of occupational fields, there are significant new developments. Journalism, for example, seems to be making much greater use of educational technology as well as of more interdisciplinary courses and reality-based experiences. Programs for the preparation of teachers have begun to stress competency-based curricula, more consistent and intimate use of materials from the liberal arts and sciences, and more field experiences emphasizing community involvement in inner-city or rural situations.

In business education, which really began substantial reforms in the 1950s, several strands can be identified. The first is the trend toward individualization of instruction, either through tightly programmed materials or through rather loose structures allowing students to sense problems of concern to them and to work on them independently. The second strand is the trend to integrate reality and academic learning more completely. The case study, which had been the basic instructional unit, was an attempt to do this, but more recently students have been sent into the field to work on real-life problems. A variation on this theme is the increased use of computer-based management games that allow students to experience many of the emotions of real-life situations without the consequences of faculty decisions.

Nursing education also has a relatively long history of curricular concern, and there has been a constant search to discover a core of underlying science and theory essential to nursing practice. As nursing education moves into the 1970s and 1980s, several additional elements have assumed primacy. There are attempts to involve nursing students outside the hospital and to help them learn to cope with family and community problems and pressures. In a number of modified nursing programs, students spend rather extensive periods living and working in a community. Since the health fields must increasingly work as a team, schools of nursing rely more on multidisciplinary courses and activities. And, since nursing, like other fields, is becoming more and more specialized, nursing students are allowed to begin their specialization earlier.

Most of the vocational fields are adopting several kinds of reforms. The first is a reform of the American degree structure so that degrees or certificates are awarded at approximately two-year intervals, with improved articulation between each degree. There is also an attempt to make the degree structure more flexible, allowing students to accelerate through early entry, stretched-out programs, or by earning considerable credit by examination. Credit by examination underlies another major effort, namely the attempt to create an external degree structure so that students who find it impossible to be in residence on a campus can nonetheless acquire a vocational

degree. In both New York and California there are statewide attempts to develop the external degree, and in the private sector the
Union of Experimenting Colleges and Universities has produced its
University Without Walls. The concept of an external degree was
brought to the foreground as many new kinds of students sought
academic degrees and credentials. The external degree, offering as it
did, a chance to work in relatively unthreatening conditions, was one
means of helping those new students. In most of the experiments,
some variant of independent study is important, although evidence is
still far from complete that independent study is widely appropriate.
One of the more widely practiced reforms is simply the quest, on the
part of institutions, to discover new and viable vocational programs.
This can best be illustrated by the case of teacher preparation. As
the number of credentialed teachers reached levels far surpassing
employment possibilities, students began to turn away from institutions preoccupied with teacher preparation. Those institutions, facing
serious enrollment drops, have begun to search both for criteria to
help in discovering new programs and for new programs themselves.

Especially revealing of institutional response to the new
vocationalism is an experimental program in the education of
prospective industrial chemists that was carried on in St. Leo College, a small liberal arts college in rural western Florida. The director
of the program had spent the bulk of his professional career working
in product development in the petroleum industry and had sensed a
need for a kind of person who understood chemistry and also understood product development. He had come to believe that holders of
the bachelor's degree in chemistry from most universities took
courses that were science oriented and ultimately designed for an
ultimate Ph.D. program. Graduates of most programs in chemistry
might understand scientific chemistry, but they did not understand
industrial problems nor could they converse easily with people
trained in more applied fields. He satisfied himself that no other
institutions in the country offered such a program and, further, that
chemistry departments in most large universities had no expectations
of offering applied work in industrial chemistry. This project was
also stimulated by the conditions of St. Leo College, which are not
unlike those facing many other invisible liberal arts colleges. It
normally enrolls between 900 and 1,000 students and experiences a

rather heavy attrition of students at the end of the sophomore year. Thus the institution is vigorously searching for ways to replace those dropouts with new students entering at the beginning of the junior year. Florida has a large and comprehensive junior college system, and liberal arts colleges hope to attract students from those institutions after the students have received the Associate of Arts degree. The proposed program in industrial chemistry represented one effort to tap this junior college market.

Doctor of Arts. A development less important from the standpoint of numbers of people involved, but indicative of the period, was the attempt to create a new doctor's degree. The Ph.D. has long been the glory of American higher education but also the object of intense criticism and even abomination. The Ph.D., as originally conceived, was rigorous, conceptual, disciplinary, and led to the ability to make significant contributions to knowledge. It was damned for precisely those same characteristics. It was judged as overly specialized and narrow and was caricatured as helping people learn more and more about less and less. Periodically, from the turn of the twentieth century onward, critics and commissions have issued recommendations for change, none of which have been adopted. If anything, by the early 1960s the traditional Ph.D. degree was more firmly entrenched than ever before as the proper crown for the American higher educational enterprise and the most ideal activity that could engage the professoriate. But partly as a result of presumed student criticisms of colleges and universities during the 1960s and partly as a result of the expansion of the essentially teaching institutions, such as the junior colleges, an alternate to the Ph.D. was once more attempted. The concept was introduced by a staff member of the Carnegie Foundation, was warmly endorsed by the Carnegie Commission on Higher Education, and was supported in some institutions by grants from the Carnegie Foundation. The new degree would be called a *Doctor of Arts degree* and would be designed to prepare people for undergraduate teaching. It would typically develop a major field and a strong and related cognate field, which when combined would allow the teacher to offer courses in, for example, the broad area of the social sciences. Explicit instruction and internship experience would be provided to prepare people for college teaching. The traditional dissertation as a contribution to knowledge would be replaced by scholarly interpretive papers or papers dealing with essentially education aspects of academic disciplines. A degree would be designed for junior college teachers and for those professors in other sorts of institutions who would be concerned for the most part with the undergraduate curriculum.

A number of institutions considered the Doctor of Arts; some actually adopted such a program; and a few developed reasonably large programs, the two most frequently cited institutions being Carnegie-Mellon University and the University of Miami. Almost from the beginning, the Doctor of Arts encountered insurmountable obstacles. An oversupply of Ph.D. recipients appeared simultaneously with the new Doctor of Arts programs, and, the prestige system being what it is, employing institutions preferred the Ph.D. over a second-class degree. Also almost simultaneously legislatures became conscious of the rapid expansion of graduate doctoral programs and their attendant costs and began to erect obstacles to prevent public institutions from creating new doctoral programs of whatever sort (including the Doctor of Arts). Within the American system, the imprimatur of prestigious institutions is almost essential if an educational innovation is to become widely accepted. Earlier, for example, general education began to spread after the publication of the Harvard report, *General Education in a Free Society* (1947). When prestigious universities examined the potentiality of the Doctor of Arts degree, they invariably rejected the concept; hence the idea did not have the support of the pacesetting institutions. The degree appeared to be most adaptable to an institution that did not have competing Ph.D. programs, that had available a reasonably large potential clientele, and that also had available a reasonably large supply of jobs into which graduates could be moved easily or jobs already filled by candidates for the degree. The University of Miami turned out to be the most adaptable for the Doctor of Arts degree. It had only one or two Ph.D. programs, and it was surrounded by the large state junior college system, many of whose faculty members wished to upgrade themselves by pursuing a doctoral program part-time. Thus the university could offer a Doctor of Arts, which did not require as intensive guidance as did the dissertation-focused Ph.D., and not need to worry about placement because the typical student was also placed.

How the Doctor of Arts degree reflects the changed conditions of the 1970s is well described by E. Alden Dunham, perhaps the chief proponent of the degree. He believed these degrees should be offered by state colleges, "Very few of which will ever become first-rate universities. . . . The time is now ripe for . . . channeling large numbers of aspiring graduate students toward programs that are relevant to the teaching tasks of mass higher education. While there is heavy emphasis on scholarship, the thrust of work is applied scholarship, and the dissertation relates to curriculum and instruction at the college level. A direct focus upon undergraduate education would be ensured, even possibly replacing expensive Ph.D. programs and university status as a lure for ambitious faculty. At the same time the professionalization of the undergraduate curriculum would be less likely to occur and . . . the now meaningless phrase liberal education might become a reality. If student activism today means anything, it means a revolt against professionalism divorced from the realities of life as students see them" (Dunham, 1969, p. 163). A faculty composed of recipients of the Doctor of Arts would offer general education but, as Dunham pointed out (p. 163), "there is likewise a great need for applied programs serving local regions. In fact, regionalism seems to me one of the major justifications for any claim of uniqueness among state colleges. Again, with a new kind of faculty there would cease to be the denigration of the importance of applied programs. So long as discipline-oriented, colleague-oriented faculty in major university graduate schools are predominant, regionalism will get nowhere. Ph.D.'s have much more interest in the national scene, in their colleagues in other institutions, than they have in the local scene or in problems of their own institutions" (p. 164). A multipurpose teaching institution staffed by Doctor of Arts recipients, "with strong lateral development in the introduction of new and different undergraduate programs in general education and applied areas, is bound to ease the pressures upon harassed college presidents who must find funds to run their institutions" (p. 164). Thus the Doctor of Arts-dominated institution is seen as a major economy in state systems of higher education.

Open Admissions. Also indicative of the 1970s, as contrasted with earlier decades, is the serious attention given to the concept of open admissions as a means of facilitating universal access to higher education. Open admissions is not a particularly new concept. In the United States, except for the period from 1958 to 1970, there have always been more collegiate spaces than demand for them. American colleges and universities have always competed fiercely for students and will continue to in the future. It is true that at one time knowledge of Greek and Latin was required for admission to college, but nineteenth-century colleges provided for an early version of academic-risk students through charitably assuming that the majority of all applicants who lacked that knowledge could be admitted and would rectify their deficiencies. In this century, high school graduation, ability to pay, and—in some regions and institutions—membership in one race and in one religion were the entrance requirements. By law, except in Michigan, the great state universities were open in this sense, and, by custom and necessity, so were the private institutions. Self-selection of applicants produced one-to-one application and acceptance ratios, and that openness continued until the late 1950s, when a sudden unexpected and unhistoric increased demand for higher education allowed the advent of rationing in some institutions. And, of course, the public junior or community colleges, in the majority of states where they existed, were open-admission institutions during the 1950s and 1960s. In California, which has the largest junior college system in the country, the admission requirement is a high school diploma or a judgment from the principal of the junior college that the applicant possessed the requisite capabilities for junior college work. However, even with such a tradition, the system of higher education in the United States continued to exclude some major groups in American society, especially the racial and ethnic minorities of blacks, Puerto Ricans, Chicanos, and Native Americans. The net effect of traditional admission standards, regardless of how modest, was to provide the greatest opportunity to those students who were the most economically and socially advantaged. Although during the late 1960s colleges and universities began recruiting talented members of disadvantaged groups, they still excluded many students of low socioeconomic status and of various ethnic groups. Thus by 1970 the American educational community faced the harsh choice of either continuing to exclude those groups or to abandon traditional admission standards. The most characteristic approach of the 1970s was the policy of open admissions, which challenged fundamental assumptions about the role of the university. "Traditionally, universities have been viewed as most essentially concerned with transmitting culture from generation to generation and with discovering new truths about man and the universe. According to this conception, teaching and research—carried out by devoted scholars and students sheltered from the pressures of the outside world—are the core functions of the university. Open admissions, in contrast, places the institution in a much broader role: that of providing an opportunity for the masses to continue to develop educationally beyond the high school years" (Rossman and others, 1975, p. 2).

A number of institutions have attempted open admissions. The previously cited California policy for junior colleges is one. The University of Illinois, Urbana, and the Federal City College, in Washington, D.C., which tried to use a lottery from a pool of all applicants are others. The City University of New York is still another and—in part because of the financial difficulties that began to plague that city and its university—is possibly the most widely publicized. The Board of Higher Education of the City University of New York announced in 1969 that it would move to open admissions in the fall of 1970. A new policy offered admission to some university program to all high school graduates in the city. The university would provide remedial and supportive services for students requiring them; it would provide for mobility of students between various programs and units of the university; it would require ethnic integration of the colleges; and at the same time it would maintain and enhance the standards of academic excellence in the colleges of the university. The policy would operate so that high school graduates in the top half of their graduating classes or having a grade average of 80 or higher would be placed in four-year college programs, while high school graduates below those levels would enroll in the two-year colleges. Within those broad guidelines, individual campuses were expected to implement the policy with respect to placement of students, providing supportive and remedial services, and developing appropriate ways for assessment of student progress.

The policy of open admissions in the City University of New York intersects with several other phenomena especially characteristic of the 1970s. The student body is racially and ethnically diverse—fewer than 15 percent come from WASP backgrounds. The faculty is completely unionized, and a no-tuition policy was in effect. Early studies of the open-admissions program provided reason for optimism. In spite of many difficulties, it allowed many of New York City's young people who were previously regarded as bad risks and unfit for publicly supported postsecondary education to achieve those self-determined objectives that would help them lead more meaningful and productive lives. However, the open-admissions policy in New York broke on a fiscal problem. In 1976 the institution was forced to abrogate the no-tuition policy and to place restrictions on admissions.

The concept of open admissions cannot as yet be fully assessed. First of all, the evidence as to how well various schemes to accomplish open admissions have succeeded in the light of stated purposes is extraordinarily mixed. During the first years of open admissions in the City University of New York, bachelor's degree graduation rates for four-year survival rates for open-admissions students approximated graduation and four-year survival rates throughout the nation. Of the open-admissions freshmen who entered in 1970, between forty percent and 50 percent had either received degrees in 1974 or were still enrolled in a City University College. The national percentage is approximately 47 percent (Rossman and others, 1975, p. 169). However, in California somewhere in the vicinity of 10 to 12 percent of students who enter public junior colleges as freshmen receive a bachelor's degree four or five years later. In neither California nor New York City have the programs substantially increased the proportion of minority group members or the economically disadvantaged (Jaffe and Adams, 1971, pp. 143–168). There can be serious question as to whether open-admissions programs can ever benefit the economically disadvantaged in the absence of financial support equal at least to replacing forgone income. This would be at least $3,000, and there seems to be no likelihood that either the states or the federal government would provide such support. Even if the basic education opportunity grants of the Higher Education Amendments of 1972 were fully funded, it can be doubted that there would be significant increases in enrollment of the economically disadvantaged.

Black and Other Kinds of Studies. During the 1960s, especially in the latter years and continuing, there have been attempts to use the curriculum to meet the needs of specialized groups of people. Numerically the largest have been the attempts to develop courses, programs, departments, or centers of black studies. These efforts have arisen to serve a multiplicity of purposes. Black studies have been viewed as an important aid to develop a sense of black identity and pride in students who were encountering for the first time the full impact of the predominant white culture. Secondly, black studies have been seen as a device to rectify deficiencies in curricula that had largely ignored the black experience in the United States and its antecedents in Africa. This parallels, of course, the earlier attempt to rectify an imbalance by bringing Asia to the attention of college students. These studies also have been viewed as a method for giving cohesion to the larger black community and providing a curricular device to facilitate interaction between the on-campus and off-campus black communities. In effect, black studies represented a counterforce to integrationism that seemed to black students inevitably to result in further strengthening white cultural hegemony. They allowed black subcultures on college campuses to express their own unique features through a curricular device. But not all black studies attempts were separatist. Some courses and programs were designed to help white students understand the black community, problems, and culture. Properly conducted, these programs could also focus attention on black problems and could indicate the magnitude of those problems as well as possible directions for resolution. These various reasons are well summarized by Charles H. Taylor, Jr. (1969, p. 2): "What we are faced with, then, in our black students' protest is not simply, in some respects not even chiefly, their proper demand to know more about themselves, about *their heritage* and *their tradition,* but rather their consciousness of how important it is for American society, for us, the white majority, to know a lot more about them. We need this knowledge to attack not only conscious prejudice, which is easy to identify, but to overcome unconscious discrimination, that simple lack of awareness, the ignorance from which we all suffer in white America."

As collegiate institutions sought to respond to the demands for black studies, they faced a number of issues that have yet to be thoroughly resolved. There was the organizational problem as to whether separate departments of black studies should be created or whether existing disciplines should be encouraged to add increments of black history, art, sociology, or whatever. Black students frequently argued for the separate department, staffed primarily with black faculty, on the grounds that such a structure was the only real guarantee of adequate treatment of black concerns. Professors in departments, on the other hand, contended that ethnicity was not a proper organizing principle for courses or scholarship, and that the proper place for expressing black concerns was in existing disciplines. A related problem was that of staffing. If universities adhered to normal staffing policies, there were simply not enough black scholars to provide faculty for more than a handful of black studies programs. For example, in 1967 only 185 black Ph.D.'s were graduated out of some 19,000 doctorates awarded in that year, and most of those were in education. Some, of course, contended that some degree of literacy and being black and concerned were sufficient credentials for teaching in programs of black studies.

A second major issue is whether or not there are sufficient scholarly resources to support an elaborate black studies program. In recent years, there have been serious attempts to collect and publish black literature, history, and the like, and there have been serious attempts to bring African materials into the campus libraries and museums, but the volume is still relatively slight as compared with other more traditional subjects, and substantial collections seem possible for only a few relatively affluent institutions. The experience of some of the colleges in the Great Lakes College Association (such as Oberlin or Earlham) in creating non-Western studies is instructive. They required institutions approximately ten years to accumulate an adequate mass of scholarship and faculty to support their non-Western studies programs.

Another issue, obviously applicable only to a limited number of people, is the problem of what specific use college majors in black studies make of their degrees after graduation. Do black studies majors prepare people appropriately to enter graduate school, and do they prepare people to cope with an economic system that is complex and highly technological?

Following closely the creation of programs in black studies are the other kinds of ethnic studies for Chicanos, Native Americans, and Puerto Ricans. Numerically there are still fewer of those, but they seem to be facing the same sorts of issues that confronted black studies.

More recent has been the expansion of women's courses in higher education. In September 1970, an anthology of women's studies contained 17 syllabi. By October 1971, listings contained over 700 different courses representing 178 institutions. Women's studies or women's courses have generally been designed to achieve several different purposes. Some seek to serve specific women's needs, such as for techniques of self-defense. Others try to serve women's traditional interests, such as child care, home maintenance, and the like. Relatedly, some seek to elaborate and make clear women's central roles; for example, their sex role in the family. The fourth purpose is to help both men and women to understand the unique character of women. A fifth purpose is to emphasize women's contributions to society, both on the contemporary and historic scene. For some, women's studies represent an instrument for women's liberation, being in a sense the female expression of the civil rights phenomena. A pervasive theme in women's studies has been a strong element of protest. "Women's courses were started because of discontent with women's status as it is reflected today in the content of college courses. Feminists note the virtual absence of women in history, literature, art and other fields as taught, or women are treated as peripheral, an appendix to the topic or as exceptions to the norm. References to women in textbooks, card catalogues, and indexes reveal a scholarly tradition in which women are virtually invisible. . . . Proponents of women's studies say that the current status of women in modern knowledge reflects a viewpoint which takes male supremacy for granted, thereby devaluing women's contribution. In addition, they assert that women have internalized these negative views of women's activities to the point where women have poor self-images and resultant lowered aspirations. Thus one of the purposes of women's courses is to restore women's self-esteem and to instill a sense of identity" (*College and University Bulletin,* 1972).

Although there is a great deal of interest and activity concerning such specialized curricula, the literature dealing with these matters has been largely polemical, descriptive, or exhortative.

There is no validated set of organizational principles or guidelines that could indicate the directions curriculum building should take. There are no criteria available to assist in deciding what courses are and are not appropriate for collegiate programs. There is virtually no evidence as to the impact of these studies on knowledge, values, or subsequent life-styles. The few bibliographies of relevant literature frequently list primarily the polemical or exhortative literature. There do not seem to be well-developed bibliographies that could assist faculty in developing courses and programs.

Interdisciplinary Study. The portion of the collegiate curricula (conceived in its broadest sense) that receives greatest discussion are the various attempts to create interdisciplinary courses or programs. This is not a new phenomenon of the 1970s, although experimentation may have reached a crescendo during that time. The general education movement of the 1940s and 1950s was essentially interdisciplinary: Faculties tried to put together courses in physical, biological, or even natural science rather than to continue to offer courses in specific subjects. The courses during the 1950s of non-Western civilization were also interdisciplinary, as were typical offerings during the late 1960s of courses and programs in black or Chicano studies. The reasons why interdisciplinary courses and programs are seriously considered and sometimes adopted are relatively easy to detect. There is the argument that life and its problems do not conform to specific subjects or disciplines but rather are interdisciplinary in character. People who seek to understand their various environments, for example, need to view them from different vantage points and to analyze them using different techniques. Thus the University of Wisconsin at Green Bay has been organized along interdisciplinary lines, and the courses students are required to take are considered interdisciplinary. It is also argued and in some cases demonstrated that as research in various fields progresses interrelationships with other fields become apparent and as these are elaborated new interdisciplinary concepts emerge. Thus social psychology emerged out of converging research efforts in traditional psychology and sociology. Similarly, genetics as a field brings together chemistry, biology, and even some of the social or behavioral sciences. Interdisciplinary work can also be highly motivational, in that courses with a broad common focus can still allow students to pursue specialized subparts and still relate those parts to other disciplines related to the broad focus. For example, a biological science course at the University of Southern California brings together students generally interested in biological phenomena but allows them to explore sociological, physiological, physical, or chemical manifestations of problems broadly related to biology. Such a course can presumably develop some basic concepts applicable to the various biological fields and still allow students to follow their own interests.

Difficult to document, but nonetheless possible, is the possibility that many new interdisciplinary courses and programs generated during the 1970s are essentially cosmetic in purpose. Particularly in some of the weaker private liberal arts colleges, as enrollments began to stabilize and then to decline, there has been a flurry of activity creating new sorts of requirements and programs—frequently with exotic or presumably attractive titles—in the hopes that such offerings might attract student enrollments. Of course, the rhetoric used to describe these interdisciplinary efforts is stated in idealistic and philosophical terms, but when discussions turn candid the fundamental question emerges: Will this attract students and reverse an unfavorable application trend? For example, Kansas Wesleyan University in 1976 announced a major new curricular arrangement, with a keystone program called Foundation For Decisions. The rationale on which the curricular issue was debated was educational and philosophical. Thus the proponent for that core argued that "the Foundations for Decisions program suggests that general education is not necessarily an entry into a discipline—nor is it an isolated entity. The liberalizing education experience cannot be separated into a dangling set of value-oriented courses in a Foundations for Decisions program, but must be integral requirements for majors, other requirements, and electives. In a liberal education mode, such articulation may be partially accomplished by a common thread woven into the entire curriculum" (Both, 1976, p. 5). However, the underlying theme in faculty discussions was that Kansas Wesleyan was suffering a high attrition rate, was not attracting enough students from the local community, and was not attracting students from densely populated regions outside of the state. What was needed was an appealing program that would attract student interest and subsequent enrollment. This point is not made cynically.

Some types of institutions are suffering losses in applications rates and in holding power and do need to find either new clients or ways of reattracting older clients. The curriculum is one obvious place to start. One can, of course, question the effectiveness of curricular changes in attracting students. One has the impression that high school seniors are more concerned with institutional reputation, proximity, cost, friendship groups, and possibly opportunities for career development than with the curriculum.

Not necessarily discrete from the reasons for a cosmetic uplift is the factor of a genuine concern for the improvement of undergraduate education. Although students during the late 1960s did not explicitly make curricular demands, nonetheless the general unrest made some faculty members aware that the quality of undergraduate education could and should be improved. As faculties began to consider seriously the developmental needs of late adolescents, it appeared that those needs might be best served by interdisciplinary courses and programs rather than by adherence to disciplinary requirements. Thus a well-received program in values and technology seems to have emerged at Stanford University out of serious curricular discussions on the part of sincere and tenured professors who had come to believe that the needs of undergraduate students in a major research university had been ignored or forgotten. Similarly the Unified Science program at MIT, which was highly interdisciplinary, came into existence in order to break what appeared to senior faculty members as an oppressively rigid set of disciplinary requirements for a highly able undergraduate student body. Equally substantive has been the growing awareness that new professional and vocational subspecialties were emerging and that preparation for those roles probably required interdisciplinary rather than single disciplinary preparation. For example, a professional role has emerged for individuals who can work both with physicians and surgeons and with engineers in the growing field of biomedical engineering. People occupying such a role need understanding of engineering, physiology, chemistry, and certainly surgery, yet do not need specialization in those equivalent to that obtained by majors. Thus the stage was set for an interdisciplinary degree program in biomedical engineering. Workers in the health fields are aware that, although health specialties differ from each other, many of them probably rest or could rest on some common body of interdisciplinary materials. Thus the search for an interdisciplinary component that can serve future nurses, medical technicians, and community health workers. Engineering schools have made a rather concerted effort to create interdisciplinary sequences to service people entering the various engineering specialties.

The interdisciplinary approach seems to be much more amenable to meeting spontaneously developed student interest. Hence those institutions that maintain a highly fluid curriculum (even deciding on courses through signup sheets on bulletin boards) are typically characterized by considerable interdisciplinary effort. The interdisciplinary mode is also encouraged by the parallel development of individualized instruction. Although individualized instruction or learning, as provided for during the 1970s, has such antecedents as the Honors Program at Swarthmore and the availability of credit by examination at the College of the University of Chicago, it seems to have attracted most attention from 1968 onward. Individualized instruction encourages students to examine a broad and amorphous domain, to define a problem that interests them, and then to pursue that problem in their own ways and at their own rates of speed. This approach is by its very nature interdisciplinary.

There are several examples of how several of these factors produced actual interdisciplinary efforts, the first being an attempt to create an undergraduate health sciences curriculum at Columbia University. This was an interdisciplinary effort to develop common or core courses that could be used as basic to six different specialties in the general area of the health sciences. It had its origin in a number of factors, of great significance during the 1970s. The first of these was clearly an effort on the part of the College of General Studies of Columbia University to develop new and self-supporting programs that could reverse a generally deteriorating enrollment picture. But it was also rooted in an interest on the part of the faculty and administration of the College of Physicians and Surgeons to strengthen work in the health sciences and to prepare people to assume a number of discrete but nonetheless interrelated medical subspecialties. Apparently the vice-president for medical education at Columbia University had developed rather pronounced interests in educational processes and curriculum and had appointed a committee to investigate various new programs that could utilize both the strengths of the School of Medicine and the other elements of the university. The chairman of that committee, a professor of psychiatry, became interested in improvement of education as a result of that experience and then drifted quite naturally into a position as associate dean for educational programs. He took particular and personal interest in this interdisciplinary effort. It was proposed to develop a core of courses that could be used with propriety as core requirements for each of a number of subspecialties: health education, health care administration, environmental health sciences, family life sciences, nutrition sciences, community mental health, and medical computer sciences. The core courses were to be developed after making a task analysis of emerging job requirements in those fields, with those requirements then being converted into educational specifications. The courses would be jointly prepared and taught by faculty members from the departments of Columbia College and by faculty members from the relevant subdivisions of medical education. Those new courses, put together in appropriate patterns, would serve as foundation work for each of the subspecialties.

A second example, reflecting other background factors, was the Unified Science Study program at MIT. The effort derived in part from some MIT student dissatisfaction with the rigid graduation requirements and in part from the need to provide some ways to meet educational needs of minority students who found the more formal course structure at MIT unsuited to their frequently meager academic background. The intent was to open up learning conditions, to modify the student-faculty ratio in order to provide a more intimate educational experience, and to involve students in a dynamic kind of education. The program consisted of a staff (typically nontenured research associates) that offered ad hoc sorts of problems-oriented seminars, assisted its students in selecting independent research projects, and then monitored student progress. MIT students could enroll in the program as a full-time activity for as much as a full year or as a partial activity done at the same time they enrolled in other courses. An interesting variation was the fact that, along with MIT students, students from nearby institutions of lesser prestige could also enroll and follow similar programs of activities. The stress was constantly on flexibility, individual work, and intimate interaction with the staff members.

The future of interdisciplinary work is obscure. There is a great deal of discussion throughout the country regarding interdisciplinary efforts. There are interesting and potentially significant experiments. Some new institutions are basing their major efforts on an interdisciplinary concept, and doubtless out of the emerging research will come new opportunities and forms for interdisciplinary effort.

However, there are significant issues and difficulties. The first is the fundamental one: What is the nature of interdisciplinary study? Is it primarily exposure of students to a number of related but still disciplinary courses, with the expectation that each student will arrive at his own interdisciplinary synthesis? Is it selecting portions from various disciplines and fashioning them into a completely new entity? Or is it identifying some complex real-life phenomenon and then searching for many different ways of coping with the problem? Or does genuine interdisciplinary work require the evolution of a discrete intellectual synthesis, such as has appeared in the field of genetics?

A different sort of issue is whether faculty members prepared in one of the disciplines can achieve the interdisciplinary sophistication needed to make them feel at home with new combinations of materials. One problem the general education movement never solved was this problem of professorial talent. Professors trained in music had difficulty feeling comfortable with philosophical, literary, and historical elements in a broad course in the humanities. Related to this matter of professorial ease in dealing with materials from several fields is the matter of career development. In American higher education, professors develop careers as historians, economists, or biologists. Promotion and recognition come from deepening mastery in those specialized fields. The professor tempted to spend several years developing an interdisciplinary course must always ask himself: Will the effort help or hinder long-term professional development? A related problem, especially in highly departmentalized institutions, is whether a department will contribute its resources for nondepartmental courses. Since salary budgets are linked to departments and since the availability of adequate external funding has decreased significantly, this becomes an especially acute problem. There is, for example, the well-received program in values and technology at Stanford that was started by concerned members of several departments with the assistance of some external funding. Students liked the program, but the schools and departments became more and more unwilling to provide faculty salary money to maintain a staff. The senior faculty members who had originated the program also had other research and professional interests and hence could not be expected to continue intense involvement at very real cost to their professional careers.

A somewhat different complexity, which is two-edged, regards the intellectual content of an interdisciplinary effort. On the one hand, developing an interdisciplinary program by exposing students to disciplinary work and expecting them to make their own syntheses may be appropriate for the academically highly capable and motivated, but for students of lesser ability, who have trouble even synthesizing a well-structured disciplinary course, the task may prove to be impossible. A rather poignant example was an attempt to transfer the Unified Science Study program from MIT to a Massachusetts community college. That effort was intended to provide ample opportunity for self-inquiry and value clarification on the part of students. They were to be allowed opportunity for project-oriented interdisciplinary and independent study. Flexibility in scheduling was to permit spontaneously organized seminars, contract learning, and individual uses of a wide variety of resource people and opportunities in that region of Massachusetts. The students entering the program were academically average or below and were not motivated academically. They floundered in trying to make sense out of the program; they had difficulty identifying relevant problems; they demonstrated inadequacies in using educational resources; and they had difficulty internalizing the various interdisciplinary stimuli to which they were exposed. In the end, the faculty members offering the program turned it into almost a therapeutic endeavor to help students solve personal problems and simply to gain greater understanding of the what the college might offer them.

The other edge to the matter is the possibility that interdisciplinary courses may turn out to be quite superficial and may produce no solid and lasting intellectual gains.

A last—and at times haunting—issue is whether interdisciplinary courses and programs will actually attract student enrollments that can be sustained over years. College and university students are motivated by conditions similar to professors. They are interested in developing marketable skills; they want easily transferable academic credit; and they frequently want the structure that comes with the familiar. The relative ease with which both faculty and students regress to the more disciplinary style of education suggests that these far from trivial concerns have not yet been accommodated.

Independent Study. Mention has already been made of independent study, but some further elaboration is probably in order, for independent study is an essential in nontraditional learning and in many of the new institutions and seems to be increasingly attractive in traditional institutions. Also, it is probably significant to note the changed conception of independent study since the 1950s and 1960s. At that time independent study, whether linked to honors programs, tutorials, comprehensive examinations, or special projects such as theses, was judged to be highly expensive if properly carried out. The one-to-one student-faculty ratio that seemed necessary to provide guidance to students made independent study too expensive for most institutions to attempt in any massive way. However, by the 1970s independent study had expanded for many different reasons. It was used to allow students to pursue topics for which there were no qualified faculty members; it was seen as economically sound because it substituted self-service for service provided by faculty members; it was viewed as a way to make the curriculum more flexible, both spatially and temporally; it was judged as a workable way to make the curriculum more relevant for increasingly heterogeneous student bodies; and it was highly consistent with the educational potentialities of the two most promising educational technologies—computers and videotape cassettes.

A substantial majority of collegiate institutions in the United States by the 1970s did make specific provision for some kind of independent study. However, the number of students who had taken advantage of those opportunities represent a distinct minority

(Dressel and Thompson, 1973, pp. 14–15). Thus to claim that independent study is a major active movement within traditional collegiate institutions is not a warrantable conclusion. However, an examination of the sorts of activities undertaken as independent study during the 1970s contributes to a profile of American higher education in the 1970s that is ideologically different from earlier periods. The University of San Francisco, suffering rather acute financial difficulties, contracted with a for-profit organization to develop degree programs for upgrading teachers to the master's degree and for upgrading police officers to the bachelor's degree. The for-profit organization developed syllabi, recruited faculty (many of whom were on the University of San Francisco faculty), and scheduled the sequence of activities. The two programs did involve periodic seminar or workshop situations. However, much of the work for credit was carried on by individual students doing assigned readings and developing projects in connection with their ongoing work for which academic credit would be granted. Through assigning academic credit for military and work experience, credit for college work done elsewhere, and credit for the independent projects, students in the police work program, for example, could receive the bachelor's degree with only about thirty hours of formal classroom work, the rest of the credit being given for independent study.

The other revolutionary freshman-year program, at Antioch College in Yellow Springs, Ohio, pushed the potential of independent study perhaps further than any other of the traditional institutions. Freshmen in the program, after suitable orientation, were allowed to contrive their own full academic year, which might include classroom work or small group work but which might include nothing but independent study throughout the year, with the exception of the time students spent in cooperative work-study. Possibly the most prevalent provision is for institutions to assign independent study course numbers to individual faculty members and to allow them the discretion for registering students for independent study if that seems appropriate.

Although independent study as yet does not loom large in the repertoire of traditional institutions, it is possible that it might come to play a substantial role. Some of the new private institutions created since 1968 have been able to survive financially by using a small core of full-time faculty, a larger number of part-time or adjunct faculty, and stressing a substantial amount of independent study. Those models could become appealing to older institutions faced with the mounting costs of conducting education in traditional ways, in addition to which the rhetoric of independent study, which stresses the need to develop self-reliance in students, is appealing.

However, future expansion or retraction will depend on how perplexing issues are resolved. The first of these is cost and effectiveness. The substantial number of experiments with carefully programmed sequences of instruction that students follow at their own rates of speed demonstrate that as much learning (as measured by cognitive tests) by students working on their own takes place as in a formal classroom setting using lectures and discussion. However, the cost of preparation of carefully structured courses seemingly precludes widespread use of this approach. Less costly, in terms of faculty time, is the more open approach to independent study, in which students find their own problem, devise their own learning activities, and check periodically with an instructor regarding their progress. This is such an idiosyncratic kind of activity that any sort of normative appraisal of education benefits is virtually impossible; students' expressions of satisfaction and professorial impressions of progress are about the only workable kinds of evaluation. If professors spend a great deal of time carefully monitoring student plans and progress, the cost factor again rises.

A minor, but potentially significant, problem involves what students expect in return for payment of tuition in traditional institutions. In a number of nontraditional institutions that stress independent study, students can tolerate tuition because degrees and credentials can be obtained in relatively short periods of time. But in traditional institutions with reasonably strict residency requirements, programs that emphasize a great deal of independent study run the danger of the students complaining that for a $3,500 tuition fee they received a library card and an admonition to educate themselves. Then there can also be the question as to how much independent study students can tolerate. Education can be viewed as a gregarious activity in which students assist and reenforce each other. The interaction between students helps clarify concepts and assigns meaning to knowledge. Independent study typically minimizes such interaction and could conceivably prove to be counterproductive if overused. This very phenomenon may account for the high attrition rate that the British Open University continues to experience. The bulk of the work in that institution is carried on independently and does prove to be too lonely for many students.

Then there is always the question as to whether all students are capable of carrying on independent study. There may be personality, motivational, or aptitude characteristics that allow some students to succeed remarkably well, while other students fail completely when placed on their own. Present knowledge only allows speculation, but it is a matter that will require exploration if independent study is to be expanded (as some proponents believe it should be).

And of course, as is true of other developments, the purposes of independent study are unclear. The rationale of Dressel and Thompson for independent study provides some help in this regard, but not enough. They point out that learning must ultimately be accomplished by the learner, regardless of ability, and that if learning is to continue throughout life students should be trained to work by themselves. Students need some kind of off-campus experience, which can best be accommodated independently. Working independently toward their own goals theoretically places students in competition with themselves rather than in intensive competition with other students, as in more traditional settings. And theoretically individuals working on their own can bring the full range of their cognitive and affective powers to bear better than in more formal situations. They go on to remark that there is little agreement as to whether independent study is properly viewed as the process through which students acquire knowledge and skills or an ability developed by instruction and through experience. If it is a process, then the results should be compared with acquisition of knowledge and skills acquired by other means. And if it is a skill or ability a similar question must be answered. The typical attempts at independent study for the most part have not yet addressed such questions (Dressel and Thompson, 1973).

Competency-Based Education. One of the most popular curricular and instructional developments of the 1970s—one intimately related to other major developments of the period—is competency-based, or criterion-referenced, education. Although a complex technological language has developed around the concept, it is essentially quite simple. It posits that the purpose of education is to develop specific outcomes, such as the ability to write, to think critically, or to perform certain kinds of experiments. It clearly draws on the model of vocational training to develop physical skills that can be described in advance and demonstration of which can be measured with relative ease. Competency-based education intellectually derives from the theories of Ralph W. Tyler, which stress stating and refining educational objectives, finding appropriate learning activities, and measuring student demonstration of the behaviors posited or objectives. Nor is such education in essence particularly new. Dressel and Mayhew in 1954 edited three handbooks showing how to state desired behaviors as educational outcomes and how to evaluate whether or not students had devleoped the desired competencies.

But during the 1970s interest in the use of objectives to guide instruction, which had waned during the 1960s, once again became popular. Several factors seem to have been related to this change. First there was the rising interest in accountability as a means of justifying educational expenditures. To prove that funds were used wisely, it was necessary to prove what educational changes had actually been accomplished. It was also related to open-admissions policies, by which institutions accepted students of widely differing traits and talents. The theory was that students might be unequally prepared on entry into college but that they should be equally qualified on graduation. Establishing such equality required demonstrating competency. Similarly, as it came to be assumed, in the nontraditional movement that people could be educated in many different ways and through many different agencies, it also became apparent that the effectiveness of different educational routes could best be shown by measuring competency.

Interest in competency-based education was strengthened by several different agencies and institutions. State credentialing agencies began to ask for more specific evidence as to the professional skills that colleges and universities actually developed in applicants for certification. Teacher licensing is a good example. Voluntary accreditation, shifting from making judgments of institutions based on inputs (number of Ph.D.s on the faculty) to using outputs (what is the educational effectiveness), began to demand evidence of developed competency. Research scholars, seeking to study collegiate impact also stressed the need for evidence of competency and suggested ways by which it could be measured. And, in a vague sort of way, the growing national preoccupation with consumerism contributed as colleges and universities came under scrutiny. Consumer advocates and possibly eventually even the courts could best be answered if institutions could demonstrate production of competency in their graduates.

Many of the widely publicized changes of this period came to be identified with a few institutions; general education—Harvard, Chicago, Columbia, Michigan State; honors work—Swarthmore and Wooster; large-scale computer-based education—Illinois and Texas; Doctor of Arts—Miami and Carnegie-Mellon; cooperative work experience—Northeastern and Antioch. Little Mars Hill College is rapidly becoming the epitome of competency-based education.

Many specific devices are combined in different ways in a competency-based program. The College Level Examination Program provides both general and special education tests that can be used; passing the test is evidence of competence. Students collect evidence in portfolios, of their growing competence, which are then reviewed by faculty members. There is actual field observation of students performing or videotape reproduction. With careful training, faculty members can observe behavior with considerable inter-observer reliability (.500/70). The traditional methods of oral examinations, display of creative products, and recitals are also used. Unfortunately it is also assumed that passing a course demonstrates competence.

The competency-based approach seems to have produced some worthwhile developments in institutions in which it is practiced. Discussion of competence leads directly to pedagogical questions as to how best develop it. It also forces a consideration as to the meaning of collegiate degrees: Which competencies does a bachelor's degree imply?

However, competency-based education reveals some issues and perplexities. The first of these is an economic one. Specifying behavioral outcomes, finding appropriate learning materials, and developing evaluation techniques are enormously time consuming and expensive. Developing a reliable, one-hour, objectively scored test of critical thinking in social science requires about 50 hours of trained professional time. If a course in social science seeks no more than six such competencies, then 300 hours of time are needed, just to construct the measuring instruments. That is seven and one-half weeks of the professor's time. Grading themes reliably requires continuous reader training, as does also judging proficiency in speaking a foreign language. And training and actual judgment are both expensive. It is argued that costs of test construction per student can be reduced through use with large numbers of students or repeated uses of tests over time. In a few institutions, this is realistic, but in most it is not.

In addition to the economic issue, there is the technical one. Professors are trained in a subject and typically have not been trained in psychology or psychometrics. Yet creating appropriate learning resources to produce quite specific behaviors requires a great deal of psychological sophistication and skill in measuring outcomes, at least in test construction. Whether needed insights can be generated through in-service training has yet to be demonstrated. Probably it can, assuming institutional ability to pay for it and faculty willingness to be trained. Both of these assumptions are highly conjectural.

Then there is the matter of professional role—and whether professors, in any appreciable numbers, will exchange the traditional role for the new one of planner, adviser, manager, and evaluator. The impression persists that this can be done in a few institutions that have a unique tradition or problem. Also, a few professors in large universities may be enough interested to embrace the competency doctrine. But if competency-based education is to become a major orientation of collegiate education, substantial numbers of faculty and of institutions must change.

Perhaps the most that can happen in higher education generally is that the concept of competency will generate a little more thought on the part of professors as to what they are really trying to do in their courses. Thus, the movement will leave a residue in the conventional wisdom, just as have other major educational trends.

On the negative side, the movement may produce in some institutions adherence to the competency doctrine, the actual assessment
being done impressionistically. This seems to be happening in some
more traditional programs as student testimony as to life experience
is used as evidence of competency.

Improving College Teaching. College teaching and the improvement of college instruction has been a perennial subject of
speeches and of polemical and exhortative literature. During the
1940s, 1950s, and 1960s, committees on the improvement of
instruction issued reports and periodically edited books seeking to
show how college teaching might be improved. For the most part,
however, institutions, especially the large complex and prestigious
institutions, did little in a formal way to express an institutional
concern for the improvement of instruction. It is true that at the
University of Washington and the University of Minnesota considerable use was made of student evaluation of teaching. At the University of Michigan and the University of Southern California, there
were courses on college teaching, and occasionally someone deeply
concerned about college teaching, when placed in a leadership role,
could gain acceptance at least of the theory that college teaching was
an important professional activity that could be improved. For
example, Sidney J. French (1956) edited a book called *Accent on
Teaching,* subsequently became the academic dean of the University
of South Florida, and was able to stress teaching as the paramount
activity of that institution. The first catalogue, for example, was
entitled *Accent on Learning* (1959). That particular emphasis, it
should be noted, disappeared toward the end of the 1960s when
French retired. It was only at the beginning of the 1970s that something akin to a movement for faculty development and improvement
of college instruction took place.

It is difficult to isolate the forces involved in this development,
although some of the changes were quite dramatic. For example, in
research-oriented universities during the 1960s, teaching ability was
rarely seriously considered in making appointments or promotions.
Yet suddenly, in the 1970s, central administration would not consider such recommendations unless specific statements were made
supported by evidence regarding instructional ability. Some of the
situations in which institutions found themselves undoubtedly con-

tributed to the new concern. The leveling or declining of student enrollment implied that conditions might stabilize or improve if instruction improved. Decreased faculty mobility suggested that improvement had to come from changing incumbents rather than through recruiting new talent. One suggestion for alleviating the economic crunch facing collegiate institutions was to make instruction both more efficient and more economical. And the increased demand for accountability by parents, board members, legislators, and the public in general forced institutions to account for their uses of faculty members and the outcomes that faculty efforts produced.

At about the same time, the educational potential of technological refinements was being more and more widely publicized. It seemed clear that if educational technology were to become important in higher education faculty members would need to be trained to use such equipment. It is possible to speculate that the inclusion of students as members of faculty committees and senates may have focused more interest on teaching. It is also possible to speculate, but by no means to prove, that the aftermath of the student protest years produced a demand for changed and improved teaching.

Institutions around the country began to experiment with one or more strategies to bring about change and improvement. Some adopted training programs to develop such new skills as conducting tutorials or small-group discussions. Some administrators began to carry on regular consultations with faculty members to discuss individual professional development and instructional improvement. A growing number of institutions made organizational changes to facilitate personal and professional development, such as the creating of special administrative officers or agencies to help faculty. Through conferences, workshops, and use of experts, faculty members were shown new techniques of instruction and new instructional materials, and were taught how to use both for optimal improvement effects. Here and there the reward system was changed to include teaching as an essential element in the promotion or tenure process. Institutions began to assume some responsibility for helping individual faculty members change teaching specialties or teaching careers, and a great deal of attention was given, beginning quite early in the 1970s, to stimulating discussion of the broad subject of professional development. The monograph dealing with faculty development in a period of declining enrollments was widely used to stimulate serious faculty consideration of developmental issues.

Many different sorts of activities could be considered part of the professional development movement; for example, allowing for lighter teaching loads for junior faculty, using more institutional funds for professional travel, appointing younger faculty as university fellows with time allowed for work on professional and institutional problems, increasing remuneration for sabbatical leave to allow career redirection, and inviting lecturers to the campus to discuss professional development. However, the most visible and characteristic elements of the movement are systematic programs to improve the instructional ability of teaching assistants and junior faculty members; widespread use of student evaluation of teaching and the use of those results for administrative decisions about faculty appointment; promotion, and tenure; and the creation of university centers for the improvement of instruction.

Attempts to improve the teaching ability of teaching assistants run the gamut from the casual suggestion that all graduate students should have some teaching experience as part of their academic preparation on to structured programs supervised by fully ranked faculty and making use of advanced educational technology. An example of the last is a project at the University of Nebraska in which six videotape presentations concerning the teaching of chemistry and six manuals to accompany them have been prepared. Those two elements comprise an instructional package designed to be used in highly flexible ways not only at the University of Nebraska but also by different chemistry departments in different institutions. The project was apparently undertaken because of growing interest on the part of a professor of chemistry in doing research on teaching rather than research in chemistry. He seems to be one of a relatively few but still a growing number of professors throughout the country who direct special chemistry programs and who are trying to make a professional role out of the position of director or coordinator of freshman chemistry. His interests were reinforced by the decisions of two major chemical professional associations to stress the improvement in the teaching of freshman chemistry. The decision to use videotape rather than some other mode of delivery seems in part due to the quite considerable television expertise available at the University of Nebraska. This particular effort is being made at four or five midwestern universities and seems to result not only in changed teaching practices on the part of teaching assistants but also in greater awareness on the part of regular faculty members that teaching is modifiable.

Many different examples of the use of student evaluation of teaching could be cited, but perhaps one best reveals the nature of what is being attempted and the factors that are involved. At the University of Rochester, a system of evaluating faculty teaching has been created that includes student judgments, administrator judgments, and the use of evidence in personnel decisions. Leaders at the University of Rochester had long been interested in stressing college teaching as an important activity; however, when a senate committee on college teaching attempted to require all faculty members to use a student evaluation form, the proposal was rejected. When exploring evaluation of college teaching was attempted under the rubric of research, however, faculty cooperation was obtained. The system consisted of a grading scale used by department heads to rank each faculty member on the categories of professionalism, visibility, research, teaching, ability to communicate, and academic good citizenship. These same elements were woven into a student evaluation form, and the results could be related to department head ratings by computer analysis and manipulation. Once the system was perfected, several of the professional schools voted to require that results go to department heads, who would use the evidence in personnel recommendations. In schools in which the faculty was unwilling to make such a decision, the deans accomplished the same end by requiring that any departmental recommendation concerning faculty must contain specific statements about teaching, as well as supportive evidence. Hence the combined department head rating scale and student evaluation forms were easily available, and, administered by a neutral agency (the counseling center), such an administrative decree ensured widespread use of the system.

There are also many models of institutional centers for improving teaching that exemplify this part of the faculty development movement. A reasonably typical one is the Center for Teaching

Effectiveness at the University of Texas at Austin, created in September 1973, in response to a recommendation from the faculty senate. The primary mission of the center was to provide assistance to the teaching faculty in making teaching and learning more effective. Originally it was to focus on support for the faculty, but gradually the center expanded its activities to include teaching assistants. The first five-year agenda for the center included offering courses on college teaching for faculty members, courses on college teaching for teaching assistants, maintaining a consulting service for faculty members who wished assistance involving teaching problems, maintaining a referral service for questions about undergraduate education and teaching, conducting periodic workshops and seminars for faculty members and teaching assistants, and examining instructional classrooms and facilities as a basis for recommending modification of existing space and the specification for new space to be constructed. (This and other centers are well described in Crow and others, 1976).

These three kinds of activities have been sufficiently examined in different kinds of institutions to suggest that they can achieve perceptible and desirable outcomes. Teaching assistants, after going through a systematic program, do change methods of teaching, do testify to greater personal comfort in teaching, and do come to view teaching as something more than a subsidy for their own graduate study. Faculty members in even the most research-oriented universities have accepted student evaluation, and in some situations faculty members do try to change after pondering the results of student evaluations. Annual reports of centers for the improvement of instruction show evidence of individual professors being helped, and centers have received favorable evaluations by committees of the faculty. However, the long-term future of the faculty development movement depends on how several issues are resolved. One of these is how seriously senior professors will take the responsibility for training teaching assistants. For example, the typical freshman chemistry course is directed either by a quite junior faculty member who is not expected to gain tenure or a quite senior faculty member approaching retirement. The work of the coordinator is for the most part logistical—ensuring enough teaching assistants for all sections and instructing them in the setup of laboratory experiments and how to obtain chemicals from storerooms. The successful programs to improve the teaching assistants seem to require the full professional energy of fully ranked professors who are willing to assume supervision of freshman chemistry over a prolonged period and who gain major professional satisfactions from that work. One estimate is that there are probably not more than twenty coordinators of freshman chemistry in the country who take such a professional attitude, and in other subjects the number is probably even smaller. An interesting question is whether, in view of a relocalization of faculty interests, this new role can spread widely. An issue involving student evaluation of teaching is that of how long a program can be maintained before faculty, administration, and even students tire of the periodic ritual. There have been programs of student evaluation of teaching going back twenty-five or thirty years, but the pattern of evolution has been quite uneven—use of evaluation forms typically decreases after initial enthusiastic attempts to use them. A program of student-evaluated teaching seems to require clear administrative assignment to some office and enough staff to take care of logistical as well as public relations problems. Relying on student groups or faculty committees may produce a brief spurt of activity but not the sustained use of forms that seems to be essential. Administration of the program does require resources, and whether institutions in a time of diminishing resources will allocate funds for such an activity is conjectural. Probably institutions will not sustain them unless clear and persuasive evidence can be accumulated showing that beneficial changes in instruction are taking place. A similar economic issue seems to be involved in centers for the improvement of instruction. The typical pattern has been for an institution to create centers with a relatively small staff supported by institutional funds. When they have expanded their agendas, these centers have typically sought external funding for specific projects. In some centers, it has even appeared that internal demands for service to faculty was so slow in developing that externally supported projects were needed to absorb the creative energies of faculty members assigned to the centers. An expanded center for the improvement of instruction creates a service that must compete with other services, such as libraries, computer centers, counseling centers, testing offices, ombudsmen, and offices of institutional research and planning. The long-term significance of these centers will undoubt-edly depend on the competitive priority assigned to them for financial support, and that, of course, will depend on demonstrable evidence of significance for the institution. Another issue is how warmly the large and distinguished universities will embrace faculty development programs and the extent to which substantial numbers of senior faculty members avail themselves of services. As has been repeatedly stressed, the American system of higher education is stratified, and there clearly are pacesetting institutions. Practices embraced by those leaders gain a respectability that can facilitate the dissemination of a practice. As yet, with the exception of the University of Michigan, the exemplary centers for the improvement of instruction are not the pacesetting institutions. (One at Cornell was eliminated five years after its inception.)

A last and quite complicated issue is whether or not a college faculty member has a definable professional role. The broad concept of faculty development implies that there is and that professional practice beyond deepening understanding of a subject can be im-proved. The acceptance of such a professional role, however, appears to be far from generally shared. Discussions with faculty members, particularly in four-year institutions, reveals a typical conception of the professor as one who knows a great deal about a subject and shares that knowledge with students through writing and through oral presentations.

Significance of Change

The important question is whether these curricular develop-ments in traditional and established colleges and universities in aggregate form a pattern and, if so, what the significance of it is. It has been argued that the large veteran enrollments in the late 1940s and 1950s sparked the proliferation of prescribed, staff-taught courses in general education that could be taught by partially trained teachers. It is also suggested that the launching of Sputnik and the heavy involvement of the federal government in supporting research produced a disproportionate emphasis on science and the replace-ment of broad general education courses with more rigorous introductory courses in various disciplines that took place during the 1960s. The event of comparable magnitude for the 1970s is, of course, the deteriorating financial situation and the slowdown in enrollments of traditional kinds of students.

There are enormous variations in developments in different institutions and different kinds of institutions, and the reason for development also varies according to individual situations. Nonetheless a composite seems to be emerging. First of all, within traditional two- and four-year collegiate institutions there have been significant changes but not radical ones. The amount of general education required for graduation has declined somewhat, and the prescribed courses in general education (frequently of an interdisciplinary character) have given way to a distribution system in which students select from introductory disciplinary courses. The amount of time devoted to a major has remained almost constant throughout the 1970s. However, students have strengthened their major preparation through using most of their elective courses in the major field or in contiguous fields to serve as a context. There have been slight decreases in overall credit-hour requirements for graduation (Blackburn and others, 1976).

Against that backdrop of relative stability, the various curricular developments of the 1970s seem fundamentally to be related to four conditions. The first of these is the deteriorating economic condition and the return of competition for students to much of American higher education. The curricular response typically appears to have been a market response—to generate new services and to try to open up new sources of clients. Although some theorists have recommended curtailment of programs in order to help solve economic problems, institutions seem to have taken the opposite course of action. New programs have been created, and only relatively few old programs have been eliminated. New vocational courses and programs have been added, and new sorts of interdisciplinary courses that might appeal to larger registrations have been contrived. In all save the most highly selective institutions, there have been developments designed to admit more students. Admissions standards have been changed to allow people of modest academic aptitude to enter; a policy of open admissions has been attempted in a few public institutions or systems; residence requirements have been modified to allow students greater flexibility to enter, leave, and reenter institutions; and institutions have sought to retain students longer and to cut down on costly attrition rates through providing better or at least more visible services to students. The increased use of senior faculty in freshman and sophomore courses is probably an example of this phenomenon. Paradoxically there has also been considerable experimentation to modify the mix of low-priced and high-priced labor and to modify the mix between labor and capital, as well as experimentation with increasing the less expensive self-service ways of coping with students' needs. These new mixes are found in programs of independent study and in the organization of some interdisciplinary problems-oriented courses.

The second condition is the anticipation of a steady state for higher education for at least the remainder of the twentieth century, a state characterized by an aging faculty. This recognition seems to be involved in the various efforts at faculty development and seems to be based on the belief that an aging faculty needs rather regular professional self-renewal. This steady state, with almost all teaching positions filled with tenured faculty, is also probably involved in the creation of new professional roles, such as heading up centers for the improvement of instruction. Of course, the creating of such roles may be antithetical to the economic goals of institutions but does appear as a way by which some academics can preserve status within traditional institutions. As pointed out earlier, others who were not able to find such a role have sought to contrive a parallel one in new kinds of institutions and in the nontraditional educational activities of other social institutions.

As institutions struggle with the economic and competitive circumstances, they seem to have striven to reconcile the meritocratic, academic, and research view of higher education of the 1950s and 1960s and the necessary egalitarianism of the 1970s. There has been a significant amount of reluctant experimentation with black studies, Chicano studies, and the like, but with the covert intention of eventually accommodating then in the traditional departmental structure. There appears to have been some acceptance in theory of some of the more prominent attributes of nontraditional learning, such as independent study or external degrees. Closer examination, however, reveals that adoption of the nontraditional, with the exception of certain specific institutions, is more verbal than real. This seems to imply that in the absence of radically new and unexpected forces traditional institutions are not likely to adopt nontraditional learning to any significant degree. The nontraditional, if it is to flourish, will probably be developed by new kinds of institutions specifically created or modified for that purpose.

FIVE

Educational Technology

Just as nontraditional learning has not replaced traditional learning (although it might) and just as new kinds of institutions have not typically been imitated by traditional ones (although this could also happen), so educational technology has not become an essential ingredient in higher education—but it could, theoretically. The potential of educational technology is characterized by the British scholar Sir Eric Ashby, who called the use of such technology "the fourth educational revolution." His phrase became the title for the policy statement of the Carnegie Commission on Higher Education. Ashby pointed out that the first revolution in education was the use of symbols to represent reality rather than the use of artifacts themselves. The second was the assignment of educational responsibilities to special people, thus removing part of that obligation from the family. The third revolution was the invention of movable printing type, and the fourth, of course, is the use of mechanical and electronic devices to carry out many different educational practices. The Carnegie Commission (1972a), in elaborating this theme, has pointed out that there is currently available an array of technological resources that, properly used, could change education substantially. Some of these had been around a long while, but others, such as computers or multimedia classrooms, are relatively new. There are devices to facilitate self-instruction, to deliver educational services to remote areas, and to enrich more orthodox instruction, and still others that can exponentially increase the amount of information quickly available on a subject and deliverable in relatively short periods of time. It is this potential that justifies devoting a whole chapter to something the actual uses of which are still relatively modest.

Educational technology is not new. During the eighteenth and nineteenth centuries, certain currents in educational philosophy urged less abstract and formalized instruction. Realists, such as Locke and Rousseau, urged reality as the primary means of instructing people. As early as the turn of the twentieth century, there was a definite educational movement in the United States labeled "visual education," which, among other things, urged the use of museums and magic lantern slides for public schools. As in later periods, use of mechanical devices was encouraged by such commercial interests as the Keystone View Company, which specialized in the production of lantern slides and stereopticons. As motion picture technology came to be perfected, other firms came into existence to manufacture and sell educational motion pictures. Despite these disparate efforts, however, there really was no definite intellectual rationale encompassing educational technology until after World War II. The experience of the military, in that war, of using filmstrips, mock-ups, slides, motion pictures, and silhouette devices contributed substantially to the growth of a fullblown movement.

Promise of the 1950s and 1960s

During the late 1950s and 1960s, the first major expansion of systematic use of many different technological devices caught the attention of the higher educational community. By 1959 serious attention was being given to mechanical and electronic devices for the storage and retrieval of information, to mechanical devices that could substitute for the drill activities of regular classrooms, to the use of audiotapes and films in language laboratories, to instruction by telephone, to augmenting the potential of radio and television, and to refinements in the use of films, such as presenting full courses on film. By 1959, the potential of videotape recordings had been seen, although the cost at that time was prohibitive for most educational institutions. Also by 1959, some institutions had initiated closed-circuit television systems and were offering full courses over them, a few courses had been offered over open-circuit television, and the potential of beaming television courses over several states had been examined. A status report of the period captured the current optimism with the title *New Frontiers in Learning* (1959).

It was claimed that educational technology could serve purposes that exhibited the general characteristics of higher education—growth and large size. Anticipated enrollment expansion required ways to compensate for a shortage of professors. It was envisioned that institutions could link themselves together with coaxial cables to bring one lecturer before hundreds of students. Open-circuit television was seen as a way of bringing credit courses to thousands or even hundreds of thousands of degree students. Language laboratories were viewed as a way of conducting drills for many, whereas, historically, language drills had been limited to a few. And the computer was seen as a utopian way of providing individual attention to a thousand or more students. Relatedly, educational technology was viewed as a way of saving scarce professorial time by using equipment to handle routine parts of instruction and to leave faculty time free for the creative acts of course preparation and counseling.

In addition, the technology was seen as a potent device for enriching orthodox instruction, through such means as films of great doctors or teachers, amplified telephone interviews with opinion makers, and pictorial representations made quickly available to professors in many different courses. Language laboratories and various kinds of teaching machines were seen as a way of providing somewhat structured but nonetheless independent study.

Because preparing films, television presentations, instructional programs and carefully meshed video materials requires sound understanding of learning and modes of teaching, the educational technology was also judged to be an important means for improving teaching and for facilitating greater understanding of learning theory. Moreover, the technology provides ways for precise study of learning and the relative significance of such things as immediate reinforcement or applications of principles to new settings.

All of these potentialities were seen as being chiefly realized in conventional collegiate institutions and as serving essentially traditional kinds of students following a reasonably academic program.

Changed Possibilities and Potentialities

Actual experimentation with educational technology and the justifications for its use during the 1950s and 1960s were conducted and expressed in the context of traditional colleges. By the end of the 1960s, a new emphasis appeared that considered technology a primary means of delivering educational services. The two chief reasons advanced were reaching new groups of students and economizing.

Expanded Access. While those potentialities were continuously examined and elaborated on into the late 1960s and 1970s, the rhetoric concerning the values of the technology changed perceptibly, and several new and distinctive potentialities were suggested. Carpenter, writing in 1968 (pp. 3–5), advanced several propositions substantially different and more egalitarian than those found in earlier writing: "The whole educational job is to provide appropriate opportunities and conditions in our society for each person to learn what he needs to know and what he has the assured right and abilities to learn, wherever he lives in this nation and whatever the time and condition of his life. . . . Education is an unlimited enterprise. There are no boundaries to the needs, uses, and desires for more learning, more understanding, more skills, more technology, and more intelligent regulation of the physical and biotic forces of the world environment. Sustained educational effort will never be outmoded. . . . The work of universities for the near and more truly for the distant future cannot be done fully and well by traditional educational operations, methods, and procedures. . . .

There has developed and matured a communication revolution which, in unique ways, corresponds to the industrial power energy revolution that is still in rapid progress. . . . The technological developments of the communication revolution are eminently appropriate and applicable to the solution of many if not most of the educational problems which confront the growing universities and the nation." Those promises could be summarized in one assertion: "The whole educational job is to provide favorable learning conditions for people who have the needs, rights, and abilities to learn." Boyer, in a similar vein (1975), suggested a radical expansion of higher education to many new groups of students, clearly implying utilization of technology in his suggestions for more flexible schedule arrangements, a greater mix of formal and informal learning throughout the adult working years, and much greater concern for older men and women, to whom educational services could be most effectively brought through combinations of educational technology.

Reducing Costs. Earlier discussions of educational technology had recognized that finances represented a problem but did not consider it an insoluble one. The virtues of the technology, compensating for teacher shortages and enriching instruction, were the prime justifications. Obstacles to the achievement of those purposes could be overcome through adequate funding, and those who considered the matter believed funds would be forthcoming. It was a time of faith in exponential increases in support for higher education.

By the 1970s, however, the media were being considered as one possible way to effect economies and to reduce the overall cost of a highly labor-intensive higher education. Throughout the 1960s, rates of increase in the cost of higher educational services exceeded those of other consumer goods. This differential seems to have resulted from inflation, lagging productivity in education, costs of enriching the quality of educational services, increased costs of administration, increased costs of providing requested or required information, and the carry-over costs of past decisions. All institutions had been seeking to bring income and expenditure into equilibrium and had tried a number of different approaches: increasing productivity through increasing class size, substituting cheaper for more expensive labor, minimizing high-cost programs and maximizing low-cost programs, modifying the length of time required for degrees, shifting much educational responsibility to a self-service mode, once again rationing higher education, and using educational technology as a means of reducing labor intensivity and/or increasing the quality of outcomes. The Carnegie Commission on Higher Education (1972a, pp. 45–46) lent its authority to the belief that educational technology was an economically sound partial solution: "Although short-run costs for the development and introduction of new instructional technology are expected to be very great, they will ultimately yield dividends. Much of the expanding technology has a potential economic effect of spreading the benefit of investment in a single unit of instruction among very large numbers of students. It therefore has an ability to increase the productivity of higher education. The earlier efforts are made to develop the expanding instructional technology fully, the earlier this increased productivity will be realized." By 1976 this potentiality had clearly not been realized. However, the quest went on to find ways of exploiting the technological bonanza and to do so in ways that were economically sound.

Another economic development, which began in the middle 1960s and which is somewhat different from other developments concerning educational technology, was the sudden entry of large corporations into the production of educational technology and related materials. IBM, General Electric, Lytton Industries, Raytheon, and Xerox, all conglomerate corporations, decided to develop special units to concentrate on producing and distributing educational materials. It was recognized that to be profitable the technology would need to receive a substantial portion of the funds being allocated for labor-intensive professional services. Some of these corporations had had considerable experience contracting with the U.S. Department of Defense and hoped to transfer some of their professional and scientific capabilities from defense to education-oriented markets. It apparently was assumed that federal expenditures for educational services would continue to increase at such a level as to make education subunits of corporations profitable. With the exception of firms producing computers and serving as linkages in computer networks, the total impact of industrial corporations on the practice of education turned out to be relatively slight, and corporations have either divested themselves of their educational subunits or allowed them to function in relatively small markets. The most significant element of that entry of business into education is that it symbolized the belief that educational technology could indeed bring about economies and that those economies could be turned to a profit for business and industrial corporations. It is this belief that represents the sharp departure from the technological dogma of the late 1950s and early 1960s.

For Developing Peoples and Nations. A review of the uses of and research concerning educational technology during the period 1945–1965 suggests that it was highly parochial, being carried on chiefly in the United States. It was in such centers as the University of Illinois, the University of Nebraska, Teachers College, Yale University, and Stanford University that major research studies were carried on concerning uses of technology, frequently in connection with cooperating public school systems. However, by the late 1960s and on into the 1970s demand for and experimentation with educational technology began slowly to catch on in many new and different places. In the developed industrial nations, there were some developments sparked by indigenous people and purposes. In Sweden all schools had projectors, recorders, and videotape recorders. The United Kingdom was not far behind. West Germany and France had lagged substantially behind, and in other Western European nations the situation was mixed. In Japan educational technology was widely used outside of schools, but the educational institutions were significantly slow in developing sympathy for technological devices.

It was in the developing nations, when aided by external funds and, more recently, by the inflated prices of certain natural resources, that there was a pronounced experimentation with quite sophisticated technologies, even though those nations lacked the technical resources and people to use the equipment wisely. For example, a $50,000 computerized typewriter was hailed as the answer to Africa's educational problems, in spite of the fact that most of the schools had no electricity. Several of the oil-producing nations of the Middle East have embarked on serious projects to use educational technology to solve deeply embedded educational problems, an attempt that has also been made in Samoa and in Central and South American nations. The motivation for adopting technology in developing nations seems to be the faith that such things as television and computer-based instruction can eliminate centuries of educational deficiency in ways that ultimately can be more cost effective than can the slower process of training larger batteries of teachers and expanding school capacity. Funds for the initiation of these attempts have come from such agencies as the United States Agency for International Development, UNESCO, and other international bodies. The technical expertise seems to have been supplied more by the United States than by other developed nations. It cannot be proven—but there is room for speculation—that the stepped-up attempts to use educational technology in developing nations derives from the same beliefs that seem to prevail in the United States, that is, that the technology might be used for groups of students previously excluded from higher education. It is also possible to speculate that the interests of American scholars and technologists in working on media systems in developing nations is not unrelated to the generally slowed-down expansion of American higher education in the United States. Perhaps, as professional work opportunities for an increasingly large number of trained American technologists began to disappear, carrying ideas and technologies to developing institutions represented a way of acquiring or maintaining a professional role and doing the things for which these individuals were trained.

A somewhat minor shift seems to be the prevailing attitude toward the number of professionals expected to work with media programs and projects. During the time when there was an intense shortage of professors, there was a serious belief that use of the technology would compensate for teacher shortages. By the 1970s, however, for the more complicated technological devices, the doctrine had become that a team of professionals was needed to make optimum use of the technique. In the British Open University, it was assumed there would be subject-matter specialists, educational programmers, and television producers and crews to create high-quality instructional programs. At Florida State University, the development of an interactive communication system for individualized college instruction required an educational psychologist and a computer programmer who could work out the system's design. This then had to be adopted by professors in substantive fields, who actually related the content of their fields to the blueprint provided them. The actual monitoring of the course, as finally produced, required teaching assistants to work with the sections. Now it is very likely that earlier experience with one individual trying to be master of several techniques was bound to produce less than professional-quality materials and that this movement toward a team has a rational base of the desire to present students with high-quality instruction materials. But it may also have been related to the oversupply of professionals during the 1970s; a team of professionals can use three, four, or five people in place of one. The hope, of course, would have been that if the device proved economical it would generate enough resources to support that team of professional and technical workers.

Supporting Other Reforms. The nontraditional movement and the most prevalent curricular and instructional developments on traditional campuses, while reflecting some differences, also reflect great similarity to the attempted technological revolution. All stress variety of individualized instruction. All stress, in varying degrees, off-campus instruction, whether it be offered in homes, temporary facilities, or in facilities of other institutions. All attempt to use increased varieties and amounts of the sorts of educational resources not normally found in traditional libraries and laboratories. All are concerned with serving new categories of new students, and to some degree the actual curricula of both appears to be somewhat more nontraditional than in the past. While overall there has been continued experimentation with a wide range of educational technologies during the 1970s, the three most prominent types are techniques highly consistent with those common curricular and instructional approaches stressed in both the nontraditional movement and in traditional institutions. This is not, of course, to suggest definite causal relationships, but the correlations are striking, and the rhetoric espousing the predominant technology developments is remarkably similar to the rhetoric espousing the common curricular and instructional developments.

The Major Technologies

Educational media include a wide range of devices such as radio, audiotape, fast dry copying equipment, amplification systems, and mechanical games; all have some educational uses. However, the most promising deliverers of large-scale educational services are computer based networks and computer based or videotape based systems of instruction.

Networks. The first of the major technological developments is called *networking,* which is a term subject to varying definitions. The concept enjoying the most widespread interest and support involves computerized networks that facilitate the storage, manipulation, and retrieval of information for the benefit of individuals and institutions often widely separated geographically.

One rather advanced example of a type of network is the ARPANET (Advanced Research Projects Agency), a computer communications system supported by the U.S. Department of Defense. It began in September 1969 by linking the computers of four western universities (University of California at Los Angeles, Stanford University, University of California at Santa Barbara, and the University of Utah) so that packets of information could be transmitted almost error-free from one computer to another. The system originally was created to avoid the considerable redundancy of equipment and approach that had developed during the time the four universities were receiving support from the Advanced Research Projects Agency. When the network was first created, the amount of real use (as contrasted with experimental or developmental use) was relatively light, mainly because the mechanisms connecting different computers that enable reliable exchange of information had simply not been perfected. Those technical problems gradually were overcome, and the number of computers linked into the system has advanced from the original 4 in 1969 to 50 in 1972 on to about 125 in 1975. The network now links different types and capacities of computers and allows the user to select the sort of computing service most appropriate for a particular need. In theory, appropriate charges could be passed on to users according to the level of service received. In practice, however, the entire network is still partly subsidized. And this problem seems endemic to uses of much educational technology.

A somewhat different example in the state of Michigan is MERIT, which links by telephone lines the computer facilities of the University of Michigan, Michigan State University, and Wayne State University. A user can submit, at a local terminal anywhere in the state, a task intended for any one of the three computers. Gradually, at all three institutions, various aggregations of data are added to and stored in computers, and these in turn become available for use through the state. The technology of the MERIT system is quite sophisticated: The different computers are able to communicate with any one of the other two, and each is able to initiate tasks. However, the dream of the system's originators—to have the appropriate hard- and software on the campuses of all or most of the four-year and two-year colleges in the state, linking the entire state educational network—has not yet been realized.

The MERIT system faces a rather acute problem that seems generic to not-for-profit installations: The three-way link-up's tremendous capacity is being seriously underused. The capacity was created with the expectation of a steady, if not exponential, increase in research and development activities throughout the 1970s. That expectation clearly has not been realized, and the network suffers a continuous deficit.

One small example may illustrate other problems. Individuals in the University of Michigan Center for the Improvement of Instruction have been interested in the concepts and practice of computer-assisted instruction and would like to see a spread of interest in such activities throughout the state. They consider junior colleges to be fertile fields for expansion of computer-assisted instruction, yet junior and liberal arts colleges do not have computer capacity, nor are their faculties knowledgable about operating computer arrangements. The MERIT system seemed an ideal solution, if terminals or telephone connections could be established on junior and liberal arts college campuses throughout the state and if instructors could be trained to use the system and to develop computer-assisted modules for their classes. After several years of continuous effort, a few people on a few nearby junior college campuses did develop instructional units and experimented with them in their classes. However, the dream of such activity greatly increasing the use of MERIT proved to be illusory.

Beyond question, the most widely publicized network for bibliographic purposes is the Ohio College Library Center (OCLC), created as a nonprofit corporation in order to provide greater cooperation among Ohio libraries and library systems outside of

Ohio. Approximately fifty academic institutions and public libraries in Ohio make up the essential cadre of system users.

The essential OCLC goals were envisioned as shared cataloguing, remote catalog access and circulation control, serials control, a technical processing system, and retrieval of information by subject. By the summer of 1970, over one third of the fifty members were situated so as to link into the catalogue production system. In that system, MARC (Machine-Readable Cataloguing) tapes were searched and appropriate bibliographic information recorded. It was then possible to derive information from the system to print on cards that could be shipped to member institutions for inclusion in their individual card catalogues. It should be pointed out that this simple-sounding act required considerable technical sophistication and modification of equipment to accommodate the idiosyncratic needs of all users. As the system became more fully operational, in the early 1970s, other modifications were accomplished so that the catalogue production system could accommodate 8,000 combinations of printing options available for user library catalogues. The original system dealt with book titles, and in 1973, a parallel system went into operation, dealing with journals and other serial publications. By 1975 OCLC had expanded its linkages to almost 1,200 libraries and emerged as the largest of a growing number of networks designed for facilitating, locating, ordering, and cataloguing library materials.

These examples exist now. However, before the real futures of this use of technology can be gauged, a number of issues must be faced and resolved. Some of these are involved in the likely future of other technological developments. They arise here because the rate of advance of networking has been somewhat more rapid than that of computerized instruction and portable video materials.

The first issue involves polar positions with respect to the values and dangers of computer-based networks. At one extreme are the advocates of networks, who see in them a revolution not only in information processing but also in the quality, intensity, and magnitude of actual uses of information. At the other end of the continuum are those who fear computer aggregates of data as a threat or as an unnecessary dehumanization of administration, teaching, or even scholarship. Opponents of networking seem to be of two general sorts: those who are sure it will not work and those afraid it will. As with so many other matters, reality probably rests some place between these extremes. The specific value of networking will depend to some extent on how other contributing issues are resolved.

One of these issues is obvious: Do networks increase productivity and efficiency? If they do, then other issues arise: For example, does the existence of a complex network actually result in more extensive, effective, or efficient actual behavior? Does an instructional network lead to more efficient undergraduate teaching that produces the same or better results than more conventional methods? Does easy access to enormous amounts of bibliographic data result in any greater use of such data or better and more balance of scholarship? Does, for example, the MERIT system result in more, or more significant, research in the three Michigan institutions than took place before the network? Do networks of management information result in more detailed planning, and does that planning produce any difference in the educational outcomes sought by the institution?

The existing literature is for the most part silent regarding such matters. Here and there is a bit of evidence regarding some economies and user satisfaction. But there is no evidence as to whether requisitions for literature on the part of professors is greater or whether the libraries are more frequently used because of the increased potential resources.

To some, this may seem an irrelevant matter, on the assumptions that the improved acquisitions function is a sufficient end and that, as libraries develop access to a larger pool of potential parts of a collection, greater student and faculty use will likely occur. These assumptions may be true, but eventually the cost of complex installations must be measured against results, especially once external funding ends and the system must maintain itself. Greater precision in the preparation of cards for a catalogue or greater speed in ordering books and periodicals may well be worth the effort, but that fact should be established.

A logical next issue is whether noncommercial networks can be made economically viable. Most of the more prominent networks have been started with external financial assistance from the federal government, foundations, or state appropriations. Now, such funding support for a potentially significant tool seems warranted. However, long-term financing would seem to require different methods, ones resulting in something comparable to self-sustaining financing. Thus payment for regular services should be built into appropriations for public institutions or libraries and should be included in the "hard money" budget of private institutions. If a network of games and computer simulation programs available in all eight general campuses of the University of California is to be orchestrated into a major resource, then funds for such services should be incorporated into budgets of individual campuses or the university system, with services then provided free to member campuses. If junior colleges and liberal arts colleges in Michigan are to use the MERIT system as a regular and major instructional device, then at some point the institutions must become convinced that the services are worthwhile and must build payment into their regular budgets.

Viable sustaining systems of financing have not yet been found, except for a few networks like OCLC that provide a valued service for a sufficiently large clientele. Whether some of the desired future developments of OCLC, such as a major retrieval of information effort, can be self-sustaining or can be supported by the care production function is another question.

Another issue involves the limits of information that can be economically stored in a network. As computer capacity enlarges and especially as new kinds of memory, such as holograms, are developed, it will be technically possible to store not just bibliographic data and reasonably brief annotations but also complete texts. However, the manpower needed to place such textual materials in computers is enormously expensive, making that level of storage unlikely in the foreseeable future. In the meantime, restricting networks to bibliographic materials alone tends to limit their full utility. Long lists of titles are not often useful to the scholar, simply because of the time and money needed to locate and read each of the cited documents.

Another issue concerns how many of each type of network the nation actually needs. One conceptualization of networks posits three distinct types of networks. Facilitating networks are visualized as mediating between transmission and user-services networks. Current thinking indicates that one, two, or a few facilitating networks might be enough for the entire country but that a large computation center would allow various smaller computers to serve the needs of departments and organizations. No long-range national plan has been developed along these lines, in part because deployment of computer resources at a national level is still threatening to many local systems.

This matter of local versus national systems is significant enough to be a discrete and complicated issue. As the potential of computers was realized, institutions began to develop large computation centers and to increase computer capacity. Then costs began to soar, just as federal research funds with provisions for computer use began to decline. At the same time, two potentially more economical alternatives became available: (1) small computers for specific purposes and (2) large-scale networking. Those involved in computation centers obviously wanted to preserve their domains, and institutions wanted to maintain control over their computer activities. Based on these needs, it seems likely that networking indicates the shape of the immediate future. However, quite specific provisions are required to accomplish the economies of the larger operations and at the same time to provide participating organizations with some control and voice in policy.

A different issue involves bibliographic networks whose listings go beyond simple author, title, and source information and whose annotations are of varying lengths. The Educational Resources Information Center (ERIC) system, funded by the National Institute of Education, is a good example. Some involved persons have questioned whether evaluation of information could be included to help users winnow through the volume of listings stored in ERIC. With no evaluative comment, users' time can be wasted. Yet obtaining qualified evaluation would be very expensive and, in the case of ERIC, contrary to public policy and the will of Congress. Yet if the volume of listings continues to increase and the scope of information sources expands, the problem of selecting the valid from the invalid or questionable becomes even more serious (Mayhew, 1975).

Computers in Instruction. The second of the predominant technologies of the 1970s involves the use of computers in instruction. The use of computers in higher education enjoyed its first initial expansion in connection with research. This was followed by limited but growing uses of computers for administrative purposes. By the end of the 1960s, however, the instructional potential had become vividly apparent, and a flood of experimental uses appeared. The elements of teaching and learning, to which computers are expected to make a major contribution, can be first seen by reviewing the traditional ways by which colleges and universities assist learning. Lectures, discussions, and textbooks have since the 1870s been the predominant mode of transmitting information and concepts. Case studies and written assignments have been the typical ways by which students manipulated and applied information received. There has been an additional effort to help students relate knowledge gained to reality through such hands-on investigations as laboratory experiments, library investigations, and real-world experiences, such as field trips or clinical activities. There have been a number of technologically based substitutes for lectures, including radio, television, tapes, cassettes, and motion pictures. There also have been attempts to simulate learning through application through such things as paper programmed instruction and carefully organized and sequenced independent study modules. It is in connection with the application phase of learning that computers are seen to be of greatest value and are most highly consistent with the reality element of other curricular and instructional developments during the 1970s.

Computers, visualized essentially as a pedagogical device, consist of hardware and software components. In a conventional computer system, there is the processor, which accepts data, performs computations, and transmits data; there is a main storage element, which holds data and instructions; and there is typically secondary storage capacity, which contains data and instructions for ultimate use after transfer to the main storage component. Then there is the input-output equipment, which facilitates communication between people and the computer system. By *software* is meant the programs that run in a computer. There are four categories of software—operating systems, utility programs, language processors, and application programs. Operating systems are typically rewritten programs for all users to utilize. Utility programs consist of sets of general-purpose programs that can be used by an individual programmer to perform specific functions—for example, programs that automatically print out specified data contained in storage. Utility programs are also prewritten and increasingly are being supplied by computer manufacturers. Language processors are also manufacturer-supplied programs that translate a particular set of programmer-written statements into instructions that can be used by a particular computer. Application programs are those written by users to do specific jobs involving quite unique steps. These, in the early days of computer-related instruction, were the typical devices and were extraordinarily expensive. Recently serious attempts have been made to utilize prewritten application programs called *packages,* which can be adapted to many different sorts of instructional situations. In the early days, each user wrote all of his own software, which restricted the widespread use of computers in instruction. There is a clear trend toward having the user create only a minimum of situation-dependent application programs.

Perhaps the most significant shift in emphasis on computer-related instruction has been the shift from author-controlled drill and practice activities toward having the computer serve an enrichment function, with much more learner control and considerably less author control. This shift is illustrated by the design of an interactive communications system for individualized college instruction at Florida State University. The individual responsible for this system wanted to develop a full, computer-managed college course that would involve an interactive system between students and the computer. He was convinced that the high costs of early uses of the computer could only be overcome by shifting from computer-assisted instruction to computer-managed instruction, the principal difference being that in computer-assisted instruction learning takes place essentially at the console of a computer and follows carefully sequenced modules. In computer-managed instruction, learning takes place elsewhere, and the computer serves in a diagnosing and prescribing role. What this person wanted to do was to develop a computer-managed course on the teaching of reading in secondary schools. The state legislature had mandated that all credentialed secondary school teachers must have credit for such a course. This mandate provided strong motivation to develop an efficient and effective course for preservice education of teachers that would be easily adaptable to in-service education of teachers. The plan was to develop an entire rationale and blueprint for a computer-based interactive college course and to develop the computer software to make such a course feasible. Once that step of software development was taken, the next task was to work with a professor of a college course who would develop the actual learning materials. The initial developer created a model and then introduced the model to a professor of education who offered the course on teaching reading to secondary school students. This collaborative effort produced lists of key concepts, lists of learning tasks, a glossary of words, hundreds of test items, and other materials needed for the course. Along with those materials, which would be stored in the computer, the subject-matter professor also developed printed instructional guides that would serve as a basic text. In this course, the role of the instructor was shifted from that of transmitter of information to a role as manager and counselor of students. Students would decide what problem was giving them difficulty and would then work at the computer, seeking solutions to that problem. After the initial refinement of the course concept and development of software, it was assumed that the course could be offered on a cost-effective basis, not only at Florida State University but also in school buildings throughout the state, thus adopting into the scheme one of the critical tenets of educational thought during the 1970s—taking instruction to where people were.

Also revealing the computer concerns of the 1970s is the work of Donald Bitzer and his associates at the University of Illinois as they created the Plato system. The Plato system, now in its fourth stage of development (Plato IV), is a large computer center located at one end of the University of Illinois (Urbana) campus. It was designed and has been modified by a staff that had worked together for years and which believed early that the computer could become a major tool for collegiate instruction. As originally developed, twenty student stations were built, each having a key set and television screen. Students send information to the computer with the key set and receive information back on the television screen. An essential of the system has always been to enable professors with little knowledge of computers to place their own instructional materials in the computer, thus keeping costs for programming relatively low.

The system has undergone steady improvement. The following example of a course created by a professor of political science for the Plato IV indicates how the system operates and what learning theories are implied.

This is an attempt to modify a beginning course in political

science through intruding six computer-based games involving contrived but frequently encountered types of political action. The
project seems to have arisen as a result of several factors, the first
of which was considerable dissatisfaction with the large, somewhat
impersonal, lecture technique used to teach Political Science 150,
which annually enrolls between 1,200 and 1,500 students. When
that number is divided into lecture sections of 150 to 200 students, a
passive situation resulted, unresponsive to individual differences. . . .

The principal investigator anticipated several possible advantages to this new style course. A game engages the student and
requires him to commit himself. It allows a student to proceed at an
individual rate, thus individualizing instruction and assessment by
virtue of the fact that completion of a game implies a degree of
mastery unrelated to the progress of other students. In addition, the
actual creation of games forces the instructor to concentrate on behavioral objectives desired from instruction and instills similar
awareness on the part of students once they have played the game.
However, at least several potential disadvantages were also anticipated, with the first being the possibility that students would tire of
the solitary act of sitting at a computer console. Secondly, the very
structure of a program could prove unappealing to the radical student wishing to discuss philosophic presuppositions of political action
rather than accepting political action as a fact of life.

The project evolved through several somewhat discrete steps.
First, the investigator and his associates prepared six games: *Leader,*
placing the student in the role of a teachers' union, who becomes
involved in a tenure case; *President,* involving the role of the United
States President and foreign policy; *Chairman,* involving a Congressional committee chairman steering a higher education bill
through committee, and *Chief,* which asks the student to play the
role of police chief confronting the problem of a radical and inflam-
matory speaker visiting a community. A sixth game differs somewhat
from the others and is called *Budget-maker,* which allows the student to approach a budgetary problem as head of a state agency, a
key legislator, or the role of governor. These games were first
written and then coded in Tutor language, which is a flexible near-
English language developed specifically for PLATO. After encoding,
the author actually places the program in a computer, which is a

relatively easy task once the exercise has been well designed on paper. As these exercises were completed, they were tried out with a small group of students who reflected on their sensations using the computer, discussed and evaluated readings, and who made suggestions regarding an ideal introductory course in American Government. Original plans called for using the new course experimentally during a summer session. However, light enrollment forced postponement until the fall of 1970. The experimental term in which 100 students took the revised course was organized into alternate weeks of formal lectures (which really were not extremely formal) and work at the computer, which required some reading in advance and then approximately three hours at the computer. As the experiment evolved, students would spend the first computer period seeking to understand how to play the game and the last period at the computer actually running through the game two or three times. A refinement of the original scheme was to schedule two students at each console rather than one, which seemed to heighten the motivation by providing some group activity as well as the more solitary thinking activities. An important part of the original design was to have been a pretest, posttest assessment. However, for a variety of reasons, including, one must suspect, some departmental suspicions, the formal assessment did not work out because of the generally poor quality of the test materials. Hence, at this point, comment about the worth of the project must be based on impressionistic evidence.

While during planning, the project experienced some difficulty in arranging enough console space for a large enough group of students to make the experiment valid, this matter was finally resolved satisfactorily. During the early weeks of the experiment, students did experience some delay because computer capacity was occupied, but this technical matter also was corrected. The students generally liked using the computer and attended sessions considerably more regularly than did students in more orthodox discussion groups. Students seemed to personify the computer and either regard it as a nurturing teacher or as a very real competitor which should be defeated. A full term after the exercise students were able to exhibit almost total recall of weeks involving computer work but had only vague notions of what took place during the weeks of lecture. They did not feel that the reading materials were closely enough related to the computer games but did sense much greater alignment between the lectures and the games. In a sense, the experiment may have been contaminated by the fact that the faculty member chosen to deliver the lectures in the experimental section was a young, popular dynamic person, whereas the lecturer for the control sections was the department head, whose voice, diction, and generally gray manner would be almost assured to repel student interest and enthusiasm. Generally, students believed that the experimental course was worthwhile, realistic, personal, and that they would be inclined to take another computer-based course if one were offered. As compared with other discussion courses they had taken on the University of Illinois campus, they much preferred the computer-based exercises. However, there were weaknesses. There did not seem to be a good mechanism by which students could obtain feedback on error, and there probably should have been considerably more done by way of orientation to the entire project as well as better orientation to each of the six games. Simple handouts indicating what students might read in preparation for a week of computer work would be one appropriate device.

This example made use of Plato III. Bitzer and his associates theorized that the Plato IV could provide a computer-based system that could reduce total cost-per-student-contact-hour significantly below costs of any other system currently available, while maintaining individual student terminals and providing for relatively easy programming by professors of any of a variety of courses. The essential elements of the Plato IV system are a large third-generation computer capable of serving as many as 4,000 student stations with several hundred lessons simultaneously, a versatile student console allowing the graphic display of pictorial images and allowing students to interact directly with the computer, and a networking system providing service to terminals located anywhere within a 150-mile radius. Each of these three characteristics represents a major theoretical and technical breakthrough for the University of Illinois group. With these three characteristics, a single Plato IV system could provide major educational services to thousands of students on the university campus as well as to students in dozens of other institutions within the service area. The Plato system seems especially advantageous for institutions without previous experience or equipment in offering computer-related educational services. Such an institution can enter the field by investing only in a modest number of student stations and company telephone lines. Their facilities could even use course materials previously prepared by the University of Illinois for other institutions.

Assuming full use of a Plato IV system consisting of 4,000 student terminals during an eight-hour day, the cost per student contact hour would range between $.31 and $.68, depending on whether telephone lines or a television channel were utilized. In arriving at such a figure, it was assumed that the multimedia student station could be made commercially available at approximately $1,500 each and that the visual and auditory components would still be commercially available at relatively low cost. It was also assumed that the costs of the preparation of lesser material could be kept to levels comparable to textbook charges that students paid themselves. For example, the cost of $600 per hour for the preparation of lesson materials, prorated over 500 student enrollments, would yield costs of approximately $.25 per contact hour. For such large introductory classes as statistics or inorganic chemistry, offered to students in a number of different institutions, the cost would drop significantly, and (assuming a way could be found to do it) rather substantial royalties could be paid to authors.

An important ingredient of the Plato model, from the standpoints both of gauging potentialities and evaluating realism of the model, is some of the educational implications that theoretically could be derived from such a system and that are highly consistent with the ethos of the 1970s. It could alleviate lockstep schedules and narrow curricula by allowing students to proceed at their own pace. It could allow for remedial instruction or tutorial assistance during regularly scheduled courses, thus eliminating the need for any tracking of students according to preparation or ability. The system could lead to a reduction in the number of large lecture classes and could also provide special instruction at home for physically handicapped students. It could provide for individual development of cognitive skills in private, away from the exposed environments of classrooms. It could be modified to provide job training or retraining as technological changes took place, and it seems to have great potential for the continuing education of professional personnel by permitting the updating of knowledge and skills in their own offices and on their own schedules.

Cross underscores these virtues and sees the greatest advantage as the facilitating individualized instruction. She also notes that these advantages are instructive because they reveal the theoretical potential and the idealism of the persuaded. However, her very words reveal just how little evidence there is to prove it can achieve its potential. Although computer-assisted instruction has not really spread, it is probably like the Wright brothers' first aircraft as the prototype for the jet and space age. The computer may reduce time required for a student to learn something. Students are intrigued with the machine and enjoy working with it. Given large enough classes and assuming steady reduction in hardware costs, it could become an economical adjunct to other kinds of instruction. Of course, it can be abused by concentrating on learning of facts and by forcing the mind to be reactive rather than creative. But, in the end, it will help understand learning and will in turn be improved through application of new learning theory (Cross, 1976a).

Videotape. The third most promising technological development is the use of videotape to create modules or even entire courses that can be used in remote places in the absence of an instructor or on campuses, to make the scheduling of instruction more flexible. The technological development of videotape equipment and film is far advanced and, as commercial television demonstrates, can bring the world live into the homes of everyone. It is theorized that its potential is just on the threshold of realization in educational settings. However, there are problems of cost and human reluctance to be overcome. Both the potential and the difficulties are revealed in the following single experiment.

This experiment was an attempt to videotape a full advanced course in chemistry and to use the videotape recordings and supplementary written materials as a full course in other institutions that did not have the faculty resources for such advanced work. The effort apparently derived from the principal investigator's concern that private liberal arts colleges facing serious financial difficulties were not able to offer the advanced courses needed by relatively small numbers of students. He became convinced that ways should be found by which the resources of publicly supported institutions could be adapted to help the private institutions. Creating an advanced course and videotape recording seemed to be one contribution that could be made without placing great strain on Washington State University and that could be of considerable value to some private institutions in the region. The videotape mode also seemed to be desirable because of the distinct likelihood that there would be a statewide microwave system developed within several years and televised instructional materials could become the life blood of that system. In addition to his concern for private liberal arts colleges, the principal investigator (who has long been interested in pedagogical processes) wondered whether adequate televised presentations could be produced without extensive preparation, rehearsals, and editing. Specifically, he wondered whether or not lectures could be televised as they were given to a live class and then used as the principal instructional device on other campuses.

This particular effort followed a relatively simple plan. Whitworth College, Fort Wright College of Holy Names, and Gonzaga University all agreed to participate by offering a course for academic credit that would be produced on videotape recordings at Washington State University. A faculty member at each institution became the liaison and local resource person responsible for showing the televised lectures, distributing supplementary materials, and being available for consultation with the students. In the fall of 1973, the project began with seventeen students at Washington State University enrolled for the course, three students at Whitworth, six students at Gonzaga, and eleven students at Fort Wright. The scheme followed was for the principal investigator to deliver his lectures in front of seventeen students at Washington State University and for the research assistant to take notes on the lecture. Immediately after the lecture, the notes were edited and duplicated, and the videotape was duplicated and shipped to each of the participating institutions. Thus, with only a modest time lag, of perhaps a week, the course offered at Pullman, Washington, would be also offered at the other three locations. As the course progressed, the princpal investigator learned a number of things. He had to tighten the organization of his lectures. He discovered that people viewing the televised version could tell whether or not the lecture had been delivered in front of a live audience (students at the remote centers did not like presentations that he had delivered in solitude). He discovered that the presence of adjunct professors on each of the campuses obviated the need for students in the remote campuses to call him with questions. However, the adjunct professors made considerable use of telephone consultations with him regarding the progress of the course.

The principal investigator judges the effort to have been successful. He completed the recording of lectures for the full course in advanced chemistry and the accompanying edited version of lecture notes. Thus this course is available for reuse should someone wish to avail themselves of it. The course was offered for academic credit at three other institutions; student satisfaction was reasonably high and the impression rather strong that student performance with respect to the course materials was comparable whether the course was pursued in a face-to-face situation or in the televised situation. The investigator demonstrated that less competent instructors for advanced work in chemistry could function quite effectively when the course was based on televised lectures and carefully edited lecture notes. He also noted his belief that the cooperative effort demonstrated a new way by which private and public institutions of higher education could assist one another.

The quality of videotape recording was quite good. The testimony from the adjunct professors was almost rhapsodic as they described the benefit of having a distinguished professor of chemistry offer an advanced course which their own institutions could not afford. And the films and notes as well as transcribing equipment were available for almost immediate reuse. However, several concerns should be expressed. Although presumably the need for such a course existed in academic year 1974–75, none of the participating institutions reused the course as was originally intended. Nor was the course offered via television at Washington State University. At one of the participating institutions, there was some plan to use portions of the course as enrichment, but for many different reasons the anticipated continuity between the first and second years did not eventuate.

Assessment of Educational Technology

Gauging the prognosis of educational technology, especially the dominant modes, does not necessarily rest on the factors and forces that produced the various devices, any more than the motivations that led Fleming to examine molds predicted the development of penicillin and the entire family of antibiotics. However, a consideration of the forces involved may deepen understanding of educational technology itself and may be suggestive of likely next steps. One of the most obvious factors involved in the use of computers, networks, and portable visual devices is simply the existence of sophisticated equipment, which was frequently designed for other purposes. The complex Michigan network designed for research purposes, just by being there and being underutilized, stimulated experimentation with the network for instructional purposes. Related to the technology are the professional, technical, and creative motivations and interests of people who became deeply involved in producing more and more sophisticated equipment. It appears that the sophistication of networks far exceeds the skills of potential users, even though such networks could be designed more simply with unsophisticated users in mind. The reason for the excessive complexity seems to be the satisfaction of those who design and program the equipment.

A second factor, to which allusion has already been made, is the need for institutions to bring income and expenditure into equilibrium and to slow the price increase for educational services to rates comparable to the price increases for other consumer goods. Several ways of accomplishing these ends have been suggested, including shortening the period of time students spend in degree programs, discouraging reluctant attenders, and bringing about some economies through better management. One important way of affecting cost is by increasing educational productivity, typically by increasing student-faculty ratios and modifying the mix of student activities. Educational technology has been seen as one device to increase professorial productivity and to facilitate self-service, with attendant lesser costs to institutions. Illustrative of the extreme hopes was the creation of Florida Atlantic University in the mid-1960s as an upper-division graduate institution. It is generally assumed that upper-division and graduate education is more expensive than lower-division education. Florida Atlantic University was part of the state system of four-year higher education, and costs at the various institutions were expected to be roughly equivalent. The plan was that the higher cost normally associated with upper-division and graduate work could be reduced to average levels of cost at institutions that had lower-division units by using a wide range of devices from educational technology. The fact that the goal was not achieved does not negate the aspiration to effect the economies and the expectation of the ability to do so. Of the three major technologies, the computer and the video cassette represent a kind of self-service that would make students much more responsible for their own education. When that responsibility was fully assumed, it was expected that there could actually be reductions in faculty or redeployment of faculty time into other activities intrinsically more valuable than the transmission of information. Networks were also seen as ultimately reducing costs by increasing volume of use and through sharing expenditures. For the most part, expectations of substantial cost reductions have not been realized. However, those expectations continue to be advanced as a reason for urging widespread adoption of this, that, or the other technological device.

A third factor is the use of analogy. Various technologies have been used in cost-effective ways in business, industry, and the military, and the reasoning goes that, if they work there, why can't they work equally in the education part of the service sector? Airline reservation procedures have been computerized and involve a network system in ways that apparently are cost effective for the airline companies. The General Electric Company maintains a computer network linking one centralized facility in Cleveland to points throughout United States, Canada, Alaska, Japan, Latin America, and most countries in western Europe. The network operates through several levels of concentration, with some 2,100 locations where people can place and retrieve business-related information. The General Electric network is a worldwide enterprise and can operate its Cleveland facility twenty-four hours a day and be available for servicing to all of its outlying offices and agencies during the time of day when their needs peak. The military services have also demonstrated effectiveness in using educational technology to serve large numbers of people with equipment that can be purchased relatively inexpensively. In view of the enormous size of the military establishment, it is reasoned that, if these examples work, could not educational institutions also be served effectively and efficiently? Those who use this analogy, of course, overlook several salient matters.

Educational institutions have no good way of passing added costs onto customers, as have airline companies, for example. While enrollments in higher education are large, enrollments in specific courses are typically small, thus denying any possibilities for economies to scale. Further, educational institutions are not standardized in the sense that various units of the Army, Navy, Air Force, Coast Guard, or Marines are standardized, hence the possibility for bulk purchasing of equipment and bulk preparation of materials typically cannot be realized. In spite of these exceptions, however, throughout the 1970s the ultimate possibility of genuine economies undergirded much of the literature urging greater use of educational technology.

The needs of new kinds of students are also involved, especially those who find it difficult to attend classes on the campus and those who find working with the traditional verbal and mathematical modes of lectures and assigned readings difficult or unrewarding. Videotape cassettes are seen as a way of sending instruction to where students are rather than expecting them to come to where instruction is delivered in traditional forms. Carefully paced and programmed courses in such fields as engineering and mathematics are seen as ways to ensure mastery of difficult subjects by categories of students, such as underprivileged blacks, who find themselves lost trying to make their way through textbooks and following rapidly delivered lectures in formal classrooms. Cross and her associates, for example, visualize a lifelong materials service center as an essential instrumentality to deliver education to new groups of students. This center would maintain a wide range of technological devices and complete catalogues of courses and modules of instruction needed by an enormously heterogeneous student body. They feel that for many of the new kinds of students television would be the key instructional device and believe it to be highly flexible. As they visualize the work, "Materials planned for taping and for ultimate presentation over television would, by the nature of the preparation, be well suited to use in any instructional setting, including the conventional classroom. Motion pictures fitting the course objectives would be previewed and chosen; 35mm slides would supply visual support when selected and ordered in the best sequence. Overhead projection transparencies would be designed, executed, and fitted into the lesson. Film clips too would be fitted in. Notes for narration, discussion, and lecture sequences would be sharpened. A given lesson would materialize on a story board and become a scripted 'production' " (Cross, Valley, and Associates, 1974, p. 108).

It is difficult not to reach the conclusion that external funding agencies represent an important pressure resulting in greater use of educational technology. The National Science Foundation provided direct subsidy for institutions wishing to develop computing capacity, and research supported by a number of federal agencies also helped to underwrite the expansion of computer use. The National Science Foundation supported development of computing facilities on individual campuses and also in regional organization like the Triangle University's computation center. Foundations, such as the EXXON Education Foundation, have been particularly interested in the potentiality of computer uses and have supported projects including the linking of ten midwestern liberal arts colleges into a network to facilitate data exchange and to improve management planning. That same foundation contributed to a complex network of large and small computers for instruction in the science and engineering departments at the University of Texas at Austin and to an effort to increase usage of the MERIT network. It seems apparent that without specific external financial support development of computers at educational institutions probably would have remained at a relatively low and unsophisticated level.

Relatedly, manufacturers of some educational technology have been a factor generating purchase of equipment regardless of whether or not the equipment actually was incorporated into educational programs. While, as indicated earlier, some kinds of educational services that momentarily attracted the interest of profit-making corporations proved disappointing, the production of other kinds of educational technology nonetheless has emerged as a growing and reasonably lucrative activity. In 1973 retail sales of media amounted to $200 million, and the proportion of media sales as compared with textbook sales has increased slightly more rapidly. Impressions gained from visiting educational conferences suggest that sales are vigorously pushed and that for most devices there are attractive and competitive examples, all being sold on the theory that possession of the devices is the best way by which a school can up-date itself and provide its student with enriched curricula.

One factor, which in actuality is not significant, although in mythology it may be, is the presumed educational benefits derived from using educational technology. Literature regarding technology is replete with claims for enrichment, more rapid learning, deepened learning, and the generating of greater student enthusiasm for learning. However, with respect to educational outcomes (typically defined as performance on tests), a considerable amount is known, whether the instructional technique be lecture, discussion, field work, motion pictures, or computer-assisted or managed instruction. And the intractable fact derived from years of experimentation is that there are no significant differences in outcome related to different instructional interventions. The 1970 edition of the *Encyclopedia of Educational Research* contains several relevant articles. One, reporting on program instruction (with and without computer hardware), indicates that, of 190 reports of original research, the large majority indicated no significant differences between programmed instruction and conventional lecture, discussion, and recitation. A longer essay, reporting studies of teaching methods, occasionally notes modest differences, but for the most part the studies do not support the generalization that methods or approaches to teaching make any significant difference. That same conclusion was also reported by Dupin and Taveggea, who stated (1968, p. 35), "We have reported the results of a reanalysis of the data from ninety-one comparative studies of college teaching technologies conducted between 1924 and 1965. These data demonstrate clearly and unequivocally that there is no measurable difference among truly distinctive methods of college instruction when evaluated by student performance on final examinations."

Portraying the full significance of experimentation with educational technology in higher education is equally, if not more, difficult than assessing the impact of new kinds of institutions, nontraditional learning, or the most recent and popular curricular changes in traditional institutions. The possibilities for distortion of perception are enormous. If one reads the papers and talks to career educational technologists, one gets the impression that the use of technology is assuming tidal wave proportions and that a fourth revolution is almost on us. However, if one strolls the corridors of most colleges and universities, one gets the impression that instruction is, with few exceptions, being carried on as it historically has been, in formal classrooms, through unidirectional transmission of information from the professor to an audience of students. For very real economic, logistic, and planning purposes, some perspective is essential, so as to determine proportion of effort that reasonably should be devoted to educational technology and to other modes of curricula and instruction.

There are rather large claims made regarding the potentiality of educational technology and some quite impressive reports concerning a few highly visible programs. Alexander Mood (1973) writing in a utopian vein but with obvious conviction that his predictions are valid, foresees typical college students spending only one year in a residence setting. Further education would take place on the job and in the home. He visualizes a video university producing and distributing videotape cassettes that students would use on their own television sets. The video university would publicize such materials and would be the agency of evaluation and record. It would ensure the quality of educational opportunity for all groups and would be based on the premise that individualized learning is the most profound learning possible. Conceivably there would be some full-length courses developed and distributed, but the more typical commodity would be segments of courses, classified and indexed to allow each student to construct a course suited to his own needs. Correlated with the videotape cassettes would be various computer programs that could help lead students to appropriate cassettes or that could reinforce materials originally learned from the cassette. There would be several large regional computers linked into a network and accessible by remote consoles located in libraries, schools and colleges, or even homes. This massive computer facility would interact with students, would handle testing and evaluation, and would even be linked to distribution centers, directing when new videotape cassettes should be sent to each student.

The third component of this nationalized move toward a learning society would be a national television network that would publicize cassettes and computer programs and that also would present synthesizing sorts of programs. An important component of the television network would be a counseling and guidance mission that would continuously present updated information about vocations and avocations, in order to produce a better match between the demand of the labor force and materials presented by the technology-based educational institution.

While Mood's vision is utopian, there are a few major projects operating on the assumption that ideas basic to that vision can be utilized for large groups of students. Mention has already been made of the Plato IV system at the University of Illinois, which anticipates linkages with any junior colleges and liberal arts colleges in Illinois that will use computer-related instruction for at least 10 percent of the total credit hours produced. A more recently developed project is the University of Mid-America (UMA), created to serve off-campus students in the four states of Iowa, Kansas, Missouri, and Nebraska. It offers curricula consisting of courses that are multimedia in nature but that stress the primacy of television, because television sets are widely available to people in the region.

Courses at UMA are developed systematically, step by step. Typically a course has as many as four or five carefully integrated components, each in its own medium, with each medium assigned an appropriate instructional goal. For example, a textbook and detailed study guide serve as a knowledge base for a course to help the learner organize the course material into units of appropriate size in a sound sequence. Audio cassettes, which may be replayed as often as desired, convey the essential elements of course content. In contrast, the supporting television productions stimulate the higher-order mental processes needed to understand and apply what is learned. Abstractions and obscure thoughts are dealt with carefully at the production stage to enable the television medium to make concrete, through visualization, those concepts which are particularly difficult to grasp in abstract form. Besides book, cassettes, and television, a weekly overview and cumulative summary of the course, lesson by lesson, is often carried in newspapers distributed statewide. Another component is an annotated list of recommended readings developed to give the learner a feel for the full scope of the subject matter covered in the course and to guide him or her to more extensive study than the more essential components of the course require. To complete the multimedia presentation of course work, study center arrangements on WATS telephone networks enable learners to reach an instructor or a mentor for help in clarification of obscure points, or for periodic discussions. All eight of these components—text, study guide, audio cassettes, television programs, newspaper features, learning centers, WATS lines, and reading lists—are actively used in various UMA programs of studies [Walton, 1975, pp. 3–4].

The applicability of the media to traditional institutions has also been claimed. Technology-based instructional programs, when properly mixed with traditional modes of instruction and tutorial instruction, can produce a varied and reasonably economical curriculum. Bowen and Douglas (1971), for example, after analyzing costs of various curricular plans, reached the conclusion that private liberal arts colleges might cut costs and improve instruction by employing a judicious mixture of educational methods. That mixture would consist of a few large lecture courses, courses requiring programmed independent study, some of which would use educational technology, courses with emphasis on tutorials and conventional student classes of thirty to forty students each, stressing lectures and discussions.

These somewhat optimistic hopes and claims for the uses of educational technology must be tested. One way of doing so is to examine exemplary experiments with the use of the technology, paying particular attention to elements of success and failure and particular issues that the examples reveal. The first of these involves a 1968–69 attempt to use computers to develop student understanding of complex biological science concepts. The attempt, at the University of California at Irvine, was made as a result of several factors. The institution, when created, planned to emphasize computer-based or computer-assisted instruction and the use of educational technology, and it recruited faculty members who were sympathetic to modifying instructional procedures through using technology. The principal investigator for this particular case had been using the computer as a research tool, to simulate complex population models, and had begun to ponder the utility of that approach as a pedagogical device. He was especially concerned by the increasing cost of laboratory facilities, which could conceivably deny students access to needed laboratory experience. He was also convinced that students would be helped if they could work at complex problems requiring data impossible to collect through normal laboratory activities, such as genetic data from actually breeding generations of fruit flies.

The undertaking consisted of developing half a dozen models of various population or genetic phenomena to serve as the basic data bank with which students would work. Then, for each model, there were developed a series of problems that students were to solve using the information contained in the computer. When the project was first undertaken, limitation of computer capacity and terminals required group problem solving rather than individual problem solving. However, it was expected that in the relatively near future the university would have sufficient time-sharing outlets so that individuals could work on their own. The actual physical setup of this particular experiment included a time-sharing outlet that was located adjacent to the instructor's office and that was staffed by a teaching assistant available to help students overcome technical problems. Although there was no systematic attempt to evaluate educational outcomes, both the instructor and students testified to considerable educational values for at least some students. In general, the better students, given adequate orientation through the computer, became quite creative in testing out various problems based on a given data bank. Less able students viewed the computer as a bother and testified to difficulty in comprehending the concepts they were intended to assimilate. As of 1969, it appeared that for less able students in this context the computer would have its greatest utility as a conventional but powerful teaching machine. For the more able students, who could assimilate basic concepts quickly and creatively, working through the computer with a data bank concerning genetic changes in organisms proved to be quite valuable.

Several economic issues are involved in this case. Developing the program required a great deal of time on the part of a senior professor, as well as the time of several teaching assistants and computer technicians. The models were actually used in a very small class, and there were no plans for using the model consistently in the future. Thus (and keep in mind the date—1969) the cost per student was substantial. This particular project was supported by a philanthropic foundation in the expectation that if such an approach to teaching proved to be feasible additional models could be developed in the future and other courses could be based on such uses of the computer. However, the staffing formula for the University of

California system did not allow for the quite considerable faculty time needed to prepare models. Hence, in the absence of continued external support there was no feasible way by which this particular activity might have become institutionalized.

Thus two of the critical issues involving the use of technology stand clear. First, large numbers of students are needed to make the technology economically sound, and, second, the preparation of software requires sophisticated professional and technical personnel, which must be paid for in some way. Unless ways can be found to institutionalize costs for preparation into institutional operating budgets, the economic problem will continue to remain; that is, how to pay for the preparation of software.

A 1970 effort to improve the teaching qualities of teaching assistants reveals other economic elements. The effort was made at Michigan State University, whose administrators had come to recognize that the bulk of lower-division instruction would be handled by teaching assistants, many of whom entered the task of teaching with no preparation and no ways of improving their teaching. The thought of using technology in such a situation came naturally at Michigan State University, because as an institution it had long been committed to innovation in education. There existed on the campus an educational development program specifically designed to encourage innovation and experimentation within the university.

A special teaching facility was created in the form of a seminar room immediately adjacent to a television deck enclosed by one-way windows, so that class instruction could be both televised and observed directly without interfering with the dynamics of the class. A group of eight teaching assistants were selected, one from each of eight departments, and asked to teach one of their two regularly scheduled sections in the special teaching facility over a one-term period (ten weeks). These teaching assistants were first given some orientation to concepts of teaching and conditioned to teach while television cameras recorded what they were doing. Thus each teaching assistant would teach his two class periods in the facility, everything being recorded on television. At the end of the class session, the teaching assistant would select clips from the television film, which would be reviewed by himself and the other seven teaching assistants each Friday afternoon, during a debriefing session. During that session, the television clips would be shown and discussed thoroughly and critically by the teaching assistants, sometimes with and sometimes without a senior faculty member present.

For the most part, the teaching assistants liked the experience and felt they had grown a great deal as a result of the videotape recording of their performances and the discussions that followed. Department heads of the relevant department also seemed reasonably satisfied, and the deans of several schools kept track of the project with a view toward possibly institutionalizing the procedure for all teaching assistants.

Several cost elements deserve comment. A special facility had to be constructed and, as it turned out, was located on the edge of the campus, hence presenting a modest logistical problem. As better portable videotape equipment became available it was planned that future efforts would be conducted in actual classrooms and laboratories rather than in the special facility. In addition to the cost of equipment, there would need to be a technician present at all times to ensure that the student performances were actually recorded. The service of a technician was paid for through external funds, and there was some question as to whether institutional funds could be redeployed to provide such a service. Additionally, the teaching assistants using the system were required to devote a full afternoon a week to the debriefing and critique session, as well as some additional time reviewing their own televised performance and selecting clips to be used. This activity was not remunerated; the experiment relied on teaching assistants seeing sufficient personal and professional value to expend that time. Conversations with the teaching assistants revealed some feeling that, for the project to be institutionalized, time spent in personal didactic activities should be compensated. Once again, in view of the somewhat precarious financial condition of Michigan State University in 1969–70, there was some doubt that the requisite funds could be provided, and without requisite funds there was some doubt that the activity could be continued.

Here is clearly an add-on situation. Teaching assistants had been selected and had taught in the past, and they would be selected and would teach in the future. The use of videotape seemed to be a feasible approach to improved teaching effectiveness. The pro-rata cost—including purchase, maintenance, and supervision of equipment; cost of a special physical facility; and cost of a supervising senior professor to improve the teaching of eight teaching assistants—was relatively high, but conceivably it could be somewhat reduced per student if more teaching assistants were included in the program. The critical question was whether the improvement in quality of teaching assistants would be sufficiently marked to persuade the central administration of the university to approve budget support for a continuation of the effort.

A 1972 study at the University of Wisconsin at Madison was a somewhat more complex undertaking. It was, essentially, an attempt to teach a large-enrollment course on the principles of economics in a self-paced mode relying to a considerable extent on computer capability and, if possible, to address the cost-benefit question. It was a somewhat unusual sort of experiment in that a young full professor of economics attempted to become conversant with the literature of educational and psychological research and to conduct an experiment that would have both educational and economic implications.

The underlying rationale was called "The Teaching Information-Processing System," which consisted of a course in the principles of economics meeting once a week for a lecture, voluntary discussion sessions, and a computerized feedback system that related the variety of background factors for each student (major, SAT scores, amount of mathematics previously taken, and so on) to student performance on biweekly quizzes, midterm examinations, and the like. The instructor reviewed the performance and fed into the computer special instructions for each individual, designed to rectify decisions or to provide enrichment opportunities. After each test, the test performance was fed into the computer, which provided a full printout for each student within two to three hours after test completion. Those printouts might tell one student that there was no need to do the next assignment but that he should attend the lecture of a visiting professor, while another student might be informed that he not only should do the next exercise but should also master several collateral readings and should make an appointment with the teaching assistant responsible for his section.

The actual full first run of the course was conducted as part of a rigorous experimental design according to which the students using the computer-based feedback mechanism would be compared with students taking the same course in a traditional mode, the criterion of success being the common final examination consisting of multiple-choice questions, short-answer questions, and a take-home essay examination. Collateral data involving attitudes and a knowledge test a year after the course were also part of the design. In general, students in the experimental group scored considerably higher on end-of-course measures than did students in regular sections. Students manifested favorable attitude toward the experimental course and testified that it had produced changes in their study habits. The normally expected attrition and failure rates of students in a course on principles of economics was reduced by 85 percent.

Essential to the experiment was a cost analysis with cost computations including such things as depreciating the cost of computer programming, test preparation, professorial time and preparing individual assignments, use of physical facilities, and teaching assistant time. This was done to determine whether teaching the course using the computer would be comparable in cost to the traditional mode and to register equal or superior educational gains. Early analysis of this $58,000 study indicated substantial educational gains for students in the experimental section but showed significantly more gain for less able students than for more able students. The principal investigator testified that once the software problems had been solved in developing an appropriate program the program could be continued as a regular offering but at equal or lower costs than similar sections taught in orthodox ways. However, it may be instructive that the course was not planned to be offered the following academic year, nor were other professors in the economics department willing to replicate the experiment. Further, when the principal investigator moved to a new institution he did not institute the same sort of course at the new location. It is true that the principal investigator devoted considerable time during the subsequent few years conducting workshops and showing others how the system might be put into effect.

Several elements in the Madison experiment are relevant to the thrust of this book. Developing the course and computer programs was moderately expensive, and it did produce a usable course. However, excluding the contribution to knowledge element (which is not inconsiderable), for the cost to be amortized the program and approaches should be used repeatedly and with larger groups of students. Since this replication was not attempted, there remains only the theoretical argument that using the system can educate students in principles of economics at the same or lower per-unit costs. Thus this experiment is not unlike some of the models cited earlier that make some assumptions and then theorize that with optimum enrollments the approach can be cost effective. Several commonsense problems also intrude. The essence of the method's effectiveness is that the professor himself must keep rather close track of student performance and must keep current knowledge of available and emerging resources relevant to the course, so that specific diagnostic and descriptive instructions can be fed into the computer and blended with student performance to produce individual assignments. The principal investigator contended this was a relatively undemanding task, yet such a claim seems a bit strained. Just the act of reviewing categories of test performance for 250 students would appear to be considerably more demanding, hence more expensive in faculty time than the traditional mode of student quizzes, namely grading and criticism by teaching assistants. The computer's potential for receiving and combining many different kinds of information is undisputed, but when there needs to be rather continuous injection of professorial judgment into the process costs logically begin to mount. These queries are not intended to be critical of the rationale nor the intent. It seems obvious that before the cost-effectiveness question can be definitively answered many such experiments must be conducted. But these queries do suggest that in this one experiment the computer mode of individualized instruction through feedback still must be judged as an add-on, the value of which can be warranted only if considerably higher educational yields are obtained consistently when the system is used not only by its advocate but also by the run-of-the-mill instructor in principles of economics.

A previously cited 1973 experiment (pp. 177–178) sought to harness the computer for educational purposes in a more elaborate way. This project was to conduct experiments training faculty members in junior colleges and four-year liberal arts colleges to develop computer-based instructional materials that could be used in connection with the rather elaborate network of computers located at the University of Michigan, Michigan State University, and Wayne State University. As of 1973 that network had been completed and represented enormous computer capacity, which for the most part was underutilized. One potential new plan would be for the two- and four-year colleges, if their faculties could be trained, to develop course software compatible with the Michigan Educational Research and Information Triad (the MERIT network system).

The experiment consisted of developing didactic materials, either at the University of Michigan or in a few cooperating colleges. From these some principles were developed and a handbook produced that could instruct people in the techniques of linking educational activities into a large computer network. On the technical side, those responsible for the network solved most of the problems of linking computer terminals in prototype colleges to the network, thus making available great computational power and access to a variety of data bases if faculty members could be trained and motivated to use the system.

Although the technical problems were solved and didactic materials produced and used by a limited number of cooperating instructors, the significant economic issues were not addressed. Junior colleges and four-year liberal arts colleges found it difficult in 1973 to find funds for the needed terminals and computer time, as well as for the requisite technical personnel on each campus to maintain active use of the computer network. Additionally, those institutions had no way of paying for faculty time in the substantial amount needed to convert courses or portions of courses to the computer mode. The prototype lessons have been subsidized by external funds. However, generating the sort of volume that the network desired implied a rather substantial redeployment of the time of many different local faculties—a redeployment that existing budgetary regulations did not allow. Moreover, the University of Michigan conducted the experiment and made a start in educating people to use the system. However, the university did not have funds to continue the education of larger and larger numbers of college instructors after external funding ended. Thus the two salient economic considerations continue to be vexing. The first is how to finance the in-service training of large enough numbers of college instructors to use in a productive way computer capacity. A second is how to reorganize college budgets to support continued use and even expansion of a rather complex albeit potentially rewarding educational activity.

Moving away from computers was a 1974 effort by American University to restructure the teaching of beginning Spanish through using films, videotape cassettes, and a specially prepared textbook, all with the purpose of economically improving the quality of foreign language instruction. It was intended to introduce systematic instruction in nonverbal aspects of language, to coordinate several sophisticated new techniques into a single course, and to generate research evidence that would be of help to the profession of foreign language instruction. It began in classic educational format by developing objectives arranged in taxonomic form and then by reducing those to statements of specifically needed competencies. A full-length movie in Spanish was selected, a portion of which would be shown each week. This would serve as a base for the course, would provide motivation and continuity, and would display the natural setting for language use. Then videotaped materials were prepared locally and correlated with each movie installment, emphasizing selected elements of the language structure. These elements were designed to repeat, in many different contexts, the 2,500-word vocabulary of the film. Then a specifically designed textbook was prepared, to be distributed to students in segments, the first segment to be handed out in class each week. The entire course ultimately consisted of 112 lessons organized into twenty-four lesson units intended to cover twenty-eight weeks or two semesters. Each lesson included classroom instruction, which involved viewing the movie and conversation about it, together with laboratory drill, during which time the videotape units were available. Each class period opened with a five-minute installment from the movie, following which the class would discuss the various twists and turns in the story.

In the hands of a dynamic female assistant professor, the first full utilization of the course seemed to produce impressive gains. Students were able to communicate in the language after only one semester of study, and they manifested a high degree of enthusiasm for the language. Accents of students approximated native accents much more than did the accents of students exposed to more traditional forms of instruction. The videotape cassette course, as compared with a similar course offered by the Defense Language Institute, required fewer instructional hours to reach comparable levels of competency. To the principal investigator, the effort seemed so successful that second-year Spanish courses at the American University have been converted to the new format, as has the first-year course of French. It is intended to convert Russian as quickly as resources allow. The course seemingly has important economic significance, for at least the professor in beginning Spanish was able to teach in one semester the equivalent of two traditional semesters. In this regard, there is one caveat that should be mentioned. The assistant professor teaching the course, as was indicated, was an attractive, young, dynamic, and talented teacher who conceivably could have recorded equally impressive gains just on her own. She, however, disputes that possibility and points out that several sections of the course were taught by more pedestrian instructors, who also produced comparable gains in student performance.

As put into effect in the American University, under the close supervision of a highly interested and involved principal investigator, the course apparently has accomplished both its educational and economic objectives. The educational gains are well recorded, and the cost of using the new approach is claimed to be no higher than regular classes in beginning Spanish. The course in beginning Spanish cost $60,000 to produce. Through lessons learned from that effort, the costs of developing similar courses in other languages should drop to perhaps the $15,000 to $20,000 level. The problem of expanding numbers has been faced with a plan to link the entire American University campus to a closed-circuit television system so that sections in foreign language can be taught not only in the foreign language building but in other classrooms as well. A modest economic issue involves the degree to which the total course is essentially teacher-proof, so that it could be extended to many different sections being taught by instructors who had not been thoroughly oriented into that particular approach to teaching.

Also based on videotape presentations was the 1976 attempt

to improve the teaching abilities of teaching assistants in freshman chemistry (p. 160). As mentioned earlier, the project consisted
of developing six videotape presentations, each by a different senior
professor in chemistry, each from a different university. Professors discussed different topics in these tapes: One, for example,
discussed educational objectives and their relevance for instructional
strategy; another discussed how to conduct effective tutoring; and
still another discussed how to conduct productive discussions. Each
presenter also prepared a manual elaborating the details of the
videotape presentation for which he was responsible. Planning the
specific topics to be covered and the selection of people to discuss
them was a modestly expensive and time-consuming task. However,
that effort did produce materials generally acceptable to leading universities offering freshman chemistry. The actual videotaping of the
materials was done by the University of Nebraska television network,
which aimed at professional quality while still featuring a practicing
professor to carry the principal instructional goal; that is, trained
actors were not used, although trained studio people worked on
production. The entire packet has been tried out in a number of
different institutions in various ways. At one institution, the materials
are used supplementary to other efforts to improve the instruction of
teaching assistants. At a different institution, the six presentations
and text materials provide the essential framework for a six-week
seminar for teaching assistants. In this latter situation, videotaping
is also employed to videotape teaching assistants conducting various
teaching situations, the videotape being critiqued by the teaching
assistant himself and by the faculty member in charge of teaching
assistants for beginning chemistry. Out of those experiments, a finally
edited package was completed and has been produced in sufficient
numbers so that full sets can be sold to colleges and universities
throughout the country. It is planned that the packets will be sold at
cost plus a small mark-up, to provide funds to be used for continued
experimentation in how best prepare teaching assistants.

The entire project was relatively inexpensive, costing in the
vicinity of $40,000. It produced a package of professional-quality
tapes and script that can be sold at relatively small cost to departments of chemistry. It is used as was anticipated. The initial production costs can be quickly amortized, and, because of the nature of

the material, the package is not likely to grow obsolete. The critical economic element here will be whether the use of this kind of material can demonstrably improve the teaching qualities of graduate students as they enter for the first time an actual classroom situation. The costs to user institutions are not likely to be high, the only costs additional to regular training of teaching assistants being the purchase price of materials and perhaps some slight increase in supervisory time on the part of the coordinator of freshman chemistry and his senior teaching assistants. The potential volume for this material, assuming that it produces generally as it produced on the University of Nebraska campus, is such that the per-unit cost, including all elements, is and will likely remain relatively modest. It is conceivable that as of the mid-1970s this particular project indicates one of the better ways by which technology can affect productivity from the standpoint both of increased quality and of costs appreciably no greater than for other ways of doing the same things.

The 1970s represent a substantial shift in economic climate from the late 1950s and 1960s. A powerful motivation for using educational technology is the hope of realizing economic savings. Achievement of this goal is actively pursued through four related but somewhat different approaches. The first of these is probably the most prevalent claim and premise for continued expansion of the use of educational technology. It is that, although the use of technology very likely will add more to institutional budgets, appropriate and well-planned uses can so increase the quality of output as to warrant the increased expenditure. The related approach is based on the economic value of student time and on the notion that judicious uses of some of the technology can reduce student time expended in achieving certain educational outcomes, thus producing a reduction in total cost of higher education. This approach very likely will not reduce institutional expenditures or appropriations to institutions, but when the full cost of education is computed there will be or can be a reduction in the total bill. The third approach, which thus far has not been successfully followed, is overtime, taking advantage of less expensive but more sophisticated equipment to reduce total institutional expenditures by stressing capital-intensive instruction (with capital decreasing in cost) over labor-intensive efforts of instructors (with steadily increasing costs of labor). A variation of this approach is the acceptance of differing costs for different kinds of technology-based instruction and searching for the proper mix so that there will be some high-cost technology-based instruction, some low-cost technology-based instruction, and some additional instruction. The search is for an optimum mix, to ensure either that overall costs do not rise or that—ideally—overall costs might drop somewhat. Available literature does not provide a basis for judging any of these approaches to have been successful. In spite of a few examples that seem to indicate that uses of educational technology can produce actual cost savings and in spite of the theoretical conclusions from several different models, the most warrantable assertion is that use of educational technology as a significant means of reducing educational costs is not a likely possibility. Whether such things as videotapes or computer-managed instruction can do so in the future cannot be known. The burden of proof for a predicted cost-effective future must rest on actual large-scale experiments rather than on theoretical formulations, and these, by the late 1970s, do not seem to be forthcoming.

The major themes and developments discussed elsewhere in this book present a number of issues that impinge directly on the likely diffusion of uses of educational technology, particularly the predominant types. The first of these is a matter of cost. A preponderance of evidence indicates that using educational technology is invariably more expensive than the traditional modes of education conducted through lectures, discussions, and laboratory and library work. Claims are made in some examples that certain kinds of technologies are cost effective, but none of these are supported with full cost figures. Now, some institutions can afford using computers, videotapes, and the like on the ground that the educational values warrant the additional expenditures. However, those new institutions that rely exclusively on tuition to operate are not likely to possess the requisite resources. Additionally, many of the categories of new students that institutions are currently seeking to serve are economically marginal or disadvantaged. They are willing to undertake educational activities if there is a clear cost benefit to them, but they are unable to pay for programs inherently more expensive. This cost factor appears to contribute to the stress on work-related activities and textbook-based independent study rather than on independent study through computer-managed styles. For many of the new kinds of students, even in well-established and financially stable institutions serving more traditional students, the cost factor still emerges as a significant barrier to widespread use of educational technology in the mainstream, on-campus curricular activities.

A second issue affecting the diffusion of educational technology is related to institutional capacity, including reputation and financial strength. Institutions suffering stabilizing or declining enrollments, mounting operating deficits, nonexistent reserve or endowment funds, and relatively weak faculties are attracted to some of the more glamorous technological devices as a means of attracting more students or effecting savings. However, such institutions lack the necessary slack resources essential if the technology is going to be used effectively. At the other extreme, institutions with high capacity all too frequently are also complacent and see no need to modify practices that appear to have been successful in the past. As many have observed, American higher education is a status-oriented system, with the visible, prestigious, pacesetting institutions serving as models for other institutions to emulate. It can be theorized that until the pacesetting institutions make significant uses of educational technology in essential ways in their educational programs the uses of such equipment will lack respectability and that very lack will affect diffusion of the potential fourth revolution.

An essential characteristic of systems using computers extensively and videotapes extensively is that they ultimately will modify student-faculty ratios and conceivably would modify the mix of high-cost and low-cost instructional personnel. A matter that is only now becoming visible is that unions, accrediting agencies, and even state legislation tend to limit the modification that could be undertaken. Since these agencies are likely to play even larger roles in the practice of higher education in the future, their postures with respect to substituting capital for labor or substituting self-service for rendered service must be modified if the more promising technological devices are to become truly essential in colleges and universities.

Widespread use of many of the techniques seems to require a change in role for the professional faculty member, from the role of transmitter of information to that of manager. Some professors who have become intrigued with the possibility of using the technology claim the new role is quite satisfying. However, conversing with large numbers of faculty members and observing the short duration of so many experiments with the technology suggest that the professoriate as a whole may be unwilling to adopt the new roles, both for psychological and economic reasons.

SIX

𝖀𝖁𝖀𝖁𝖀𝖁𝖀𝖁𝖀𝖁𝖀𝖁𝖀𝖁𝖀𝖁𝖀𝖁𝖀𝖁𝖀

Issues in Governance —Conflicts in Values

Quite likely the most lasting changes are those significant modifications in control, administration, governance, and adjudication of differences that have come about mainly during the late 1960s and 1970s. The actual substance of formal education and the processes by which it is delivered are sturdily resistant to change. While some of the curricular and instructional developments conceivably may make significant differences, it is equally or more plausible that they will not. However, administrative, organizational, and governance structures have not proven to be quite so intractable. This is intriguing, since organizations do tend to resist change and to protect well-routinized roles, processes, and procedures. It may be, of course, that many recent changes are superficial and that the continuing

215

conduct of tasks and the real organizational structure remain the same. However, that possibility must for the moment be rejected.

The magnitude of these changes is best revealed by exemplifying higher education in 1958 and again in 1970. In 1957 the individual autonomous campus, with its own board of trustees and its own president and administrative staff, was typical. Ten states maintained suprainstitutional coordinating or controlling agencies, and a few institutions, public and private, maintained several campuses. Stanford, for example, maintained its medical school in San Francisco; the University of Illinois maintained its medical school in Chicago. The Board of Higher Education in New York City maintained four campuses, and in each of several states the state board of education operated a system of teachers colleges. But these were the exceptions.

On these individual campuses, presidents exerted considerable authority, although for the most part they did so within the constraints of generally recognized but uncodified values and beliefs. The faculty was a rather amorphous body presumed to have certain responsibilities (for example, the curriculum), and it met monthly or once every term or semester, just barely achieving a quorum. There were faculty committees, although their relationships to the total faculty or administration were frequently unclear. There was little interest in unions or collective bargaining on the part of the faculty, the general belief being that unionism was incompatible with the professionalism and spirit of collegiality prized by college and university professors. Budgets in even large institutions were relatively simple and were produced incrementally each year. Budget making and budget control were typically highly centralized. Indeed, in many institutions even deans did not know what salaries were awarded professors in their administrative unit. A few institutions had begun to use mechanical methods of data processing (for example, using IBM card systems for registration), but typically data collection and uses of data for administration were handled manually and more in a spirit of validating hunches than of producing a data base on which decisions could rest. Students were not even considered to be part of the administrative or organizational apparatus. John Corson (1960), for example, does not include the word *student* in his first study of academic governance. Courts typically refrained from involving themselves in internal differences in colleges and universities.

By the 1970s that tranquil and symmetrical uniformity had changed radically. All states maintained some kind of suprainstitutional control or coordination of publicly supported institutions. Nine multicampus universities, the largest maintaining fifty-two separate campuses, enrolled 25 percent of all students enrolled in public four-year colleges and universities. There were close to 2,000 consortial arrangements between collegiate institutions, ranging from quite casual cooperative agreements between two institutions to a denominational board of higher education that maintained power over individual campuses comparable to that of a public coordinating board, such as the Board of Higher Education in Illinois. The number of campuses whose faculties had elected union bargaining agents had increased from 11 in 1966 to over 500 in 1976. Both on campuses that had collective bargaining agents and on those that did not, there were typically formal faculty organizations, typically called *senates,* operating on a clearly specified constitution and set of bylaws. Committee structures were carefully linked to faculty senates, and the prerogatives of administrations, senates, committees, and commissions all were clearly specified in writing. The size of central administration had increased at a faster rate than had faculties. As the need for new administrative specialties emerged, such specialties included officers in charge of space utilization, administrative planners, lawyers, ombudsmen, directors of institutional research, and computer specialists charged with constructing budgetary models.

The courts had begun to move into various areas previously regarded as exclusively the province of institutions, especially such matters as institutional relationships with individual students and their rights and procedural rights of faculty members. Students were typically members of faculty committees, were legitimate members of some senates, were members of board committees, were actual members of some boards of trustees, and had at least advanced a claim to the right of participation in collective bargaining discussions. Voluntary accreditation, the means by which institutions have historically maintained some standards of intrainstitutional quality, continued to be important, but there was a growing involvement of state and federal government in accreditation activities. Computers had become an essential element of administration, and each year demands for additional and more sophisticated data grew more and more insatiable.

A relatively simple explanation for these changes can be advanced: The administrative, organizational, and governance developments of the late 1960s and early 1970s were logical extensions of structures created earlier. Thus the movement toward statewide coordination was already well advanced by 1968, and the courts had already begun to concern themselves with some internal affairs of institutions as the civil rights movement crescendoed, from 1964 onward. And the emergence of systems of institutions, complicated management information systems, the shifts to more formal systems of faculty involvement in governance, the creation of new kinds of administrative roles, and the increased demands for more data and better planning could all be attributed to the increased size, complexity, and cost of higher education in the United States. The conventional wisdom in 1968 assumed continued expansion of higher education and held that surveys of higher education were designed to produce data that would aid in making more rational decisions about expanding higher education to meet the needs of people. Coordinating agencies were intended to ensure proper deployment of resources so that growing educational missions might be accomplished. Master plans were intended to chart the direction in which institutions should move in order to accomplish state educational purposes. Control agencies were responsible for the conduct or operation of institutions, singly or in groups, on the ground that some centralized authority could do better than individual campuses.

However, that simplified explanation does not hold up. By 1968, although there had been a great deal of planning activity and many statewide coordinating or controlling agencies had been created, there was no evidence that they had been particularly effective in producing more rational and more economical statewide educational programs. California, for example, had a highly developed system, whereas Michigan had not. There was no evidence that Michigan or California were serving their people educationally any better or worse, although new and more formal systems of faculty involvement in governance had been created. The performance of faculty structures by 1968 was not particularly promising for the future, bogged down as senates were in procedural matters of organizing and coping with the outburst of campus disruption. Although program planning and budgeting had come to be heralded as a way of reaching more rational decisions, they were actually in effect in no institution by 1968, and decisions were still being reached incrementally or as a result of political maneuvering on the part of the different campus constituencies.

In view of the lack of evidence on the effectiveness of newer structures or devices, other models could have reasonably emerged. Since states such as Alabama, Michigan, and Kansas had accommodated enrollment increases during the 1960s without statewide systems, they could have continued their pattern of institutional independence, and other states could have abolished recently created coordinating or controlling systems and returned to complete individual institutional independence. Indicating the precariousness of some systems in 1968 was the remark made by the Chairman of the Colorado Coordinating Commission that the biggest achievement of the commission's first two years of operation was that it survived. Certainly there appeared to be no greater reason for states to move from statewide coordination to statewide control than for states to return to institutional independence and autonomy. To be sure, there was the growing belief on the part of students of higher education that centralization of some sort was good, and various policy-recommending groups adopted that particular point of view. However, beliefs of theorists and positions of policy-recommending groups are not necessarily adopted generally unless they are congruent with forces stressing the same things. In 1958, for example, the Eisenhower Conference on Education Beyond High School urged increases in faculty salaries, and those increases did come about, in large measure because of the increased demand for college professors during the early 1960s. Similarly, in 1968 the newly created faculty senates could have taken a form that would have safeguarded the economic conditions of the professoriate and thus obviated the growing desire on the part of college and university teachers to embrace unionism and collective bargaining.

Factors Affecting Change

The structural changes in higher education during the 1970s—including statewide systems of control, expansion of multicampus universities, more vigorous consortial arrangements, unionism and collective bargaining, use of complex data systems, and expansion of administrative bureaucracies—came about because of a number of factors. Legislators and governors were demanding better planning, more efficiency, and greater accountability, and they saw, in new organizational structures, ways of bringing these things about. Various commissions such as the Carnegie Commission on Higher Education urged greater rationality in the planning of higher education and the allocation of financial resources. The successes of using computer-based systems in such other enterprises as the space program or in some commercial ventures suggested that using similar devices in higher education could produce more economical operation of institutions while at the same time enhancing institutional effectiveness. To those rational and plausible contributing factors, however, must be added several more fundamental forces that added the power to institutionalize changes that otherwise might have remained superficial or that might have disappeared entirely.

Antiprofessionalism. The first of these is a growing spirit of antiprofessionalism in the society, which seems to be reflected in several of the changes in governance. As noted in Chapter One, what Jencks and Riesman (1968) describe as a successful academic revolution produced a professoriate responsible for the selection of its own members, for setting its own goals, for evaluating its own performance, and for being accountable primarily to itself. Whether that revolution finally failed because of the turmoil of the late 1960s, because of the failure of universities to produce all they claimed they could produce, or because of the general skepticism concerning major social institutions that became pronounced in the society by the early 1970s cannot be known with any precision. However, by 1971 the ability of academics to govern themselves had become highly suspect. Gross and Grambsch (1974, p. 3) point out that "An ominous cleavage has grown up between outside power holders (regents, legislators, state government, citizens) and 'insiders' (chairmen, deans, faculty, students), which very much affected the goals of universities." This distrust of the academic as a professional is expressed in the demand for accountability and in the beliefs of political leaders that only some strong, suprainstitutional organization could control academics and force them to attend to public needs. Indicative was the serious effort on the part of some Kansas legislators to create a separate fact-finding body reporting directly to the legislature on the ground that only such an agency could or would report honestly. There was the strongly expressed feeling that faculty, administration, and even boards of regents could not be trusted to report accurately on their own activities. Also indicative was the belief expressed by the chancellor of the California state university and college system that only a strong system office could ensure diversity of educational activity within the system. Left to their own devices, he believed faculty would invariably try to emulate the state university system, even though that system was inappropriate for the mission of the state colleges.

This antiprofessionalism is also involved in unionism and collective bargaining. Within the system of American higher education, there is a definite continuum extending from the most highly professionalized, prestige research institution at one end to the low-prestige, invisible, and slightly professionalized public junior college at the other. When unionism and collective bargaining began to be of considerable significance during the late 1960s and early 1970s, those institutions that were relatively low with respect to prestige and professionalization of faculty became the most highly unionized. The phenomenon could almost be described as substituting unionism for professionalization on the ground that the former would most clearly attend to the personal and financial needs of faculty. Kemerer and Baldridge (1975, pp. 55–56) epitomized this phenomenon when they remarked that "In general, institutions are more inclined to faculty collective negotiations if (1) they are public rather than private; (2) they are community colleges rather than state colleges or universities; (3) their faculties have fewer Ph.D.'s and their admissions policies are not selective; (4) they are not wealthy in terms of income per student and are more recently established; [and] (5) they experience more interference by outside authorities. This portrait clearly fits two-year colleges and the less prestigious state colleges—institutions where most faculty unionization has occurred."

Egalitarianism. Difficult to reject but also difficult to prove is the belief that strong egalitarian sentiment is involved in a number of the structural changes of the late 1960s and 1970s. Historically, at least in theory, the American system of academic ranks and award of tenure was based on a meritocratic belief. Individuals judged best trained, most able, and most productive were favored over less-qualified individuals. While in a few public systems salary scales ensured equal financial treatment for individuals once accepted into the system, the more typical pattern was to emphasize merit, if only through initial placement at different levels on the salary scale. Among public institutions, there were also salary differences based on presumed qualitative differences. Thus salaries in the flagship state universities were higher than in state colleges, and those in state colleges in turn were somewhat higher than in public junior colleges. Within institutions, there were salary differentials between various categories. Women, for example, typically held lower rank and received lower salaries than males. As higher education moved into the 1970s, several factors merged. First, the general slowdown in enrollment increases meant fewer new hires, which worked particularly hard against newly prepared, young, minority or women professionals. During the 1960s, the proportion of faculty holding permanent tenure across the country had increased from slightly less than half to almost 70 percent, with predictions that the proportion would rise to 80 percent by the 1980s. To stave off the rigidities that such a high proportion on tenure would produce, institutions began to exercise restraints in the granting of additional tenure. This tightening was expected to operate most seriously against blacks, Native Americans, people with Spanish surnames, women, and people under thirty. Concern over such a situation appears to be one of the factors leading to unionization and to negotiated contracts that base job security on longevity rather than on judgments of merit. The egalitarian or leveling motive is implied by an examination of who has gained the most when union contracts have been negotiated. "The most disenfranchised—the nonteaching professionals at most institutions, community college faculty, and junior faculty at four-year and graduate institutions—will receive very real gains from collective bargaining. As a result of unionism, for example, the pay of community college faculty within CUNY rose sharply when parity with senior institutions in the system was achieved. Further, status differences between the disenfranchised and regular faculty are likely to be reduced as militants strive to dominate the union and establish union goals through the 'majority rules' procedures" (Kemerer and Baldridge, 1975, pp. 197–198).

Egalitarianism also seems involved in the intrusion of the federal government, through enforcing various provisions for affirmative action, and this intrusion is reflected in increases in institutional administrative staffs through the appointment of affirmative action officers and the appointment of lawyers to assist institutions in coping with the increase in complex legislation. This same egalitarianism seems involved in changes and suggested changes in accreditation of collegiate institutions. Throughout the twentieth century, assessments of institutional quality have been made by voluntary regional accrediting associations and by special accrediting associations concerned with such specialized schools as medicine, law, or library science. Judgments were typically made on the basis of a limited number of measures such as training of faculty, size of library, and the like. The sudden increase in interest in new students, in nontraditional study, and in the creation of new kinds of institutions (all based on egalitarian principles) raised the question as to the appropriateness of assessing those developments with traditional criteria, and accrediting associations responded by making some modifications in procedure and even in criteria. But, in the eyes of some, those modifications did not go far enough, and as a result both state and federal governmental agencies began to involve themselves more and more in accreditation activities. A clear illustration is the Western College Association, which accredits California and the Pacific islands of Hawaii and Guam. The association had made a number of changes in its procedures and criteria to accommodate new and nontraditional programs, but it still refused accreditation to institutions that appeared to lack a secure economic base or to lack quality. In the eyes of the lieutenant governor of California and of several legislators, such denials were really denials of educational opportunity to new groups of students. To ensure that opportunity, legislation was proposed that would make responsibility for accreditation a state affair, in the belief that the state bureaucracy would be more inclined to validate new programs and hence to aid previously unserved groups of students, such as the working, the poor, and the elderly.

This egalitarian sentiment is one of the, if not the most powerful, links connecting the variety of significant changes during the 1970s. A growing concern for new students (typically previously excluded from higher education) has led to experimentation with nontraditional modes of learning. When traditional institutions have appeared slow to embrace those ideas, new kinds of institutions have been created that focus on new students and nontraditional methods. Reaching new students, many of whom cannot readily attend classes on existing campuses, has led to an interest in technological developments, especially in television, videotape cassettes, and computer-based, programmed lessons and courses. When those new developments do not receive instant approval through voluntary accreditation, a movement is made to involve governmental agencies, on democratic, populist, or egalitarian grounds. When legislative or administrative remedy does not appear imminent, there increasingly is an appeal to the courts. Although a proprietary school called Marjorie Webster Junior College lost a suit to force the Middle States Accrediting Association to examine it, the aftershock of the case forced regional associations to reconsider the position of not examining proprietary institutions, and institutions increasingly began to threaten legal action to force attention to their concerns with accreditation.

And, of course, the egalitarian sentiment is involved in those university senates that extended membership to all campus constituencies, including faculty, administration, students, and nonprofessional staff. It is also involved in using students on faculty committees and in the creation of new offices to ensure protection of the rights of individuals.

Much easier to observe and document as a force producing structural changes was the breakdown of traditional mechanisms in the face of challenge and crisis that institutions faced from 1964 onward. The first of these was clearly the outbreak of student dissent, which revealed that existing administrative structures in many institutions were inadequate to respond. In both Harvard and Columbia University, for example, faculties had been allowed great latitude to proceed with their own work and interests, while the management of the institution rested in the hands of the president and key administrative or board associates. No mechanisms had developed that could allow faculty and administration to work in consort when the institution was presented with the demands of frequently intractable protesting students. That sort of failure appears to have been most involved in the rather rapid adoption of senates during the last half of the decade of the 1960s. To be sure, there was also other factors involved. Senates had long existed on the campuses of the University of California, and senates were created as a result of administrative awareness that new techniques were needed for new times. That same crisis period also produced increases in institutional administrative staffs, increases in formal statements of rights, responsibilities and procedures, and the increasing interest in internal institutional affairs.

Deteriorating Finances. The second crisis that found traditional mechanisms wanting was, of course, the financial condition, which began to deteriorate in approximately 1968. Educational leadership had acted as though American higher education had entered a period of continuous expansion and perpetual prosperity. Almost without warning, institutions found themselves in what Earl Cheit (1971) called "the new depression in higher education." Expenditures exceeded income in increasing amounts each year, and some private institutions faced possible bankruptcy. When this condition became generally known, institutions began to take emergency steps to correct their financial conditions and then to prevent such emergencies in the future. This led institutions to develop more complex data systems, more complex budgeting systems, more modeling of institutional finances for planning purposes and, of course, increases in administrative staff to provide these services. In the public sector, the financial condition led legislatures and state agencies to involve themselves more deeply in financial matters in higher education; for example, by requiring evidence of accountability and scrutinizing budget requests ever more closely.

Student protest and financial difficulties appeared as rather sudden crises. However, throughout much of the 1960s, with their enormous expansion of American higher education, a continuing crisis existed that involved equitable and effective deployment of state resources, the appropriate location of new institutions, expansion of needed programs and restriction on unnecessary ones, extending equal access to higher education, and ensuring that collegiate institutions functioned for the benefit of the public good. Early attempts to deal with those matters resulted in the creation of statewide coordinating agencies. However, as the decade wore on serious weaknesses in many of these committees or commissions stimulated a search for new structures. In California, the coordinating council proved inadequate to the task envisioned for it by the legislature, and, after several exhaustive studies, a new postsecondary education commission was created. In Wisconsin, apparent failure resulted in the creation of a single board of trustees for higher education in that state. A similar development took place in North Carolina, and debates go on in other states as to advisability of moving from coordination and cooperation to outright control of institutions. Among the perceived failures were failures to keep costs within reasonable limits, to prevent expansion of expensive and lucrative programs, to provide fully for universal access to higher education, and to keep institutions sensitive and responsive to changing public needs.

Structural Changes

A more intensive examination of six major structural changes of the 1970s will help underscore differences of the 1970s from earlier periods and may imply something as to future structural change. These six—multicampus systems, statewide control, university or faculty senates, unions, court intrusion, and centralized and governmentally related accreditation—make the profile of organized higher education in the 1970s radically different from what it was during the 1950s and 1960s.

Multicampus Arrangements. Probably most important are the various multicampus arrangements, which, while begun earlier, now took on new form and exercised greater power than earlier attempts to coordinate activities of different campuses or different institutions. By the 1970s there had emerged several major types of multicampus organizations and a number of minor variations, which, when combined in different ways, produced a variegated national pattern, no one organization exactly resembling any other organization. As has been indicated, many different forces have helped produce multicampus arrangements, including the professional aspirations of administrators, political distrust of academicians, ideas of theoreticians, influences of the federal government, accidents of history, and strident demands for enriched educational programs. However, the two forces that predominate are economic and egalitarian, and, of the two, the desire to minimize cost or to maintain financial viability appears to be the stronger.

Among publicly supported institutions, there has been a steady drift toward some form of suprainstitutional agency or organization possessing at least some of the prerogatives previously enjoyed by individual campuses, each having its own board of trustees and chief executive officer. As the number of such bodies began to increase during the early 1960s, the most prevalent forms to be adopted were coordinating commissions or committees, of which the coordinating council in California was in a sense prototypic. That agency was created in 1960 as the culmination of fifteen years of study and restudy of the needs for higher education of the state of California. That council was assigned responsibility to generate data, to conduct and coordinate long-range planning, to review and comment on budget requests from the three sectors of public higher education (University of California, state colleges, and junior colleges), to review and approve or reject locations for new campuses, and to conduct studies regarding higher education as needed. In varying degrees, that model was followed in such other states as Colorado, Texas, Missouri, Illinois, Virginia, and West Virginia. Some councils (in part because of characteristics of their chief executive officers) became quite influential in the state and made recommendations that were accepted regularly by the legislature, while others evolved into relatively impotent agencies, advising the governor and the legislature but having no assurance that their recommendations would be attended to. While coordinating agencies differed, state to state, the typical scope of their responsibilities consisted of collecting data from individual institutions, conducting long-range studies, and coordinating institutional master-planning, reviewing and commenting on institutional budget requests, reviewing and commenting on requested new major programs desired by individual institutions, and approving or disapproving sites for new institutions. And these coordinating agencies were typically created to facilitate achievement of the state's educational roles at costs that the state could afford. Awareness of prospective large increases in student enrollment led educators and political leaders to seek some mechanism that could undertake rational planning to help avoid costly duplication of educational services, yet meet the very real needs of the people. Almost without exception, coordinating agencies accepted the idea that some opportunity for higher education should be provided for every qualified person and that the number of qualified people could rise to approximately 80 percent of high school graduating classes. With some greater variation, coordinating agencies also assumed that there was a need for some differentiation among types of public institutions in the state, that individual institutions would cooperate in long-range planning, and that decisions about higher education could be rationally arrived at through consensus.

During the 1960s, statewide coordination enjoyed varying degrees of success or failure in different states. Overall coordination seemed to succeed in publicizing the need for higher education in the state, in educating legislators regarding higher education and its intricacies, in obtaining better data, and in stimulating somewhat more sophisticated planning within institutions and throughout the state. However, with respect to several major goals, coordinating agencies proved to be inadequate. They were unable to reduce costs below costs in states in which coordination did not exist. With few exceptions, they were unable to deny program expansion if, for example, the senior state institution really wanted to created a new dental or medical school. Nor were they particularly successful in locating new institutions or branches of new institutions where they could most likely extend access to large proportions of segments of the population that had previously not been well served by public higher education in the state. Except for generalized recommendations that institutions should be located in the most populated areas, scant attention was paid to the needs of the central city; new junior colleges, state colleges, and branches of existing institutions were typically established in the suburbs and in the periphery of large cities rather than in central city locations. Thus it was only at the end of the decade of the 1960s that a junior college was located in metropolitan Minneapolis-St. Paul or that a branch of San Francisco City College was established away from its main campus, which is located on the western perimeter of the city. Willingham (1970, p. 36) underscores this failure by noting that "Twenty-eight states added one or more free access colleges in 1968; in only eight of those states was any college opened in the general location where it could serve the largest number of people."

As weaknesses of coordinating agencies became apparent, states began to experiment with suprainstitutional agencies that had much greater power. Rhode Island created a single board responsible for all of education in the state, similar to what had long existed in Idaho and Montana. Wisconsin created a single board of control for all public higher education in the state, as did also North Carolina. By 1975 twenty-two states maintained single consolidated boards actually controlling all senior public institutions and eight states maintained multicampus universities, each with boards controlling the individual campuses. Only four states persisted in the historic practice of allowing each individual campus to be governed by a single board of trustees, having direct and unrestricted access to the governor and the legislature. The magnitude of this shift is illustrated by the fact that in 1940 70 percent of all public four-year campuses were governed by their own individual boards, whereas in 1975 only 30 percent were so governed (Carnegie Foundation for the Advancement of Teaching, 1976, p. 85). As of 1976 it is still too early to judge whether more centralized control through a statewide board typically appointed by the governor will succeed in the areas in which coordination demonstrated weakness. However, the Carnegie Foundation for the Advancement of Teaching saw reason for skepticism. It believed that centralization of authority "reduces the influence of students and of faculty members and of campus administrators and of members of campus governing boards—all persons who know the most about institutions of higher education, and are the most directly involved in their operations. It also reduces their sense of responsibility. The governance of academic institutions should include an influential role for academics and for those in close relations with them. This centralization seems to have had no measurable direct impact on policies or on practices. No provable case can thus far be made that higher education is in any way better because of the centralization, except, where it has taken place, in the one area of careful advance academic planning for higher education as a whole. It is, of course, not possible to know, however, what would have happened in the absence of the centralization that did occur. The governance processes are worse. They are more costly, more cumbersome, more time consuming, more frustrating, and place more power in the hands of those who are the furthest removed and who know the least" (1976, pp. 11–12). This last point certainly is related to the previously mentioned antiprofessionalism that seemed to expand during the 1970s.

One specific form of centralization of authority, which evolved earlier but which has intensified its activities during the 1970s, is the multicampus university with a single board of trustees and a chief executive officer responsible for two or more campuses within a state. Nine of these systems (University of California, California state universities and colleges, University of Illinois, University of Missouri, State University of New York, University of North Carolina, University of Texas, University of Wisconsin, and the City University of New York) enroll approximately 25 percent of all students in public four-year colleges and universities. These, although created in part out of indigenous state concerns and traditions, all came into existence on the assumption that grouping specific types of institutions under one board allows more effective and efficient planning and operation. "The multicampus university is designed to promote specialization, diversity, and cooperation—a division of labor and alternative approaches to education in a coordinated, intercampus context. Thus . . . the peculiar values of research-oriented university campuses can best be protected if they are grouped together but separated from responsibility for exclusively undergraduate campuses . . . the state colleges can best play their important role as teaching institutions if organized into a separate system" (Lee and Bowen, 1971, pp. 9, 37). These had all come into existence by 1970 but were struggling to define a workable role. There was uncertainty as to what responsibilities should be assumed by the system office and what by a single campus. There was uncertainty as to how staff officers in the system headquarters should relate to the chief executive officer on individual campuses—whether a system-wide chief academic officer should have veto power over programs developed on a local campus. No effective device had been worked out to allow for faculty or student involvement in system-wide discussion and decisions. There were varying opinions as to the role of the system office in appointment, as to promotion and granting of tenure to faculty, and as to whether budget appropriations should be made to the system or to individual campuses. In short, the picture was ambiguous, confused, and differed from system to system.

By 1976, although considerable confusion still existed, some significant developments could be detected. The size of system administrative staffs increased, as did budgets for systems operations. All multicampus university headquarters had been able to establish the requirement that individual campuses do careful academic master planning and to establish the principle that the headquarters could review specific programs and accept or reject new ones or eliminate existing ones. "System-wide review of new academic programs had become more intensive, based on academic quality and campus mission, in six or more of the nine systems and on fiscal criteria rate" (Lee and Bowen, 1971, p. 9). Systems headquarters seemed to have developed new and possibly more effective quantitative measures for resource allocation, as well as more sophisticated budgeting techniques. They had also seemingly been able to relate more closely budgeting and academic planning. In each of the nine systems, procedures and policies had been developed for dealing with state budgetary officials and legislatures, which allowed somewhat greater governmental intervention but still protected the system from overburdening political and governmental intervention. However, systems headquarters had not been particularly successful in facilitating redeployment of students, faculty, and programs as needed. They had had only limited success in creating large, innovative, and nontraditional programs. Their success in facilitating intercampus offering of programs had been limited. Only two of the nine systems had given more explicit attention to racial matters than individual campuses had given. First, the entire system of the University of North Carolina is under mandate from the U.S. Department of Health, Education and Welfare to eliminate duplication of programs that tend to perpetuate segregated institutions, and, second, the City University of New York adopted a policy of open admissions that lasted until the fiscal crisis of 1976 forced a retreat from that position.

An overall assessment of multicampus systems is difficult to make, and informed people express widely divergent opinions. Harold Enarson (1973, pp. 18–19), president of the Ohio State University, argued that "The state colleges and universities have been formally merged into a single new all-embracing state university. It is a triumph of system—a new empire, a new total bureaucracy." He believed the system had triumphed because of the impulse of government itself to extend its domain and control, because of the rapid movement toward the development of a powerful system of higher education, and because of excessive reliance on management and development tools. A much more charitable attitude is taken by Lee and Bowen, who have done the most systematic study of systems. They remark (1975, p. 148) that "Multicampus systems are currently in midstream. The expansionist dreams of the 1960s have been left behind and the harsh reality of the 1980s lies ahead. But a major objective of multicampus administration has emerged from the experience of the last five years: For the foreseeable future, creative use must be made of the unique organizational structure that combines coordination and governance. Coordination implies a continuing high level of campus autonomy—the prerogative of the campuses to promote their own institutional stamp and style. Governance, on the other hand, implies that central administration has direct operational responsibility and is accountable to the state for the sum of activity across campuses. The tension between campus and central responsibility cannot be resolved by abandoning either. We believe we have shown that fiscal enrollment pressures, such as those expected over the coming decade, need not inevitably lead to inappropriate centralization at the expense of desirable campus authority."

As to the future of centralized control of public higher education, exact forms cannot be predicted. However, no force or organized sentiment on the horizon is likely to produce decentralizing tendencies. Indeed, virtually all developments and pressures of the 1970s are converging to encourage greater centralization both for public and private higher education. State involvement or interest in disbursement of federal funds, providing some support for private institutions, collective bargaining, accreditation, and, of course, the main financial support of public institutions all contribute to this trend.

Paralleling the growth and intensification of multicampus universities in the public sector is the expansion of consortial arrangements between institutions primarily in the private sector but including a substantial number of publicly supported institutions. There are over 2,000 arrangements of some sort, but for this analysis a *consortium* can be defined as a voluntary formal organization consisting of three or more institutions offering multiacademic programs, administered by at least one full-time professional, and in part supported by annual contributions of participating institutions. In 1967 thirty-one consortia of this sort could be identified, sixty-six in 1971, and eighty in 1973. These arrangements came into existence in the belief that through cooperation academic programs could be substantially enriched and made more diverse and economic gains could be made. These beliefs became especially appealing by the late 1960s, as it appeared that a new era in the organization of American higher education was emerging, in which multicampus arrangements would assume more and more prerogatives and responsibilities previously exercised by individual campuses. There was almost a feeling of inevitability concerning this matter, many educators believing that either cooperation and coordination would be developed voluntarily within academic institutions or state and national government would dictate suprainstitutional arrangements.

Among those consortia that possess the five characteristics mentioned, there are still enormous differences in size, resources, and scope of program. There are a number of three- or four-institution consortia such as the Consortium for Free Institutions in Salinas, Kansas, which are supported primarily by grants from the federal government. There are the somewhat larger consortia of colleges located in a larger region, such as the Great Lakes College Association or the Associated Colleges of the Midwest, and there are

still larger, more specialized consortia, such as the Regional Council
for International Education, which consists of approximately twenty-
five institutions. Some consortia focus on a limited concern, such as
offering urban or religious studies, and others attempt to offer an
expanding array of services as needs and resources appear. A
sampling of activities provides an indication of consortial possibilities: assisting each of ten colleges to develop specialized library
holdings available to each other, maintaining a campus or facility
abroad to be used for foreign studies programs by each of the member institutions, providing for students at one institution to take
courses at another institution without extra charge, facilitating the
exchange of faculty, cooperative book purchasing, cooperative recruiting of students whose homes are abroad, conducting cooperative institutional research, offering joint programs for faculty development, and administering an admission exchange program. Although differences do exist, consortia are generally governed by a
board of trustees that typically consists of presidents of member
institutions and are administered by a chief executive officer and
whatever additional clerical and professional assistance the budget
will allow. Basic operating funds are supplied by contributions from
participating member institutions, together with whatever grant
money the consortium can generate.

Consortia are viewed theoretically as one of the most promising innovations in American higher education. They quite naturally
are viewed enthusiastically by individuals who direct them and
who see a reasonable professional future in them. They seem to have
attracted the support of presidents of member institutions and the
respect of faculty members and students who have been intimately
involved in some one or several programs that a given consortium
maintains. And consortia have produced some quite tangible results,
such as enriched library holdings and well-received faculty development programs. However, the literature reveals no evidence that
consortia have effected institutional economies. They have typically
not generated widely accepted and utilized innovative educational
programs. They have not eased the problems of academic administration and governance, and their executive leadership continuously
reveals a sense of uncertainty regarding the long-term future of any
specific consortium. This uncertainty is illustrated by the career of

Lewis Patterson, one of the acknowledged leaders in the consortium field. He directed the Consortium of Kansas City Institutions, established a newsletter to enable exchange of information between consortia leaders, organized annual conferences for consortia leaders, obtained a modest grant from the Danforth Foundation to establish a national affiliation for consortia as part of the American Association for Higher Education, and then was forced to become almost a mendicant when the grant funds ran out and the American Association for Higher Education elected no longer to be an asylum for the consortium. Conversation with consortium directors has revealed annual anxiety as to whether participating institutions would still continue to make the annual contributions on which the organization must rely.

With the exception of the Ford Foundation and, to a lesser extent, the Danforth Foundation, consortia have not attracted much philanthropic foundation support. Some federal support has been made available, especially from the Fund for the Improvement of Secondary Education, and in Illinois the legislature asked for legislation providing financial assistance to consortia, which could bring about more effective use of educational resources. Thus the financing of most consortia has been and likely will continue to be a precarious, hand-to-mouth existence.

In 1969, the author remarked in a speech to directors of consortia that the time for cooperative arrangements such as consortia had passed. The achievement of those consortia to date are not at all part of the central concerns that produced the consortium movement. Outright merger, it seemed to him, was the only way those central concerns could be achieved, and merger seemed appropriate only in such situations as in Greensboro, North Carolina, where several institutions existed in close proximity to each other. In 1974, Franklin Patterson, who had been president of Hampshire College, a member of a consortium, and who had studied consortia intensively, reached somewhat similar conclusions without minimizing some very real accomplishments of individual consortia. He judged that "The performance of consortia up to this point has not measured well against the real opportunities and needs that have existed in American higher education in the past several decades. The general failure of the movement to deliver significant academic complimentarity or significant planned cooperation in capital outlay or significant attention to the operating economies that might be achieved through cooperation or any substantial long-range planning of change and development—together with the continuing preeminence of institutional autonomy regardless of the redundancy of results—reflects a major opportunity thus far lost by consortia in terms of higher education as it has been" (Patterson, 1974, p. 90). He, however, saw major needs that consortia theoretically could meet.

The collective rationalization of economic operations should include ways to optimize the income base of institutions from student payments and other sources, ways to match educational program with student consumer demands, ways to economize in operating costs, and ways to plan capital outlay with reference to carefully selected priorities and without redundancy.

The collective rationalization of academic operations should include ways to provide programs that are complimentary rather than competitive, ways to adapt the old institutional model to new requirements of openness and flexibility, ways to encourage institutional and faculty self-renewal, and ways to increase quality and opportunity beyond capability of the individual institution working alone.

The collective development of new modes and alternatives in postsecondary education should include ways to go beyond the old institutional model to new programs that are not necessarily campus-bound or limited to students from eighteen to twenty-two years old, ways to utilize the available technology of communication more productively, ways to provide self-paced learning for students of widely varying backgrounds and abilities, ways to help faculty toward greater pedagogical effectiveness and redefinition of role, . . . and ways to create new curriculum designs and materials appropriate to the last quarter of the twentieth century [Patterson, 1974, pp. 94–95].

Consortia seem to have been somewhat less than a resounding success for several reasons. They have provided no incentives for faculty or students to participate actively and in large numbers in realistic exchange programs. Only if that participation could be ensured could the role of curricular enrichment be realized, except for a very few individuals. Without powerful incentives, to expect faculty members from an Indiana school periodically to teach in a

Michigan school is demanding too much. Similarly, to expect large numbers of students to relocate themselves for a term, semester, or even a year and go to another member campus, in the absence of clearly perceptible rewards, is to expect unrealistic educational idealism. For the most part, consortia have not reduced costs to students nor perceptibly increased educational effectiveness. Given this situation and the absence of other valued incentives, the fundamental potentiality of consortia appear unrealizable. Given the financial straits endemic to consortia, they are clearly unable to respond to such egalitarian needs as greater service for minority and economically disadvantaged students.

This overview of multicampus organizations would not be complete without paying some attention to two other developments that clearly emerged for the first time during the late 1960s, although a few examples had been started in an earlier period. The first of these is a kind of academic colonialism, by which an established institution creates, all over the state, country, or world, centers that offer highly specific programs to people in different regions. Examples abound, but a few indicate the variety. The Pennsylvania State University has established centers for upgrading of teachers in many parts of the state. These are administered centrally, are located in rented facilities, and are staffed by people from the locality of each center, who also typically hold appointments in an existing institution in the region. Because of the vagaries of the Pennsylvania system of higher education, Pennsylvania State University can offer a course in one of its centers and charge less tuition than a state college that exists in the same city. The faculty, teaching courses as an overload, costs Pennsylvania State University less than would its own faculty members, because the state college in the region is responsible for retirement, health benefits, and other fringe benefit costs. Chapman College, LaVerne College, and Pepperdine University in southern California all have created centers on military bases and in public school systems. These centers offer degree-credit courses in sufficient variety as to enable individuals to secure a bachelor's or master's degree entirely through part-time attendance. The teaching staff typically consists of a resident director recruited in the locality. Some faculty members are from the home campus, teaching on an overtime basis, and other faculty members are recruited in the locality, frequently individuals who are teachers in the school system in which the degree programs are offered. The University of Northern Colorado has established centers, both in the East and Far West, that offer doctoral programs in urban affairs and educational administration. The format is similar to other sorts of colonial activity. An institution on the West Coast, for example, contracts with University of Northern Colorado to recruit students, develop courses and seminars, and conduct the resident instruction. Twice during the duration of a doctoral program, those matriculated go to Greeley, Colorado, for a reasonably intensive summer session. Antioch College, in Yellow Springs, Ohio, is possibly the best known of the colonizing colleges in the private sector, having expanded from its Yellow Springs campus to approximately eighteen centers and campuses scattered throughout the country, which range in focus from a law school in Washington, D.C., to programs designed for cultural minorities on the West Coast. A rather flamboyant colonizing venture, which, although now defunct, nonetheless clearly exhibits the motivations for colonizing and how such efforts operate, was the United States International University in San Diego, California. This started as a traditional liberal arts college, located overlooking the Pacific outside of San Diego, that developed a sound reputation for teacher preparation. To this was added a law school, a business school, a school of performing arts, and a graduate program in psychology. The institution adopted the name United States International University and developed the rationale that it would make internationalism the focus of all of its efforts. It developed a scheme that envisioned students alternating between attendance at centers located throughout the world and attending the San Diego campus. The university then acquired a second campus to the east of San Diego, a campus in Steamboat Springs, Colorado, another outside London, still another in Africa, and then, in rapid succession, a campus in Mexico City, one in Hawaii, and finally a research installation in Oregon. While there was a persuasive educational rationale for this expansion, there is also reason to suspect a rather central economic reason. Beginning in about 1960, the university began running operating deficits. It would then acquire a new campus and recruit local faculty and students, with the idea of operating the local campus at a profit through tuition, the profit to be channeled back into the operation of the full university. Typically the campuses were purchased with relatively small down payments and with the assumption of additional capital, yet with an obligation for heavy debt service. This general procedure finally led the institution into such severe financial difficulties that it was forced to dismantle the empire.

This colonizing pattern is an amazing phenomenon, developing as it did during the period when the rate of collegiate enrollments had to slow toward an eventual absolute decline. The primary motivations very likely include a desire to render service, but also, and more importantly, include a desire to build up off-campus enrollments to replace the declining enrollments on the home campus. In view of this motivation, several conditions must be met if the colonizing venture is to be successful. The effort must be in a field judged to be expanding or likely to expand, such as urban affairs or environmental concerns. Or it can be in an established field, such as teaching or educational administration, in which increased credentials are needed by practitioners and in which a financial gain is associated with increased credentialing. There must be available a critical mass of people who are already employed but who are powerfully motivated to acquire academic degrees. Military bases are ideal examples, given the increased emphasis the military forces are placing on academic degrees for promotion and given the military retirement policies that permit and even encourage large numbers of people to retire after twenty years, at approximately age forty, people who therefore want to prepare themselves for second careers. The school systems represent another ideal center, as do large corporations wishing to upgrade their management staff. Then there must be available, in the vicinity of each center, individuals who are sufficiently trained and credentialed to offer course work and who will serve part-time, thus augmenting their basic salaries. This condition allows for adequate instruction to be provided at relatively low cost since the parent institution is not obligated for substantial faculty overhead costs. Lastly, tuition income must be ensured, either through the operation of formula-based appropriations, the availability of tuition funds from various federal programs, or a tuition that is high enough to cover expenses and yield a profit and that individuals will pay because the program permits them to save time and gives them the opportunity to attend while working.

A last and quite new structural development, which re-

sembles the colonial pattern, is the rise of profit-making organizations that contract with colleges and universities to create and
organize degree programs, recruit students and faculty, conduct
instruction, and maintain student records. The contracting college
or university awards academic credit and confers the actual degrees.
The institution receives a percentage of income for this service,
which in a few situations has proven sufficient to enable the institution to balance a previously seriously unbalanced budget. One
such arrangement allows a police officer to acquire bachelor's degrees in approximately one year, with considerable credit given for
previous work experience, military service, college, or on-the-job
performance. This program has a tuition of $3,000, much of which
is paid by the municipality in which the police officer is employed.
A class of 400 the first year yielded income of $1,200,000, which
netted the degree-granting institution $300,000, thus contributing
substantially to a reduction of the previous year's deficit of $800,000.
This growth of such contractual arrangements is such a recent phenomenon that no estimates are possible as to how widespread it has
become. It has, however, become sufficiently visible as to force the
various regional accrediting associations to reexamine their accreditation policies.

Representative Senates. The second major structural change,
although its long-term significance is open to serious question, is the
sudden rise of representative senates during the late 1960s and early
1970s as a device of academic governance. While there had been
senates prior to this period, the senate of the University of California being perhaps the best known, faculty involvement in governance had been much more casual and had been expressed through
such things as the total faculty meeting as a collectivity or through
advisory responsibilities assigned to standing committees or administrative units such as divisions and departments. The sudden interest
in senates seems to have arisen for several reasons: First, as institutions increased in size, the use of a full faculty in meeting proved
cumbersome and really only permitted governance by the small
minority of administratively concerned faculty. For example, at
Stanford typically under 100 faculty members would attend the
quarterly meeting of the academic council, which consisted of 900
faculty members. It became apparent that if the faculty was to have

a real voice in the overall concerns of the institutions some representative organization was essential. Secondly, the movement toward senates was produced by campus unrest from 1964 onward when the sudden impact revealed that there were no good organizational devices that could allow faculty and administration to act jointly in maintaining order on the campus. Possibly stemming out of the same soil, employee unrest and faculty desire for greater choice in institutional affairs that affected them produced additional pressure for a senate. As is true of so many other innovations in colleges and universities, presidential initiative was frequently involved in the creation of the senate or council. Out of 688 institutions having created senates, in 213 the idea was initiated by the president (Hodgkinson, 1974, p. 18). The intensification of the senate idea seems to be particularly related to the budgetary questions that arose in the 1970s, as institutions had to effect restrictions on expenditures. Since those restrictions directly affected personnel, especially when cuts in faculty were proposed, faculty interest in senates increased.

Representative senates or councils manifest considerable variety, institution to institution. First there is the matter of representation. Some—for example, Stanford and Wisconsin—created a faculty senate that inherited the powers of the previously existing academic faculty, which had been created at the time of the university's founding. Others are university senates or councils that have representatives from faculty, administration, staff, and students. It is difficult to tell from existing studies how many of each type there are. However, inferring from Hodgkinson's data, it would appear that somewhat over half are of the institution-wide variety, with the remainder representing the faculty alone. Senates also differ with respect to the powers they possess. Typically they play an advisory role and serve as a mechanism by which administrative decision makers can hear campus-wide opinion. In a minority of institutions, senates have been assigned definite policy making or legislative authority legitimatized by boards of trustees. When such authority has been granted, it has chiefly to do with academic programs, curriculum review, and rules for campus social conduct. For the most part, other areas, such as student fees, faculty tenure and promotion, admissions policies, and institutional budget, are not routinely assigned to faculty senates. When faculty involvement is present, it is so through other mechanisms such as a presidentially appointed admissions committee or an elected faculty personnel committee that makes recommendations regarding appointment, promotion, and tenure.

Senates also vary as to the role of the president and the participation of administrative officers in senate activities. Hodgkinson found that in 138 institutions the president chaired the senate, in 51 he was a member of the executive committee, and in 129 he had absolute veto over senate actions. In 109 institutions, he was a voting member of the senate. In 58 he was not a voting member, and in 40 institutions he was not a member (Hodgkinson, 1974, p. 28). Other administrative officers, such as vice-presidents and deans, served in some senates as ex officio members (with or without vote); in some they may be elected; and in some they are excluded from membership.

Faculty or university senates or councils seem best suited to a single campus, but, as multicampus universities have increased, there has been considerable experimentation with ways to involve faculty in advisory and even in legislative roles. However, the larger multicampus universities reveal considerable variety, both with respect to the presence or absence of a system-wide senate and the length of time such organizations have been in existence. The University of California and the University of Wisconsin have a long history of faculty power, and, as they became systems, the faculty senate was expanded so that there were campus senates and university-wide senates, both operating on principles of representativeness. The City University of New York, the State University of New York, the University of North Carolina, and the California state university and college system all have created comparable organizations only recently, while in Texas and Missouri no such statewide bodies exist. The University of Illinois relies primarily on campus senates. However, there is a small faculty group that coordinates the several campuses and that does review university-wide matters (Lee and Bowen, 1971). In 1971, it appeared that system-wide faculty representation was expanding and becoming stronger. Such groups were being encouraged by system administrators, boards of trustees were authorizing them and prescribing bylaws to govern their conduct, and faculty and administrators were actively encouraging greater faculty involvement in system-wide affairs. However, four years later this promise seems to have aborted. "Changes in the structure or role of the organized faculty in system-wide governance has not been substantial, an increased role for faculty senates is reported in only two systems—the California state university and colleges and the University of North Carolina. In two others, the city and state universities of New York, system-wide faculty organizations have held their own in retaining influence over academic affairs, as opposed to the bread-and-butter issues negotiated by collective bargaining agencies. On the other hand, at the University of Wisconsin a strong tradition of campus autonomy and the complexities of possible collective bargaining legislation are delaying and may prevent the establishment of a system-wide faculty organization. None of the system's chief executives expects the role of a system-wide faculty organization to increase in the future, in some instances because of collective bargaining" (Lee and Bowen, 1971).

Senates also differ as to the role accorded students. This ranges from denying membership in the senate to students to assigning a fifth or more senate spaces to students. At Stanford and the University of California, students are not members of the senate, although they may serve on senate committees. The Columbia University senate has a fifth of spaces reserved, while at the University of Kansas the previously existing student senate of approximately 100 members was combined with the somewhat larger faculty senate to create the new University of Kansas senate. Very little is generally known as to how various patterns of relationships with students have worked out. There is some evidence that student participation in the Cornell senate has so irritated the board of trustees that the senate itself may be abolished. On the other hand, observers of the Columbia University senate note that it has survived its formative years and that it is functioning quite effectively.

Assessment of senates or councils must be tentative and impressionistic. They have not been in existence long enough to establish a record, and no evaluative evidence in aggregate form has been accumulated, although John Millett (1977) has collected thirty case studies of academic governance, which, when published, may provide some answers. However, several observations seem warranted. Senates were typically created at a time when institutions were being pressured by student and faculty protest. They were new kinds of organizations, with few good models after which to fashion responsibilities and procedures during the formative period, when senates seemed to be preoccupied with developing procedures and with putting out brushfires of campus disruption. As procedural matters were debated and as more and more emotionally laden issues emerged, there was a tendency for senates to proliferate the number of committees without any sound rationale indicating committee relationships to the senate, to the president, or to the board of trustees. No sooner had senates come into existence and begun to work out relationships with administration and board of trustees than the possibility of unionism on campus became very real. Although senates coexist with unions on a number of campuses and have taken on union characteristics elsewhere, nevertheless in the long run it appears that as campuses are unionized the powers and effectiveness of senates decrease. This conceivably might not happen on the campuses of prestige universities that have long traditions of faculty voice in governance. Unionization has more frequently taken place in junior colleges and state colleges in which faculties have had little voice in governance. In such situations, the union absorbs the power and influence that had begun to devolve onto the faculty senate.

Even in large universities that have quite well-developed senates, the bulk of faculty participation in policy making and decision making takes place in the separate schools and colleges and in departments rather than in the senate and its related committees. Kemerer and Baldridge (1975, pp. 139–140), after considerable study, reach the conclusion "The importance of senates has been overstressed in the literature on academic governance. . . . It is very doubtful that senates at most institutions deal effectively with substantive matters. The critical issues are generally handled by the *faculty* at the departmental level (curriculum; student relations; faculty hiring, firing, and promoting) or by the *administration* at higher levels (budgets, overall staffing, physical plant, long-range planning). The average academic senate, we suspect, deals with relatively minor issues and readily responds to administrative rather than faculty leadership." This main point is reflected in a number of the case studies collected by Millett. At Stanford, for example, the faculty in the professional schools concentrate their governance efforts in those schools, and the faculty in humanities and sciences have their biggest say in departments.

The future of faculty senates is still in some doubt. First, several issues typically have yet to be resolved in any consistent way throughout American higher education (see Corson, 1975, p. 284). The first of these is, Who shall be represented? Should the senate be representative of faculty alone, should it include librarians or teaching assistants, or should it represent all constituencies? Added to that is the technical question, How and in what proportion should each faction be represented? Illustrative is the remark made by a student that five students out of a forty-member senate was tokenism. When asked what would not be tokenism, he replied, "Forty student representatives." And lastly is the substantive matter, What authority should the senate or assembly have? But the real imponderable is the likely impact on senates, first of unionism and second of the increased bureaucratization, especially of public higher education. Lyman Glenny, for example, claims (1971, p. 1) "That the leaders who will actually control the direction of higher education in the future and who already do so to a large extent are not likely to be the visible or highly articulate presidents or the governing boards. Certain officers, who are virtually unknown, both within and without the institution, often set directions and make more important policy for the long-range welfare of the institution than do the highly visible policy councils and chief administrators. A new leadership is emerging, but it is as anonymous in personality as it is awesome in power."

Unionism. It is entirely possible that, along with centralization of authority in multicampus institutions and in statewide boards of control, the most significant structural change of the late 1960s and 1970s will be the unionization of faculties and the advent of collective bargaining throughout most of American higher education. Such a possibility, of course, relegates senates to a transitory role, with the likelihood that they will disappear as significant instruments of governance. To understand this possibility, the roots of the union movement should be comprehended. In important respects, faculty interest in a movement toward unionism is related to the other significant developments of the period: nontraditional study and concern for new students, the creation of new kinds of institutions, serious consideration of educational technology, the rise of statewide coordination, and control and experimentation with new forms of governance. That relationship exists, in that two of the major forces, economic and egalitarian pressures, are common to all. Just as nontraditional learning is intended to increase enrollments of new kinds of students, just as statewide systems are intended to produce economies, and just as educational technology is intended ultimately to reduce costs, so unionism is primarily seen by faculties as a means of gaining and preserving economic benefits. Similarly, just as nontraditional learning and some kinds of new institutions are egalitarian, in that they try to bring higher education to groups previously excluded, and just as state systems accept responsibility for ensuring universal access to public higher education, so unionism has been seen as (and has been particularly successful in) improving the economic and professional lot of younger faculty, part-time faculty, semiprofessional workers, and faculty in relatively weak institutions—all of whom were previously somewhat ill treated and who existed as second- or third-class citizens.

Unionism clearly grew out of the environmental forces operating on and in higher education in the late 1960s. Although the specific causal relationships cannot be clearly established, rates of enrollment increases began to stabilize, new job opportunities began to disappear, inflation rates had wiped out the quite impressive salary increases that had begun about 1958, state and federal intrusion through such things as demands for accountability became more intense, and other segments of the public service sector of the work force began to unionize, thus setting a precedent for college and university faculties to follow. Two quite specific environmental factors were the enactment, in a number of states, of permissive legislation enabling faculties of public institutions to unionize and the extension of the National Labor Relations Act to be applicable to private higher education. Garbarino, after making an intensive survey and case study of faculty unions, generalized three broad faculty aspirations that could be met by the union and a negotiated contract. The first of these was to increase faculty status in institutional governance; the second, to preserve job security, especially as tenure came under attack; and the third, to secure adequate salaries and other improved economic conditions (Garbarino, 1975, p. 251). The opinions of faculty in both unionized and nonunionized institutions as to the importance of factors promoting unionism supported those observations. Ranked in order, from the most powerful to the least powerful factor, they were (1) desire for higher wages and benefits, (2) fear of budget cuts, (3) desire for job security, (4) fear of teacher surplus, (5) desire for more influence in campus governance, (6) desire for fairer governance procedures, (7) weakness of existing faculty governance structures, (8) presence of experienced bargaining groups, (9) permissive government legislation, and (10) desire for more professional standing (Kemerer and Baldridge, 1975, p. 40).

How these various factors interact as unionization takes place is indicated in several examples. The State University of New York was created in 1948 by combining eleven state teachers colleges, six agricultural and technical two-year institutes, a maritime academy, and a college of forestry. During much of the following decade, it was not a true university system with respect to functioning or regard. By the 1960s, however, it had become well established and had come under the leadership of a vigorous chancellor, who, with the enthusiastic support of the governor, led the university system into a period of intense expansion and influence. Four major university centers were developed, three medical centers expanded, and a new one established. Major support was given to two-year community colleges, and the former teachers colleges were shaped into colleges of arts and sciences, in which several different professional areas were also established. Enrollments, construction, and appropriations increased rapidly, and many believed exponential increases would continue indefinitely. However, by the 1970s that creative chancellor had departed, the state system was severely attacked by a spokesman for private higher education, and the legislature began to scrutinize expenditure more intensively and to inaugurate a period of general retrenchment. Although actual amounts of appropriation continued to increase because of inflation, state appropriation did little more than maintain the status quo. Then came a stabilization of applications for admission, with the possibility that on some campuses actual declines would be expected. Faced with the consequences of that set of circumstances, the faculty turned to the permission to organize contained in the 1967 public employment relations act, generally known as the Taylor Law.

Stephens College in Columbia, Missouri, entered the 1960s with a new president, plans for enrollment and physical plant expansion, a completed self-study calling for some quite innovative new educational programs, and the promise at least that the historically low salaries paid to the faculty would be increased to the level of salaries at other strong liberal arts colleges throughout the country. And salaries were increased but at lower rates than had been expected and so differentially as to produce marked salary discrepancies between people doing substantially the same sorts of work ($13,000 and over $20,000 being salaries paid to different division chairmen). Uneasiness over salaries was exacerbated by growing conflict between the president and his chief administrative associates and a relatively small group of militant faculty who were becoming increasingly influential. This group first exerted pressure for the creation of a faculty senate, which, when finally created, began to expand beyond curricular and instructional concerns into budgetary and other financial matters. When that interest failed to yield significantly improved salaries for some faculty, the next step was to exert pressure for a revised administrative structure that might be more sympathetic to the senate. When those changes took place—at about the same time that serious enrollment declines became apparent, with the attendant need for financial retrenchment—the faculty, again led by the same group that had produced the senate, attempted to unionize and elect a bargaining agent. In New York, St. Johns University, a Catholic institution with a faculty of about 1,100 and student body of approximately 13,500, ran into censorship by the American Association of University of Professors following a 1966 decision of the Board of Trustees summarily to discharge twenty-one faculty members without specific charges or hearings. Out of this widely publicized confrontation and at the urging of the American Association of University Professors (AAUP), the board of trustees and administration gradually yielded, by adopting several of the AAUP policies regarding academic freedom, tenure, and governance. When in 1969 the New

York State Labor Relations Act was amended to allow collective bargaining at private nonprofit institutions, the St. Johns chapter of AAUP polled the faculty, which overwhelmingly endorsed the idea of a union, and the following year, after an acrimonious series of elections, designated a local group, the faculty association, and the AAUP as a joint-venture bargaining agent. Central Michigan University had formerly been preoccupied with teacher preparation but underwent enormous expansion of enrollment, support, faculty, and physical plant during the 1960s. The state of Michigan is decidedly a union state and has legislation allowing for unions and collective bargaining in public institutions. All save two of the state's community colleges had become unionized during the 1960s; hence there was an appropriate model to follow. As the institution expanded, it recruited some new faculty who wished a greater role in institutional governance and who were able to cause the creation of first a university and then an academic senate. The experience of bringing that development about prepared the faculty for the next step, which was precipitated when a totally new administration came into power in the space of two years. The new administration, in charting its own course, broke radically with long-existing practices and processes, which produced enough anxiety within leading elements of the faculty to prompt them to call for an election. This election resulted in the designation of the Michigan Association for Higher Education as the bargaining agent.*

Several different organizations emerged during the 1970s to compete for the role of bargaining agent for the growing number of unionized institutions. The first of these was the American Association of University Professors, which had been established in 1913 and which had devoted most of its history to protection of academic freedom, safeguarding tenure, and focusing on professional concerns of faculty. Faced with possible declines in membership and growing interest in some institutions in unionization, during the 1960s AAUP gradually shifted away from rejection of collective bargaining and the sanction of a strike and toward a new

---

* These last two and several additional cases are described in Duryea, Fisk, and Associates (1973). Also, a penetrating analysis of the State University of New York experience is contained in Duryea and Robert Fisk (1975).

profile resembling in most elements a full-fledged union. The second was the American Federation of Teachers (AFT), which had been chartered in 1916 and which by 1960 had 60,000 members at all levels of education. During the 1960s, the AFT increased so rapidly that by 1974 it claimed almost 400,000 members and in 1967 had formed a college and university department with approximately fifty college local unions. By 1974 AFT, alone or in collaboration with the National Education Association (NEA), claimed approximately 240 locals involving perhaps 45,000 professors. The National Education Association is by far the largest educational association in the United States, with approximately 1.5 million members. It had long viewed itself as an umbrella type of organization, in which various sorts of educational workers could be accommodated, ranging from classroom teachers to researchers, audiovisual specialists, and school administrators. Gradually the classroom teachers assumed more and more leadership and adopted policies that would force out all departments and divisions unwilling to move in the direction of unionization. Within the NEA was a department called the American Association of Higher Education (AAHE), which accepted faculty, administrators, board members, students, and anyone interested in higher education. Through modifications of dues and membership practices, the NEA sought to force the American Association of Higher Educatoin to drop its nonteaching members and to adopt a unionlike posture. This the leadership of AAHE was unwilling to do, so it took itself out of the NEA, which replaced it with a National Association of Higher Education specifically designed to be the collective bargaining representative for faculty in two- and four-year institutions of higher education. This reorganized NEA enjoys its greatest strength in the community colleges and in former teachers colleges, strength that it typically exercises through its system of state education associations.

In addition to these three, there are a number of independent units, such as faculty associations, which function like unions and which may in the future become significant in the collective bargaining arena. Each of these organizations is concerned with either or both of two functional types of faculty unions—guild unionism and comprehensive unionism. There are more guild unions, but comprehensive unions have more members. Guild unions are typically located on single-campus institutions and are composed primarily of teaching faculty. They have generally been created in the aftermath of some form of crisis as, for example, the censorship exercised by St. Johns University over the discharge without cause of faculty members. After the crisis, the creation of the union, and the planning of the contract, things typically settle down, and the union and older organs of governance coexist for at least a while. Comprehensive unions, on the other hand, may include different levels of institutions, such as would be found in a state system, and may include all professional staff in the institution, including nonteaching professions. Both of these types must deal with older organs of governance, such as senates, and at least three general models have emerged. The first of these is cooperation between the union and the senate, a form that is most likely to appear in a single-campus institution at which a guild-type union is recognized. A competitive model, found more frequently in state systems having comprehensive unions, places the senate and the union in an adversary relationship, with the administration generally siding with the senate. The compromise model can be called *cooperative,* which simply means that the senate and union agree to contract for a clear division of responsibility.

By 1976 there were approximately 500 colleges and universities that had faculty bargaining agents, and slightly less than a fourth of all full-time teaching faculty were represented. The vast majority of unionized faculty members are in public institutions, mainly two-year colleges and former state teachers colleges. Very few private four-year colleges have opted for a union. Most unionized institutions are in the states of New York, New Jersey, Michigan, and Pennsylvania, states that have laws favoring collective bargaining among public employees. The National Education Association represents the most campuses, followed by the American Federation of Teachers and then by the American Association of University Professors. A movement of this magnitude, which has appeared so suddenly, must be judged as an important new development. However, in spite of its potential significance, the long-term future of unionism cannot be gauged. Some partial judgments can be made and some speculation advanced, but this all should be regarded as conjectural.

The Carnegie Commission on Higher Education believed that faculty members should have the right to organize and to bargain collectively if they so desire. It did not take a position on whether faculty members should unionize and bargain collectively. However, the commission (1973) pointed out several possible consequences. Collective bargaining could affect such traditional areas of academic concern as instruction, research projects, selection and promotion of colleagues, determination of grades and degrees, admissions, academic freedom, and the selection of academic administrators. Unionization of faculty members could be followed rather quickly by unionization of students, and this could have quite serious and unanticipated consequences. Unionization may strengthen managerial authority and probably will reduce campus autonomy and elevate decision-making power to higher and higher levels of government. Also unknown is how unionization will affect such matters as flexibility for the treatment of individual cases or contriving innovation. Also unknown is what the differential effects of unionization would be on junior and senior faculty, and, of course, the great imponderable is to what extent the strike will be a frequently used tool.

Ten years of experience with collective bargaining on American college campuses has demonstrated some benefits and also posed some dangers. Overall unionism has helped the young, the part-time, the marginal, and the professors in weaker institutions more than it has helped well-established senior individuals in strong institutions. Almost invariably, increased economic benefits for those former groups have immediately followed the planning of a contract, with the more senior and better paid individuals receiving less benefit. Through retrenchment clauses and through specifying procedures for dismissal, contracts have strengthened job security. Contracts have also clarified and legitimatized the powers and authorities given to administration and have at the same time somewhat increased faculty influence in governance, especially in those institutions in which faculty had previously been denied real participation. Certainly the bargaining table, the negotiated contract, and the provision for handling grievances represent a recognized and accepted way for managing conflict that other systems of governance did not accommodate. And the contract typically has been able to remedy past discrimination and to eliminate salary inequities.

Angell advances an optimistic view on how unions will affect traditional academic mechanisms. He considers that a seniority system could make such matters as dealing with grievances more efficient, by specifying procedures and deadlines. Further, the bargaining team is a much more efficient way for a faculty to express its will in a binding manner than is full faculty deliberations. Because a contract is a legally enforceable document, administration of its provisions is generally more straightforward and efficient than the administration especially of personnel decisions without legal guidelines. A contract also probably in the long run will produce better personnel decisions as professional administrators, as contrasted with traditional deans and department heads, are appointed and utilized.

But the other side of the matter reveals dangers. The adversarial relationship that is fundamental to the unionized faculty may lead to intense polarization of administrators and faculty and may thus destroy the collegial sharing of academic values. Detailed contracts may assign disproportionate power to unions, which, when combined with power that already had evolved to statewide governance agencies, could leave a campus executive powerless to govern. Unionization in state systems clearly leads toward centralization of authority, and it does introduce new bureaucratic factors to governance itself. First there are the complexities of the union, and second there is the ripple effect of increased bureaucratic activity up and down the line of a state system. By complicating dismissal procedures, the unionization of a campus could limit the qualitative strengthening of a faculty. Also, increased procedural complexity could seriously hamper institutional innovation and change. And there is the very real but as yet unanswered question as to what effect unionism will have on that important but somewhat abstract factor called *quality of education* (This appraisal is derived from Kemerer and Baldridge, 1975).

Not at all inconsistent with these observations are the judgments of Garbarino (1975). In institutions with undeveloped systems of faculty participation, unions have increased faculty influence in decision making but have not extended the range of subjects or decisions. In the long run, unions will probably diminish the role of senates. Perhaps the most important change unions have produced is making the concept of effective grievance procedure available to all members of a bargaining unit on a wide range of procedural and substantive issues. "The most important effect of faculty unionism on job security so far has been the extension of the near equivalent of tenure to groups of academic employees who had previously not enjoyed security of employment" (p. 257). And the influence of unions on salaries has in general been inversely proportional to salary levels before unionization. The lower-paid faculty, part-time faculty, and lower-paid nonteaching professionals have benefited the most, while faculty at the upper levels of the range have been fortunate if their remuneration kept up with the general increases for state employees as a whole.

Extrapolation from developments of the first half of the decade of the 1970s suggests that by 1980 as many as a thousand campuses involving a quarter million faculty members will be organized in unions. Of course, it should be pointed out that extrapolation is only one way of anticipating the future. However, extrapolation does suggest polarization of faculties and administrator-trustees into adversarial positions. Governance is likely to become more explicit, uniform, proceduralized, and centralized. Management with prerogatives granted by contracts is likely to inherit greater power and authority. Autonomy of public institutions is likely further to be reduced as contracts are negotiated with state-wide agencies, and the kind of faculty leadership is likely to change as the egalitarianism of unions wipes out the factors that have granted distinction and status to faculty leadership in the past (Corson, 1975, p. 202).

Court Intrusion. The next change is partly real and partly potential. This involves the gradual intrusion into higher education of the courts, which have been considering an increased variety of cases. The historic pattern has been for colleges and universities to enjoy a large degree of autonomy, and the courts have typically refrained from interfering with the internal administration of institutions of higher education. There were, to be sure, landmark cases that contributed to the American pattern of higher education. The Dartmouth College case established the validity of a charter and, in a sense, ensured the perpetuation of an important private sector of higher education. In *Sterling* v. *The Regents of the University of Michigan,* the considerable autonomy of constitutional universities was established through precedent. *Plessy* v. *Ferguson* gave judicial approval to separate institutions for blacks and whites as long as facilities were judged equal, but that eventually came to be modified, first in *Gaines* v. *Canada,* which forced the University of Missouri to accept a black law student, and *Sweatt* v. *Painter,* which forced the University of Texas to accommodate some black students. But for the most part the tradition until the 1960s was for courts to view collegiate institutions as not liable for damages for injuries to their students, to support institutional freedom to maintain voluntary accrediting associations, to allow institutions to deal with students rather much on the institution's own terms, and to refrain from substituting the courts' wisdom for the professional judgments of academicians.

In actions that are in large measure related to the civil rights movement, student and faculty protest, the changed financial outlook by the 1970s, affirmative action, and increased concern for openness of records, the courts (with considerable inconsistency, to be sure) have begun to intervene more and more and to deal substantively with a number of matters that a decade earlier would have been rejected for judicial review. In *Hammond* v. *South Carolina State College,* the right of students to assemble as a means of protest was upheld. In *Soglin* v. *Kaufmann,* the court called into question lateness of institutional regulations but still allowed the institution time to correct the deficiency. And in *Dixon* v. *Alabama State Board of Education,* the court held that institutions must provide at least a modicum of due process. Increasingly courts have heard cases involving dismissal of faculty and in several cases have prevented dismissal. In the case of Margorie Webster College, although the Supreme Court ultimately upheld the right of the Middle States Association to refuse to examine the institution, the case had sufficient repercussions to stimulate accrediting bodies to extend purview to proprietary institutions.

These brief citations are simply straws in the wind. In aggregate, the body of recently decided cases does not bring the courts deeply into the affairs of higher education. Of much greater significance is the general climate of litigousness that began to characterize higher education by the end of the 1960s, that has led institutions to add legal counsel to their administrative staffs, and that has caused all sorts of proposed decisions to be examined closely from a legal standpoint. These include whether students can serve on admissions committees, what evaluative comments can be put in a faculty member's file without fear of suit, what decisions board members can take without fear of being held personally accountable at law, and whether an institution questioning the academic credit of another institution can be sued.

Other structural and organizational changes took place or were seriously urged during the 1970s, all consistent with those previously discussed. Federal involvement in pursuance of more affirmative action in institutional admissions policies intensified both centralizing tendencies and the likelihood of court intervention. Similarly, the "1202 commissions" mandated by the Higher Education Amendments of 1972, if funded, would give centralized state government great power over both public and private higher education. State experimentation with radically expanded university extension programs, as exemplified by the legislative efforts in California to create a fourth segment, could not only erode institutional power but could alter significantly the entire concept of higher education. The university, state colleges, and junior colleges in California have each provided some forms of extension services or adult education. Populist members of the legislature believe those services too limited and have proposed a statewide fourth segment that would offer almost any kind of educationally related service any group of people wanted, much in the way nontraditional educators would.

Accreditation. One last change should be mentioned because it is symbolically so reflective of the mood of the 1970s. During the twentieth century, minimal standards of institutional quality have been maintained by voluntary regional or special accreditation. Those standards were created by representatives of established institutions functioning in such capacities as voting members of associations or commissions, members of visiting teams, or members of review boards of various sorts. Those standards have been expressions of conventional views of quality, such as preparation of faculty, presence of a general education component of the curriculum, size and variety of library holdings, economic strength, and the nature of the campus. Since they were voluntary and given legitimacy by the prestige institutions, accreditation associations maintained considerable influence but without legal or legislative intervention.

By the 1970s, however, accreditation came under attack by representatives of the same forces producing other changes. Adherence to traditional academic standards was challenged as elitist and as restricting innovation. Because federal and state agencies were using accreditation status as a basis for agency decisions concerning institutions, voluntary accreditation was seen to possess a quasi-public character that should be subject to governmental supervision and control. For example, the U.S. Office of Education began to accredit those accrediting associations whose judgments the agency used. Because accrediting association decisions did affect the life of institutions and the livelihoods of people, the courts began to take an interest in the processes used and to judge whether or not due process and fair procedures had been followed. Within voluntary accreditation itself, concerns about seeming lack of uniformity region to region or special field to special field led first to a loose confederation and then to a centralized organization that presumed to represent voluntary accreditation throughout the country and especially to the federal government.

These and other pressures have forced such changes in voluntary accreditation that in sum they exemplify the major changes in higher education generally. Accrediting agencies have been forced to consider as educational a range of practices that would have been rejected out of hand at an earlier time. These include heavy program reliance on part-time faculty, often without traditional credentials; institutions rejecting the need for a core library; awarding of academic credit for work done as part of a paid job; and complete degree programs pursued by students almost completely independently. Accrediting associations have been forced to comply with both state and federal guidelines with respect to the processes of accreditation used. They have been forced to retain legal counsel and to maintain liability insurance to protect association officers against suit. And the associations have been persuaded to adopt a national organizational structure, for most of the same reasons states have adopted statewide reforms of higher education.

SEVEN

Financial Patterns

Changed financing patterns, attitudes, and underlying theory between the 1960s and the 1970s are intimately related to all other changes. Whether changes in finance have helped produce those other changes, have been in part produced by them, or are correlated with them and derived from some common set of causes is probably unknown and unknowable. However, careful examination of the rhetoric and behaviors of collegiate presidents, administrators, professors, board members, officials in the higher education bureaucratic superstructure, and educationally concerned political leaders allows the inference of strong economic motivation. It can be argued that—among many motivations leading to the seeking of new students or the creation of new institutions, senates, unions, or state boards—individual and institutional survival or improvement is perhaps the strongest. Such a thesis is difficult if not impossible to prove, because education is such a complicated social institution, inextricably bound up with all other elements in society. Thus any

258

major institutional behavior as, for example, a decision to enter graduate work is complexly related to individual professional aspirations, major tenets of social policy, political considerations at all levels of government, international relations, and the state of development of academic disciplines in which graduate work is to be offered.

Financial Health

It is generally recognized and accepted that the period from the end of World War II until the quite late 1960s, and more especially the period from 1958 until 1968, was one of rapidly expanding financial strength of higher education in the United States. The indices of these "golden years" can be quickly summarized. The percentage of the gross national product devoted to higher education rose from under 1 percent to almost 3 percent. The cost per student credit hour produced increased approximately 5 percent per year, as compared to a 2.5 annual increase in cost of all other consumer goods and services. Privately supported institutions increased available cash to be used to raise salaries, to improve facilities, and to expand physical plant, typically through doubling enrollment and doubling tuition over a ten-year period. This usually allowed slight excesses of income over expenditure to be accumulated each year, which contributed to a general feeling of financial well-being. While tuitions did not increase quite so rapidly in publicly supported institutions, enrollment increases and enlargement of per-student support from state appropriations accomplished the same end. Throughout the period, there were significant increases in federal contributions to higher education, principally for such categorical purposes as support of research and research training, the preparation of especially needed technicians, and the creation of needed academic facilities. There were parallel increases in private benefaction from foundations, corporations, and individual donors, and, while the total percentage of state support for higher education declined, relative to federal and private resources, the actual dollar increases doubled, tripled, and in some states actually quadrupled. Professorial salaries, which until 1958 had actually lagged behind those paid in 1939 in constant dollars, began to increase at approximately 7 percent a year, toward a goal of being doubled between 1958 and 1970. The flourishing academic economy was for the most part justified by the twin beliefs that educational level and state or regional economic level were positively correlated, as were individual economic well-being and the amount of education acquired.

These and other developments that began to take place after 1957 have been summarized by Howard Bowen (1974, pp. 24–25):

1. Grants to students, based on a systematic means test rather than on scholarship, became common, especially among the private colleges.
2. The use of loans in financing students was expanded sharply.
3. With the increasing number of married students, a legacy of the GI period, spouses became a major source of support for students.
4. The federal government became a growing supplier of funds for both grants and loans to students.
5. The federal government became an important contributor to institutions through a wide array of grants, contracts, and loans designated chiefly for research, training, and buildings.
6. Philanthropic foundations grew in numbers and resources.
7. Profit-making corporations became patrons of higher education.
8. Colleges and universities became more aggressive and professional in their fund raising.
9. State and local governments greatly increased their appropriations to public institutions; some established state scholarship programs and some made grants to private institutions.
10. Tuitions were raised year after year by both public and private institutions. The percentage increase in tuitions averaged about 5 percent a year for public and 7.5 percent for private institutions. Educators were amazed that these tuition increases called forth so little reaction from patrons.

Causes. The causes for this sharp improvement in the financial condition of higher education (although almost a century of somewhat steady improvement is involved) were several unexpected developments. The first of these was the essential condition of a reasonably sustained period of postwar affluence and prosperity. To be sure, there were fluctuations and periods of recession, but for the most part reasonable prosperity continued in spite of generally accepted expectations that a major postwar depression should have struck sometime within the decade following cessation of hostilities. This affluence allowed for rising expectations throughout the society and especially in the unexpectedly large population born after World War II. Rising expectations in that group, in the somewhat less than economically advantaged groups, and ultimately in the racial minorities produced the enormous demand for higher education that could be met because the general level of the economy permitted it. Federal involvement in research also seems to have come about unexpectedly, partly as a result of the successful combination of university research talent and federal dollars in such World War II developments as the atomic bomb, radar, and the proximity fuse. It is significant in this regard that federal efforts during the 1960s were in large measure a cold war phenomenon, undertaken when the Russian achievement in launching Sputnik appeared to threaten the ascendency of the United States in science and technology.

Institutional Behavior. Institutional and individual behavior during most of the 1960s seems clearly to have been affected by the overall economic condition of higher education. There was enormous program expansion within institutions as existing and newly created institutions moved toward the ideal of a comprehensive university or a modified version thereof. State teachers colleges first became state colleges and then state universities, creating or planning to create reasonably full complements of professional schools and graduate programs. Even relatively weak state teachers colleges with no traditions of graduate education and research straight-facedly sought to be renamed as universities and sought appropriations to support entry into doctoral work. The president of the University of California visualized a nine-campus system, eight of those campuses being comprehensive universities. Similarly, in such disparate states as Massachusetts, Florida, and Alabama plans were made for multiple campuses, each being a comprehensive and research-oriented institution. Even liberal arts colleges caught the fever, as over 200 of them adopted master's programs and a handful, such as Wesleyan, actually began offering doctoral work.

An essential element of this drive toward comprehensiveness was the enhanced value accorded to graduate education and research.

Within institutions and in the minds of the professoriate, graduate education, generally considered to be considerably more expensive than undergraduate education, came to be regarded as the most desirable form of education for institutions and professors to offer. Further, new forms of federal, state, and private subsidy of research led institutions and individuals to believe that the time would come when subsidized research would consume 50 percent or more of the time of faculty members in all save the exclusively teaching institutions, such as community colleges and the quite invisible liberal arts colleges. There really was considerable naiveté throughout American higher education during the 1960s regarding graduate education and research. The fact that several states appropriated token amounts of direct support for research led professors and administrators to believe that future state appropriations would contain enormously expanded amounts for such purposes. In states that in the past had never supported a single nationally regarded graduate and research university, all state institutions received encouragement to quest after that sort of stature. Despite what reason should have told academicians regarding limits to exponential growth, throughout the 1960s, both tacitly and explicitly, exponential growth of higher education into the foreseeable future was constantly being assumed.

The behavior of faculty members was especially revealing as well-trained faculty members found themselves in extraordinarily short supply. Their demands for continued increases in salary were met, as were their demands for reduced teaching loads. Particularly sought-after professors or professors in particularly needed subjects were able and did set demands that when met made the professoriate an extraordinarily privileged group. Instances could be cited of professors appointed but with no teaching responsibility assigned, or with the question of whether to teach or not to teach left to professorial discretion. In some respects, the downturn in the popularity of the general education movement during the 1960s reflects another kind of professorial behavior in the presence of affluence. General education courses in larger institutions were typically staff-developed courses that when taught distracted professors from their individual specialties. When faculty members were in oversupply, as they were from approximately 1952 to 1958, they were forced to accept institutional requirements that they teach general education courses. When professors became in short supply, individuals could and did make as a condition for accepting appointment that they would not be required to teach in the general education program. As economic conditions and conditions of work improved, the professoriate also made demands, which were typically met, for a greater voice in academic governance, for specific and written provisions leading to relative early achievement of tenure, for complete control over the substance of academic curricula, and for the sole and absolute right of the professoriate to evaluate its own performance. While here and there voices of concern were raised (as, for example, Beardsley Ruml in the book *Memo to a College Trustee*) and boards of regents sought to regain control over the professoriate, the 1960s saw in at least some institutions the almost full accomplishment of an academic revolution. This revolution produced a reasonably affluent professoriate, no longer primarily loyal or responsible to a given institution, which had finally gained the power of controlling its own membership, of setting its own goals and objectives, and of evaluating its own performance without particular recourse to administrators, boards of trustees, or the general public. This revolution was clearly not completed or even seriously initiated in some institutions. In public junior colleges, in some liberal arts colleges and teachers colleges, and even in some of the weaker universities, central administration and boards of trustees still exercised considerable authority. Yet even in those institutions the goal of professorial hegemony had been glimpsed, and efforts would be made to achieve it. In this connection, the flourishing of unionism in the weaker kinds of institutions by the late 1960s may be considered in some respects an attempt on the part of professors to garner the fruits of the academic revolution by other means.

Related to such professorial aspirations and made possible by expanding demand for higher education was the increased selectivity of institutions, even those which had previously typically accepted all applicants who at least had graduated from high school. During the 1960s, state universities that had previously been open-access institutions began to limit enrollments based on previous academic record of students and performance on admissions tests. During the 1960s, admissions directors in private institutions would report with pride each fall on the increased SAT scores of the

entering freshmen class. Of course, related to this selectivity was the
expansion of resources and programs of the Educational Testing
Service and the College Entrance Examination Board and the creation of the new and competing American College Testing Program.
The rationing of higher educational services was universally judged
appropriate, and professional testing agencies provided and administered one reasonably effective technique.

Several other characteristic behaviors should be mentioned,
all related to the general economic condition. There was the post-
Sputnik emphasis on academic rigor, which is reflected in the
Dressel and DeLisle (1969) finding that no significant reductions
in requirements took place between 1957 and 1967. There was the
more than doubling of professional and scholarly associations, the
substantial increases in their budgets, and the proliferation of programs they offered. During the same period, considerable educational experimentation took place, supported in part by foundations
and in part by various federal programs. What is unique is that so
many experiments, such as the creation of house plans or cluster
colleges, attempts to use language laboratories, and primitive attempts to use computers in instruction, were conducted in the
absence of normal efforts to evaluate. One almost had the feeling
that resources were so plentiful that no other evaluation, other than
completing the experiment, was needed, for there would be additional funds if someone wished to redo the experiment or to attempt
something else if the particular project proved to be uninteresting.

It should be pointed out that these behaviors, in addition to
serving institutions and individuals within the system of higher education, also possessed considerable financial value for the entire
society. The Carnegie Foundation for the Advancement of Teaching
(1976, pp. 1–2) has observed that American higher education
"provides relatively more student places than any other nations and
has supplied more of the new discoveries of high importance in the
natural and social sciences. . . . The greater costs to American
society would have been incurred if the teachers and the Ph.D.'s
had not been trained in the 1960s; but because they were trained
the 'tidal wave' of students was accommodated at all levels of the
educational system, and the United States maintained and even increased its supremacy in research. Much was done well. The trium-

phant responses to the GI baby boom and to Sputnik—once grave national concerns—now have some relatively minor continuing costs."

Financial Decline

Just as suddenly as higher educational affluence and support had come, it began to go, between 1968 and 1970. And, as was true of the "golden years," the indices of changed conditions can be quickly enumerated and are for the most part well known. Suddenly institutions found that their rates of expenditure began to exceed rates of increase of total revenue, and the reserves that had been built up during the 1960s were quickly eliminated through deficit spending. Cheit (1973) estimated in 1971 that perhaps as many as 71 percent of collegiate institutions were either headed for financial trouble or were already in such financial difficulties as to require elimination of programs and services essential to the generally accepted mission of the institution. Private institutions, particularly the less strong, discovered that their steady tuition increases had reduced their ability to compete with lower-tuition, publicly supported institutions. Thus a downward spiral was initiated, with lower enrollments generating less income with which to support fixed and increasing costs. Lower enrollments in residential colleges lowered occupancy of newly constructed residence halls built with loan funds in the expectation that debt service could be easily taken care of by constant or expanding demand for residence hall facilities. When lower-than-needed debt service funds were acquired, those obligations had to be paid out of operating funds, thus intensifying already acute cash problems.

Jellema (1973, pp. xi–xiii) pointed to the plight of privately supported institutions and indicated a few of the factors contributing to a situation in which annual deficit spending had become or was about to become the rule.

While severe financial stress has fallen on all institutions—large and small, simple and complex, northern and southern—it has severely hit the very small undergraduate institutions in the Midwest. Very small institutions—especially those enrolling fewer than 500 students—

have a relatively high fixed cost per student and, unless they have endowment for a buffer, are more vulnerable to adverse trends in enrollment than are larger institutions. A drop in enrollment means that the cost per remaining student rises more precipitously than it does in larger institutions. This fixed cost includes a basic plant, a basic administrative structure, and especially a basic academic program, whose proportions cannot be scaled down indefinitely. You can cut in half a recipe that calls for two eggs but how do you cut it in half again? To be an institution of higher learning, an institution must offer a minimum of basic educational services.

The financial crunch has been felt in large, complex institutions because of conditions they share with smaller and less complex institutions—inflation, decline in the rate of income increase, rapid expansion of plant, deceleration of enrollment, expansion of student services, increases in security costs—and also because of their considerable involvement in research and their extensive expansion of program offerings to match the explosion of knowledge. Both research and program expansion require the commitment of institutional funds beyond those available from outside sources and, if outside support declines, an added burden is laid on institutional funds.

If private colleges and universities continue to run deficits of the magnitude they have been running in current accounts, many deficits will soon equal or exceed the total liquid assets of the institution (one quarter of the private colleges and universities are already dipping into their endowments). The loss of liquid assets means the loss of flexibility and financial credibility; and the probability of further borrowing, additional debt service, and more retrenchment is increased. An institution, however, can make only so much educational retrenchment without losing its identity in the academic world. Much of it, moreover, is one-shot retrenchment. After you do not wash the windows once, William Bowen has asked, what do you do for an encore? How do you not wash them again?

At the same time that institutions began to experiment with deficit spending, there came about a rather abrupt change in federal funding of higher education. From the mid-1950s to approximately 1968, federal funds flowing to colleges and universities had increased annually. This suddenly was reversed, as amounts for research were reduced and large fellowship programs eliminated or modified. By the early 1970s, some stabilization of federal support seemed to be emerging but in a spurious sort of way. A large proportion of federal aid is designated as student aid, only a portion of which goes directly or even indirectly into institutional budgets. Thus, in constant dollars, with the exception of funds for student aid, there has been a steady decline in federal support to institutions during the first half of the 1970s, and even including student aid there is only a precarious stability of federal support.

Somewhat harder to document but nonetheless real is the index that reveals first a slowdown in rates of increase of state support for higher education, followed by a stabilization of support, and then, in some states, actual declines in constant dollar support. By the late 1960s, legislative and executive state leaders were expressing concern about high costs of colleges and universities and provided much smaller increments than had been true earlier. While appropriations in real dollars did continue to increase during the 1970s, the proportion of total state and federal budgets devoted to higher education began to decline in 1969 and has continued to decline in most regions of the country since then. Even the incremental increases in actual dollars, however, are a bit spurious, because during the 1970s steadily increasing amounts were appropriated for suprainstitutional coordinating and controlling mechanisms; hence the actual amounts received by individual institutions reveals a definite and genuine decline. This overall picture is illuminated by specific examples of requested appropriations reduced to equal only previous appropriations, with no provisions made for increased responsibilities. Also, appropriations tied to enrollment figures gradually were being reduced as enrollments in some kinds of institutions stabilized and then declined (Glenny and Kidder, 1974). Even M. M. Chambers, who normally looks to the bright side of things and who especially praises state contributions to higher education, has demonstrated undersupport of state universities, especially in view of the missions they are expected to accomplish. He uses examples to illustrate his generalization: CUNY, Washington State, Southern Illinois, Colorado State, and the University of Washington received less in 1971–72 than in 1969–70, the University of California gained 1.75 percent in appropriations yet saw enrollments increasing at a substantially faster rate, Auburn University requested $36.8 million and received only

$22.8 million, and the University of Michigan and the University
of Minnesota reflected a similar pattern (Chambers, 1972).

Additionally, foundation giving to colleges and universities
began to decline, and by the mid-1970s annual giving by individuals and corporations also had begun to decline. The precise
amounts of decrease in foundation funds going to higher education
is difficult to judge, because there are no good aggregate figures reflecting such matters. However, one major foundation deliberately
shifted its interests from higher education to urban affairs, including elementary and secondary education. Most of the major foundations reduced their contributions in the 1973–74 academic year as
the market value of their investments declined precipitously, and
what income was available had to be used to continue long-standing
commitments. Another major foundation decided to withdraw
general support of higher education in favor of massive support for
just two private institutions located in the city in which the foundation had its headquarters.

Indicators of Decline. Two major indicators of the changed
condition of higher education are (1) the sudden oversupply of
potential college instructors possessing the doctorate and (2) slowdown of enrollment increases overall and the actual drop in enrollments in some kinds of institutions. As late as 1967, responsible college and university officials were predicting that the shortage of
college faculty would continue on through the 1970s. Among
scholars of higher education, only Allan Cartter (1967), after re-
analyzing data from the National Education Association and
the U.S. Office of Education, predicted an end to the oversupply of
faculty and a significant surplus by the early 1970s. By 1969 those
predictions began to come true, as young Ph.D.'s found no available
positions in all save a few fields. By the mid-1970s, there was a
serious oversupply, and Cartter (1976) in his last analysis showed
that by the early 1980s only aproximately 2 percent of the annual
production of doctorates would be needed to fill professorial posts.
This oversupply, of course, is related to the slowdown in enrollment
growth and to the anticipated actual drop in enrollment, which
should become apparent in the early 1980s. It is also related to the
institutional exuberance of the 1960s, when both developed and
developing institutions rapidly expanded doctoral programs and

planned to expand them even further. Mayhew, for example, in 1969 observed that if individual institutional plans of 1967–68 had materialized there would be an annual production of doctorates of between 65,000 and 70,000 by 1980. Those plans, of course, were not realized. However, there were relatively few significant program reductions, hence the unbalanced market for college teachers.

Thus, beginning in approximately 1968 to 1970 higher education found itself in a distinctly different situation from the one that had existed just five years earlier. Expenditures continued to rise, stimulated by general inflation, while income began to decline, both relatively and absolutely. At the same time enrollment began to slow, thus helping to produce an oversupply of professionally trained faculty and administrators. The reason for this changed condition should be noted, because they do bear on the kinds of responses made by government, institutions, and individuals.

Causes of Decline. Many different forces have coalesced to produce the steady and growing cost pressure. Clearly a major factor is the rate of inflation, which has accelerated during the 1960s and 1970s. This inflation, which affects all elements in the society, seems to have affected educational institutions even more seriously, as is illustrated by the difference between the increase of the consumer price index from 8.4 percent to 17 percent from January 1973 to January 1974; the price increase of goods purchased by a major collegiate system was 22 percent in the same period. And educational institutions have no good way of passing along increased costs to customers. Educational institutions are also adversely affected by techniques used to combat inflation, especially restraints on governmental spending.

To inflation must be added lagging productivity in education—a result of education being a labor-intensive enterprise. In earlier times, the labor intensivity of education at all levels could be tolerated, because teacher wages were relatively low and remained that way. Thus cheap labor obviated the need to increase productivity or to design more productive means of delivering educational services. However, since the late 1950s the cost of educational labor has increased rapidly, first as enrollment increases outran the supply of teachers during the 1960s, and more recently as teachers and professors have solidified their economic positions through widespread tenure regulations, and even more recently through collective bargaining. Those factors are reinforced by the fact that wages of teachers and others in the service sector of the economy tend to follow and compete with wages in the nonservice sector, which are growing relative to inflation, but service wages are not offset by increases in productivity.

Although productivity has not increased, quality has (somewhat), and this in turn contributes to the economic plight. In colleges and universities, libraries have been expanded, new and complex research equipment purchased, and the qualifications of faculty increased, all of which lead to still higher wage costs. In addition, new kinds of programs and services for special groups of people have been adopted, and it seems likely that demands for qualitative improvement will persist. The already detectible trend of college enrollments away from low-cost humanities programs to high-cost programs in the health professions and computer sciences, which require sophisticated equipment, augurs for continued cost increases.

Two related forces interact and gain strength reciprocally. The first is a fairly substantial increase in the amount and cost of administration as institutions become larger and more complex and as more new programs are created that require administration and coordination. As late as the late 1950s, the central administration of reasonably complex universities consisted of a president, several assistants, and the deans of the constituent colleges. By the late 1960s, that changed by adding a tier of four or five vice-presidents, each with complex professional and secretarial staffs, and the addition of many new administrative positions, such as directors of institutional research, of planning, and such other positions as legal counsel and ombudsman. It is difficult to know precisely how much, but it is certain that some of this expansion is directly attributable to demands both internal and external for information. As the public and public officials demand greater accountability, more information will be demanded, and the cost of information is substantial.

The steady increase in demand for information and its attendant cost is also part of another force that is relatively new, but the significance of which is bound to grow. This is the growing number and magnitude of mandated social welfare programs, each of which places more intensive cost strains on educational institutions than on the nonservice sector. Consider the cost implications of just a few programs, such as equal employment opportunity, affirmative action, occupational safety and health, minimum wages, unemployment insurance, social security increases, and environmental protection.

A last factor, while rarely discussed, nonetheless exists: the carry-over costs of past decisions, which range from the overconstruction of new schools in districts that suddenly experienced enrollment drops to excessive numbers of graduate programs to well-equipped, expensive, but lightly used luxuries, such as language laboratories.*

Responses to Changed Conditions

Response to the changed economic situation can be observed from a number of vantage points. Immediately before, during, and immediately after the appearance of adverse indicators, six higher education policy groups issued reports dealing with financial matters. Bowen (1974, p. 36) has summarized the conclusion agreed to in varying intensity by the six reports.

1. The efficiency of higher education should be improved.
2. Tuitions of public institutions should be raised to perhaps a third or even half of instructional costs.
3. Access should be available to all qualified students. Student aid should be extended in the form of grants to low-income students and loans to low- and middle-income students.
4. Loans should become a more prominent part of the student aid program. Practical long-term loan programs should be invented and adequate capital to fund them should be raised.
5. Student aid should be portable.
6. Private institutions should be assisted by any of several types of tuition off-sets, which would have the effect of narrowing the tuition gap, and possibly by institutional grants.
7. Tax incentives for charitable giving should be strengthened.

* This analysis has been based in part on material by William W. Jellema, *From Red to Black: The Financial Status of Private Colleges and Universities* (San Francisco: Jossey-Bass, 1973), pp. 1–29.

8. Federal fellowships and traineeships for graduate students should be restored at least in part, and basic research should be supported at rising levels.
9. Methods of financing lifelong and recurring education should be developed.

On the surface these may not seem particularly radical, although several recommendations, if carried out, would change appreciably the nature, form, and structure of higher education. The support of increased tuitions for public institutions and the emphasis placed on loans represents a significant departure from the twin traditions of low or no tuition public higher education and of the older generation providing for the collegiate education of the younger generation. The full impact of a substantial loan program is, of course, to transfer costs from parents, philanthropy, and the public to the student himself. The recommendation to encourage lifelong and recurring education is, of course, an equally significant departure from the tradition that held that higher education is to prepare the relatively young for adulthood. Taken seriously, lifelong and recurring education opens the way for such a massive redefinition of education that traditional concepts would be no longer valid. That encouragement is closely involved in the nontraditional movement, the creation of new and different types of institutions, and the quest of established institutions to find new markets for their services.

Federal Legislation. Overly simplified, the federal response to changed conditions can be found in the higher education amendments of 1972 as contrasted with the National Defense Education Act of the 1950s.

Until 1958, federal involvement in higher education was in a sense limited to support of land-grant colleges, experiment stations, and extension services programmed under the National Science Foundation, research programs under the Department of Defense, and a modified version of the World War II GI Bill of Rights to take care of the needs of veterans of the Korean War. Then the Russian launching of Sputnik suddenly forced a Republican administration away from its restrictive view of support to higher education and into a large and varied effort called the National Defense Education Act of 1958. The essential purpose of this legislation was to produce an educational program from which could come the scientific, technological, and scholarly leadership needed to catch up with the advances in Russian science. Suggested full scholarship provisions were eliminated because of Congress' strong opposition to giving students a free ride to attend college. The overall meritocratic thrust of the legislation was continued in the Higher Education Facilities Act of 1963, which provided loans and grants for the construction of specific categories of academic facilities and a program of student loans. While the focus was still on academic quality and merit, the negotiations leading to the passing of the legislation and the creation of nonreimbursable loans for some students did seem to stress an egalitarian principle. That principle also flavored the Higher Education Act of 1965, which followed in the wake of President Johnson's program to achieve the "Great Society." It featured the first program of federal scholarships for undergraduates, which were to go to students of exceptional financial need. However, the bulk of aid funds still was in the form of insured loans and student support deriving from categorical federal research and training programs. The egalitarian elements of that legislation were not expanded during the next three years, as the federal government attempted to finance the Vietnam War, as disruption came to characterize the campus, and as the honeymoon of the Johnson administration and Congress ended. By 1968, federal higher educational policy had reached a plateau that contained a few egalitarian elements and that was fundamentally academic and meritocratic.

By the 1970s, however, an entirely different orientation became perceptible. The higher education amendments of 1972 epitomized the changed ethos. Either implicitly or explicitly, that legislation expressed themes characteristic of all of the significant new developments or attempts described in this book. Higher education was renamed *postsecondary education,* and stress was placed on equal education opportunity, innovation, and accountability. The legislation was intended to remove financial barriers facing students and both to allow access to the postsecondary system and to allow choice among institutions. A program of basic educational opportunity grants were intended to enable every student to start out with at least $1,400 to defray college expenses. That amount could then be augmented by any of all of such other student aid programs as supplemental educational opportunity, college work-study programs, or national direct student loans. The legislation clearly enunciated the principle that students, not institutions, were to be the first priority in federal support for higher education. Some direct institutional aid was provided but was linked directly to programs of support to students. The education amendments of 1972 encouraged or mandated a broadening of the educational mainstream to include types of students and institutions not previously included, with the clear intent of breaking the stereotype that education beyond high school meant a four-year academic program leading to a baccalaureate degree. Thus recognition and legitimacy was accorded to occupational education, proprietary institutions, and part-time students. Not only scope but also method was to be extended. Congress was convinced that something was wrong in higher education and that too much of it was too traditional and poorly managed. Not wanting to enter into academic specifics, Congress provided mechanisms to encourage innovation and change. The Fund for the Improvement for Postsecondary Education was a device to provide seed money or experimental and creative ideas, including alternative types of career training, cost-effective instruction, and more flexible patterns for entering and reentering higher education. The legislation also contained more than an element of suspicion of academics in its attempt to establish the principle of accountability. The National Institute of Education was to facilitate the gathering of needed information, and the U.S. Commissioner of Education was mandated to develop guidelines and regulations to enable close evaluation of federal education programs and projects. For example, it authorized the commissioner to require institutions to provide data on the cost of educating students. Especially significant for the growing centralization of higher education in the states was Section 1202, which required the states to create commissions that would administer the many federal programs authorized by the amendents.

This legislation was so all-encompassing and so complex that its full significance cannot be gauged. Almost immediately after its passage, a Republican administration attempted to emasculate it. The federal bureaucracy of the U.S. Department of Health, Education and Welfare and the U.S. Office of Education created confused and confusing regulations, such as an elaborate needs test for students applying for a guaranteed loan. Appropriations for the basic Educational Opportunity grants were insufficient to support the full intent of Congress. The National Institute of Education in turn encountered sharp opposition in the Congress and was but modestly funded, as was also true of the Fund for the Improvement of Postsecondary Education.

Regardless of prognosis, the higher education amendments of 1972 spoke directly to the major changes of the 1970s. In intent, it was clearly egalitarian. It legitimatized a concern for new students and experimentation with new kinds of institutions. It provided incentives to experiment with new modes of education, especially technological devices. Its very complexity and focus on controversial issues sets the stage for future litigation. It emphasized the primacy of centralized state concerns for higher education, including concern for the private sector. It called into question traditional ways of accreditation, thus opening the way for federal and state involvement in accrediting activities. By broadening the concept of higher education to postsecondary education, it obscured the definition of education, and, in addition, by allowing for many people to become involved in offering education, it may have contributed to unionization as a means of establishing parity between radically extended segments of postsecondary education. (An extended treatment of the Higher Education Amendments of 1972 is contained in Wolanin and Gladieux, *Congress and the Colleges,* 1976).

Regional Responses. Consistent with those study recommendations and the new federal policy was the response of such regional organizations as the Southern Regional Education Board, which, in its 1976 statement of priorities for postsecondary education in the South, stressed the same things. (It is significant that the term *postsecondary education* is used rather than the traditional term *higher education.* The new term allows consideration of many things previously beyond the pale of traditional colleges and universities.) That statement of priorities called for statewide planning, including more precise ways to decide on deployment of resources and quite precise ways for monitoring institutional performance (accountability). Because the Southern Regional Education

Board is the creation of the various state governments in the South, it cannot be too specific with respect to recommendations regarding finance. However, the board appears to approve a market model of higher education, in which competitive forces determine individual costs and benefits. Federal support of the kind anticipated by the higher education amendments of 1972, with its emphasis on funneling aid to students rather than institutions, is approved. Support for public institutions should come from state and local government and from students and their parents, augmented by some categorical support from the federal government. The fact that the amount borne by individual students may well increase in the future is accepted with equanimity. Also accepted in principle, but with some reservations, is the use of public funds to support the private sector. The board seems to prefer indirection in this matter, with funding provided to students, who may then expend those funds in the private sector. The statement of priorities is a cautious document. However, its main tenets are consistent with other developments in higher education during the 1970s. It accepts the fact that resources available are limited and must be efficiently used. Undergraduate programs, traditionally the heart of collegiate education, should be reexamined and, when so indicated, drastically revised and restructured. There should be greater use of nontraditional approaches, and the postsecondary opportunities should be provided for minority and ethnic groups.

State Policy. The states, to varying degrees, have also responded to changed conditions, and reports, recommendations, and actual legislation are beginning to clarify the reactions of state governments. Illustrative is the report of the Joint Committee on the Master Plan, a committee created by the California legislature. After exhaustive inquiry, analysis, and public hearings, in 1973 the committee issued its report, which revealed the same themes found elsewhere. It stressed equal and universal accessibility to higher education, particular emphasis being given to lifelong learning opportunities for persons with the capacity and motivation to benefit. It also stressed the accountability of institutions and their professional staffs to students and to the general public. With respect to financing, the committee accepted the fact that the amount of money that could be devoted to postsecondary education was limited and that institutions would be forced to live within quite rigorous constraints. It also accepted the concept of portability, which in effect funds students directly, letting them then choose the kind of education they wish. It accepted the notion of reasonable tuitions that would be set by the legislature rather than by the systems of institutions themselves. The committee's approach to financial aid ratified in principle the state's two-fold purpose of aiding needy students and assisting in the survival of independent higher education. However, recognizing that existing programs had been underfunded, it recommended significant increases.

A response that seems to be related to changed economic conditions but that is difficult to relate to the policy recommendations just mentioned is the increased questioning of the economic values attributed to higher education. During the 1950s and 1960s, there was general acceptance of the premise that investment in higher education was economically good for the individual and economically good for the society. The optimistic view is well captured in the summary of a 1965 report.

Education yields a high rate of return on investment—that is, the monetary returns exceed the costs of education by a considerable margin. This is true from the point of view of society as a whole as well as that of the individual who invests in education for himself. The benefits to society are impressive; for example, in 1949 an investment in education would have permitted male first-graders to complete high school, would have produced a 13.6 percent return on the average. An investment through four years of college would have returned 12.1 percent on the total investment. Even more striking are the economic returns to individuals. For example, the male first-grader in 1949 could expect a 25.6 percent return on the private funds required to see him through high school, and a return of 18 percent on funds required for him to graduate from college. . . . It is quite possible that society (as well as individuals) is making an underinvestment in college education. This contention rests upon the fact that the rate of return on a college education is clearly in excess of 10 percent while the rate of return on alternative investments is considerably lower (approximately 5 percent) [Innes, Jacobson, and Pellegrin, 1965, pp. 40–41].

However, beginning at approximately the same time as the financial condition for higher education changed, a different point of view began to be expressed by economists and by some critics of higher education, such as Carolyn Bird (1975). The new doctrine is that higher education is not a particularly good financial investment and that, with the exception of medicine and law, investment in postbaccalaureate education is an even poorer investment for the individual than for a bachelor's degree. P. Taubman and T. E. Wales (1974) generalized that there has been an overinvestment in education in view of the quite modest returns. Freeman and Holloman (1975) noted that between 1968 and 1973 the rate of return on college investment fell from between 11 percent and 12 percent in 1969 to between 7 percent and 8 percent in 1974. Such judgments, were they to become widely accepted, would prove somewhat inconsistent with the increased emphasis being placed on tuition (which assumes the individual will get something of value for paying the tuition) and with the efforts on the part of institutions to create new clients, efforts that are at least partially based on the notion that continued education has a distinct economic payoff. If institutions, administrators, and faculty members vigorously attended to this new point of view, they probably would refrain from some of their new practices, such as seeking increases in tuition and finding new markets for collegiate programs—especially vocational ones, which are touted for, among other reasons, their contribution to enhanced earning capacity. The only explanation is that the older conventional wisdom, that a collegiate education contributes to increased earning power, still prevails, not only in the minds of prospective students, parents, and the general public but also in the minds of professional educators.

Institutional Responses. As institutions or systems of institutions, both public and private, encountered the deteriorating economic situation, they undertook a number of changes, each justified with its own rationale. First they increased tuition, both in absolute amounts and in the proportion of income used to maintain institutions. Tuition, of course, has historically been one of the principal sources of funds for the private sector and, as noted earlier, doubling tuition during the 1960s produced the income for almost a renaissance of large numbers of private institutions, especially the relatively unendowed liberal arts colleges. However, during the 1970s tuition assumed an even greater significance for the survival of private institutions. Not only were tuitions increased steadily for fully matriculated regular and/or residential students but new programs were also created, in the expectation that new tuition generated would be sufficient not only to cover expenses but also to produce excesses, which could be applied to other parts of the institution operating at a deficit. This search for tuition income lies behind many of the more widely publicized innovative new programs. The creation of new private institutions is also based on the assumption that tuition income is adequate to maintain an entire institution. The examples are myriad; many of them have been previously mentioned. The School of Education at Stanford University began to emphasize relatively low-cost master's degree programs to generate income to underwrite the more expensive doctoral level work. The New College of California prematurely created a law school, in the expectations that high demand for entry into law schools would produce enrollments and generate income that could help underwrite the college administration and the deficit-producing humanistic undergraduate program. The University of St. Louis and Dayton University created new units to offer instruction to part-time students. These units were expected to remedy the steadily increasing deficits being registered by the residential units. The rationale, of course, was couched in the rhetoric of public service, extending equity to disadvantaged groups, and experimentation with nontraditional and presumably more effective education. The fundamental motive, however, seems to be the economic survival of the institution, whether it be a recently created one or one of longstanding and distinguished reputation. It is this definite perception of the student as a paying customer that so distinguishes the 1970s from earlier periods. Not that private institutions during the twentieth century have been independent of tuition income—clearly, tuition was important. However, other economic bases, such as contributed or low-cost services of faculty, denominational contributions, and annual development programs to meet deficits, were relied on more than were increasing charges to students. In some respects, the difference is attitudinal: The generation of tuition income clearly motivates precise calculations as to what students would pay, and potential new programs are examined from the standpoint of income production.

280 Legacy of the Seventies

Public institutions have also assumed a different posture regarding tuition. The low or no-tuition doctrine had long pervaded
the thinking of officials in publicly supported institutions, the tradition of no tuition in the City University of New York and of modest
fees in California being perhaps the most notable examples. However, as public institutions by the late 1960s saw other sources of
income, such as state appropriation, grants and contracts, and, to
some extent, gift income, dry up, they turned more and more to
tuition. Land-grant colleges and universities, for example, increased
resident tuition and required fees by 102.57 percent between 1966
and 1976 and increased the median amount of $311 to $630
(National Association of State Universities and Land-Grant Colleges, Washington, D.C., 1976, p. 8). This attitude toward tuition
on the part of public institutions is justified theoretically by several
different arguments. The first of these is that tuition to cover total
educational costs could properly be charged to students who could
afford to pay (presumably a substantial proportion of those currently enrolled), so that public subsidies might be more precisely
focused on helping needy students and supporting those categorical
and expensive programs the states most critically require. A related
point is the growing belief and argument that low or no tuition in
public institutions is essentially regressive. It benefits the children of
economically advantaged families, who would attend college any-
way, at the tax expense of the economically disadvantaged, who pay
taxes but who are less likely to utilize the services of colleges and
universities. The inequity thus maintained would best be modified
by charging those who can afford tuitions and subsidizing those who
cannot. Then, too, there is the claim that cost or near-cost tuition
paid directly by students and their families or by loans or tuition
grants could improve the effectiveness of college education. The
market model is here advanced with the claim that if students are
not tempted by one institution as compared to another by low tuition, they may choose a college on the basis of program characteristics and demonstrated quality of the education offered. Related to
this notion is the desire, at least on the part of legislators and other
political leaders, to aid private higher education. Administrators in
public institutions are much less likely to advance this argument,
except in the most abstract terms. The discrepancy between tuition

charged by a private institution and that charged by public institutions has been increasing to the point that private institutions, especially the less prestigious ones, have ceased to be seriously competitive. The choice has become payment of $1,000 tuition at a public institution or $3,000 to a private institution for essentially the same quality of educational service. Those who believe that private higher education in the United States should be maintained, for whatever reason (tradition, possible innovativeness, greater flexibility, or the fact that private institutions serve those whom the state would have to serve if the private institutions did not exist), argue that the gap between public and private institutions must be closed. The private institutions are not likely to decrease tuitions, if for no other reason than the continued inflation. This leaves two potential remedies, the first being some form of price equalization subsidy, such as is embodied in the various state scholarship programs. The other is, of course, to increase public tuition to at least the historic ratio of private tuition—no more than double that charged by public institutions.

Without disputing the potential validity of such claims, it increasingly appears that, fundamentally, substantial increase in tuition charged by public institutions is a matter of institutional and individual professional economic survival. The only public system of higher education that seriously has proposed tuition reduction is the University of Wisconsin, and that recommendation was made in the hopes of increasing enrollments that would yield larger amounts in formula-based state support than would be lost through a tuition reduction. Given the choice of eliminating cherished programs, such as a graduate center for the City University of New York or increasing tuition, the choice in recent years has been to raise tuition. And the public institutions, just as much as the private ones, have seriously investigated additional sources of tuition revenue that might come from serving new kinds of students.

The other side of the tuition matter is the effort to increase enrollments, including finding new sorts of enrollments, to compensate for enrollment declines in some programs. It may well be that the decade of the 1970s will prove to have been one of the most active periods in the creation of new programs and the search for new students of any decade in recent times. The fact that—just as enrollments of the college-age group began to decline, due to earlier drops in the birthrate, and as the number of college graduates prepared to enter many occupations greatly exceeded the number used—there should be strenuous efforts to create new programs and enroll new students does suggest an underlying economic motivation. With respect to program development and search for new kinds of students, there does not appear to be a significant difference between the behaviors of public institutions and private institutions, although the private institutions may have entered the quest earlier. Since they typically did not have the basic support of specific appropriations, even this matter of timing, however, is conjectural, for the outward reach and colonizing efforts of Southern Illinois University, Pennsylvania State University, the University of Maryland, and the University of Northern Colorado were made at about the same time that Antioch College was developing its system and Chapman College was intensifying its efforts on military bases, in public schools, and eventually its University Afloat program. The variety of institutions and their efforts to increase enrollments may be quickly indicated. California junior colleges, campuses of the state university and college system, and campuses of the University of California all advertise over television to attract enrollments into degree programs. Troy State College, in Alabama, has created centers throughout the state and even in adjoining states in direct competition to existing public and private institutions explicitly responsible for providing the same service. Similarly, the Pennsylvania State University has created centers directly competing with publicly supported state colleges, and the University of Southern California has taken its doctoral program in educational administration into the close proximity of the University of California at Los Angeles and Claremont.

The search for new enrollments is cloaked in a rationale of egalitarianism. There are many categories of individuals who have educational needs previously not served, and new programs are explicit efforts to meet those needs. Thus the various external degree programs bring education to individuals who find it inconvenient if not impossible to come to a campus or to pursue regularly scheduled academic work. Secondly, new programs and innovative modes of instruction are seen as important ways by which institutions and individuals can adapt to a rapidly changing world and thus renew themselves. A shift of program emphasis from the preparation of elementary school teachers to the upgrading of law enforcement officers thus indicates institutional responsiveness to changed social conditions. Such a rationale was succinctly expressed in a report of the University of San Francisco explaining several external degree programs. "As part of its commitment to meaningful change while at the same time preserving and building upon its own traditions, the university has developed a variety of nontraditional, external degree programs. The goal and objectives of these programs are: (1) to make postsecondary education opportunities available to populations which have traditionally been excluded from such learning experiences; (2) to provide opportunities for the faculty to expand their knowledge and talent by creating and teaching innovative educational programs; (3) to experiment with new organizational structures and delivery systems to ensure institutions' revitalization; (4) to apply the Jesuit spirit of innovation, its spiritual principles, and educational values to an ever-changing world" (*University of San Francisco External Degree Programs,* 1976, pp. 6, 7). The fact that those programs produced the revenue to remove an almost million dollars annual deficit is not stated but would appear to be relevant.

Even more revealing are the arguments in the public sector, especially the junior college segment, for radical extension of community service and community education. Gollattscheck and his associates (1976, p. 7) have called for colleges for community renewal and have advanced high social purpose for them. The community renewal college would deliver whatever kind of service community members want, where and when they want it. It would seek to rectify technological obsolescence, accommodate the needs of women and the culturally and economically disadvantaged, and address directly the major problems of the cities. "It is a true people's college not confined to the campus but decentralized and flourishing in the real world of the total community. Its mission is to help people grow in a variety of ways—from finding maximum employment to acquiring the skills necessary for renewal of their neighborhoods and the attitudes for the creation, at last of a learning society."

However, perhaps a more fundamental purpose follows the enumeration of these and similar goals. "Doomsday forecasts of declining college enrollments are based on the traditional delivery system of higher education developed in the late nineteenth and early twentieth centuries and basically unchanged since. This system assumed that a college or university required a physical location where students and teachers met and that a college education consisted of four years of courses. *Expanded access will result in a larger market and a new breed of students, thus exploding the experts' predictions of declining enrollments"* (Gollattscheck and others, 1976, p. 7; emphasis added).

The funding for such an extended agenda is important, and the sources suggested help explain the economic motivation to increase enrollments. The federal government is an obvious source, as are gifts from local businesses, foundations, professional organizations, and individuals. Potential clients must be shown the great values to be derived from participation so that they will contribute financially, and some who can afford to pay full cost should be persuaded to do so, to underwrite costs to the economically disadvantaged. Additionally, the institution itself will prosper by staffing many courses and programs by part-time staff with stipends considerably less than those paid to regular faculty members.

Examined independently of the supporting rhetoric, the public junior college adopting the concept of the college for community renewal behaves in an economically rational way. It seeks to expand its share of the market by (1) helping clients to obtain the price (federal and state programs), (2) offering loss leaders (low-priced courses supported by high-priced courses), (3) creating demand (advertising techniques stressing economic security or the good life), and (4) offering attractive bargains to already established groups (much as oil companies offer lower-cost goods to credit card holders, offering convenient degree packages to a corporation, church or public school). It further seeks to reduce expenditure through (1) less expensive labor (part-time and volunteer faculty), (2) self-service (independent study), and (3) low- or no-cost physical plant (homes, schools, or other public buildings).

Programs such as those of the University of San Francisco also illustrate another major response of institutions to a worsening economic future. That is the search for and utilization of the least expensive techniques of instruction, rather than using a mix of expensive and less expensive techniques, which has been the rule in the past. The three most frequently attempted are the greater use of cheaper labor (part-time faculty, adjunct faculty, or already employed officials to supervise on-the-job educational activities); self-service, in the form of independent study or groups of students working on projects without supervision; and the use of low- or no-cost facilities and services such as libraries maintained for the general public.

It seems quite likely that many of the newly created private institutions could not survive economically did they not require that students do much of their academic work independently, guided by primarily part-time—hence less expensive—professorial assistants. There have also been experiments with using less expensive or free physical plants rather than creating or using permanent and costly physical plant space. Conducting off-campus classes on military bases and in high schools is one example, as is expecting students to do a good bit of their work in their own homes. Now, obviously there are other justifications for using storefront instructional centers and centers in public schools during off hours or for expecting considerable home study, but it is not insignificant that the popularity of such devices coincides with the deepening fiscal depression. As was indicated earlier, many institutions have begun to experiment with a variety of technological devices in the hopes that equipment can be substituted for labor or that equipment can aid the productivity of labor. Some institutions have sought to eliminate high-cost programs and to substitute low-cost programs for them. This does not appear to have been a particularly effective device, because, more than some of the other economies, it runs counter to institutional tradition, organizational lethargy, and departmental vested interests.

The fourth response is the paradoxical one of the emergence of the concept of a managed institution. As Cheit pointed out (1975a, p. 64), "To one not familiar with academic institutions, the declaration that the acceptance of the managed institution is a new attitude might at first seem strange. Are these institutions not managed? To a large extent, they have not been. In considerable measure, that has been one of their great strengths. They have been decentralized, largely autonomous institutions relying on shared values and assumptions for their coherence and their ability to operate and relying on individuals' academic entrepreneurship for innovation and development. These values and assumptions worked well. Colleges and universities went through their period of remarkable growth despite the fact that they had been severely undermanaged. In some excellent institutions, budgets were weak tools— if they existed. The institutions made little effort to study themselves, and their members felt very little need to be managed." When that older conception of a collegiate institution proved to be inadequate, many new approaches were attempted, first among which was the effort to develop better information on which to base decisions. Information was sought as to enrollment trends, faculty utilization of time, space utilization, and the like. Even quite small institutions thought it desirable to develop elaborate management information systems, in the hopes that somehow more precise data would make their financial problems go away or at least become easier to cope with. As data became available and as managers became more sophisticated, modeling and simulation planning emerged in many different types of institutions, from junior college districts to privately supported research universities. The use of modeling and simulation planning was, of course, intended to help managers examine many different alternatives and to gauge the likely consequences of each preparatory to building a flexible long-range plan. The budget began to evolve from the relatively weak incremental budgeting based on assumption of continuous growth to a rather complex process and document that forced each operating unit to examine and present alternatives and priorities for every budgetary request made. The portion of central administration enlarged, as more managers were appointed to put into effect a quite complex process and to monitor the operation of a budget over the stipulated period. Words that would have been anathema in the 1960s when used in connection with academic programs, such as the phrase *cost-benefit analysis,* became commonplace and, in some institutions, gradually became determining concepts.

Two other responses should be mentioned, although they typically are suprainstitutional responses and indeed are frequently resisted by institutional officials. The first of these (already described in greater detail) is the movement toward suprainstitutional boards of control and administrations in the public sector, created for the most part in the hopes that centralization could improve planning and, in the long run, reduce costs. As has been indicated, they have come into existence for many reasons, but the chief one is to try to keep ballooning higher educational costs within limits. The related response is the concept of accountability, which represents an effort to insist that institutions present persuasive evidence as to the economic and educational utility of their programs and the legitimacy of fund expenditures. Accountability is clearly an ideological child of the 1970s and distinctly represents an erosion of public faith in higher education. Accountability seems to have been demanded by at least three major groups, the first and most visible and influential being state legislators. Faced with continued increases in the cost of higher education, runaway inflation, and, at the same time, recession, legislators quite naturally wish to expend resources for only programs and activities of warrantable value. Similarly, private benefactors of higher education, frequently unfavorably impressed by the higher education profile of the late 1960s, have seriously demanded an accounting if benefaction is to continue to support higher education. The third group, of course, are students and their families, who have been making and are asked to continue to make impressive personal sacrifices to obtain an education, the value of which has come to be suspect. The urgency of feeling about accountability is reflected by Philip Lang, a member of the Oregon House of Representatives, who warned that (1971, p. 19),

The future of higher education will rise or fall with its ability to respond effectively to the public demand for accountability. The typical defenses and justifications of the status quo, the rationalizations of why things cannot or should not be changed, or the lip service and double talk that are so familiar to all of us are not effective or satisfactory responses. The expectation is for deeds and not words and for results and not excuses.

Colleges and universities, in fact all schools, do not belong to the administrators and educators; they belong to society and are merely held in trust by the academic establishment for the benefit of society. Adequate evaluation and reports of the stewardship of this trust have not been made. It should be obvious to us all that society, the public at large, is dissatisfied with the system and its outcome and that they have been increasingly so for some time. Finally, they are demanding an accounting. An accounting not just of *what, where,* or *who* expends the resources, but also of *how* and *why.* Even more important, the public also wants to know what the results and products are that are generated by higher education's programs and services, so they can compare the successes and value of its operations. In other words, they expect what I call a *cost-performance analysis.*

Significance of Responses

In aggregate, these responses to changed economic conditions present a pattern highly consistent with changes in organization and structure, curricular changes, and the other salient higher education characteristics of the 1970s. In many respects, they reveal a powerful tension between surging egalitarianism in the society and institutional and professional behavior seeking organizational preservation in the fact of mounting adversity. Federal, state, and regional policy all stress the need to extend higher educational services to previously denied individuals, and special attention is paid to the major and previously disadvantaged minority groups and institutional policy, for at least the rationalization is concerned with the same matters. The various specific attempts to cope with economic uncertainties all contain the qualifications to ensure that the economically disadvantaged are not overlooked. Thus increased tuition is urged, with the proviso that adequate support for the poor be ensured. But the fact remains that there is a fundamental incompatibility between economic viability of the system of higher education and achievement of the complete egalitarian goal, unless, of course, there comes about a radical reformation of public attitude and willingness to support a system of higher education that has a new and major role—social meliorism. That this change is likely to come about seems somewhat doubtful, in view of the seeming public skepticism reflected in demands for accountability and increased centralization of authority in higher education.

The major responses to the new depression in higher education may and probably do have considerable value and may solve a number of temporary difficulties. However, many of them may, in the long run, prove either counterproductive or of limited value in solving long-term problems. The efforts on the part of institutions to identify new clientele is illustrative. If institutions expect individuals in new groups of potential students to pay the full cost of programs, there is good reason to believe that the number willing to do so would be considerably less than the number for whom a need can be claimed or demonstrated. If full costs are charged but with compensation provided by shortening time required and by using less expensive systems of delivery, the possibility of consumer dissatisfaction developing is not inconsiderable. Already criticisms of many of the new external degree programs is beginning to mount, and both voluntary accreditation and public agencies are being asked to investigate. If public funds are expected to be made available to new clients, other difficulties can be expected. Programs designed for quite atypical sorts of students are easy to caricature (for example, courses in basket weaving or macramé). Such caricatures are not lost on public officials, Senator Proxmire perhaps being a prime example. In a different vein, it seems likely that there will be public and legislative reaction if institutions continue to graduate and credential people for vocations in which there is an oversupply of qualified individuals.

A particularly serious problem for institutions seeking out new students is whether the institutions have the intellectual resources to respond to every need. The land-grant college ideal is frequently used as a model of a collegiate institution reaching out for new groups of people. But the land-grant ideal was most clearly and fruitfully expressed in agriculture. The academic program in a college of agriculture, the adjacent federally supported experiment station, the county agents, and the agricultural extension service all interacted reciprocally, so that what was offered in extension derived directly from the intellectual strength of the school of agriculture. During the 1970s, many institutions have begun to offer services for which their resident faculties are unprepared. Some have attempted to serve the role of educational broker and have sought to recruit people with specialized knowledge. However, the brokering function raises some interesting questions regarding quality control. Quality control in traditional subjects taught on a campus is maintained by a complex web of interaction between many different people and groups of people, each sharing the same values and quite comparable experiences. Thus a dean trained in mathematics is quite prepared to make judgments about work being offered in history. But that same dean is probably unequipped to make judgments about an off-campus program in public safety taught primarily by practitioners who never have the opportunity to interact with faculty members on the home campus.

A broader problem is also involved. The search for new clientele is expressed in egalitarian rhetoric, yet that egalitarian rhetoric, if applied too broadly, may conceal the real failures of collegiate institutions with respect to orthodox students. To illustrate, Cross (1976) recently affirmed that higher education had run out of new clients because all such groups were now receiving attention through various forms of nontraditional study. The very complacency of such a remark conceals the fact that the proportion of young minority-group members entering college has begun to stabilize and in some regions actually to decline.

The rather steady increases in tuition in both public and private institutions raises a number of perplexing problems. In the private sector, expectations that increases in tuition will be partly defrayed by various forms of publicly provided price equalization seems destined to produce more intensive public scrutiny. Many of the newer institutions expect that most of their students will be receiving federal or state funds of one sort or another. Currently voluntary accreditation is expected to vouch for the worthwhileness of programs. If, however, as seems to be a distinct possibility, voluntary accreditation refuses to perform that role or is rejected by government, then governmental agencies can be expected to get into the accreditation process itself—an event that likely would be hurtful in the long run for all of higher education.

If public and private institutions continue to increase tuitions (as they seem to be doing), this should produce a further drop in enrollments of undergraduate degree-seeking students, thus aggravating the economic necessities that are forcing tuitions up. Already weaker private institutions have experienced enrollment declines directly related to tuition increases. Student refusal to pay increasing tuitions is likely to intensify as the economic returns to education decline still further. As the oversupply of people trained in many different vocations continues, the continuing drop in the economic value of higher education seems certain.

During the 1970s, although in aggregate there have been slowdowns and even declines in enrollments, there have been pockets of potential students that could be recruited through quite specialized appeals. The appeal of conservative evangelical Protestant institutions have seemed to persist by serving a small but dedicated conservative segment in the population. In the search for new students able to pay tuition, institutions have searched for such specialized groups. The sudden entry into legal education by liberal arts colleges is an example. However, the number of these pockets of potential clients is limited, and those limits are already being approached.

While recommendations for increases in tuition are accompanied by plans to accommodate the economically disadvantaged, this may in the long run be an impossible goal. Various combinations of scholarship, loans, and work rarely approximate the actual costs of attending college, and the differences to be absorbed by students from the lower quartile of family income are still too great to be tolerated. Thus the problem of equity will continue to plague higher education.

Efforts to effect economies similarly must be scrutinized carefully with respect to long-term effectiveness. Plant maintenance can be deferred briefly but not forever. Use of educational technology in aggregate seems to be invariably more expensive than orthodox modes of instruction and does not produce significant educational gains. Increased class size can produce some economies, but there appear to be limits to what students will tolerate, especially as tuitions rise. Similarly, there are limits to the amount of independent study students will do willingly before they begin to question the uses made of their tuition dollars—witness the bitter remark of the student in a high-cost private university that stressed independent study, that he had received a library card in return for his $3,500 tuition.

Nor do economies to scale seem to promise much for alleviating financial distress of collegiate institutions. Economies to scale can be achieved through mass purchasing and through assembly-line organization of simple routine tasks. However, education is and has been, labor intensive, and is likely to remain so in the future, and the substantial bulk of institutional funds go for costs of labor-intensive activities.

Better management and better management information are distinct possibilities for alleviating—but not ending—financial problems. The best management information system in the world cannot increase the size of the pool from which a particular institution draws its students, nor can management affect inflation, which is one of the more important ingredients of financial distress. Further, management systems are for the most part powerless to affect the consequences of past decisions, as is well evidenced by the relatively insignificant value that programs for early retirement have had. Then, too, management using quite expensive kinds of information or intelligence is a manifestation of a bureaucracy, which very quickly takes on a life of its own and which assumes its organizational continuity as a major objectivity. Lastly, improved management techniques thus far have been relatively powerless to affect the major cost element in higher education, namely staff and faculty. This does not suggest that managerial decisions cannot be made that will reduce expenditure for salaries. It does suggest, however, that decisions regarding faculty appointments are either acts of desperation (as when a system faces bankruptcy) or acts of will, difficult to summon in a collegiate setting.

Accountability, in the sense of presenting evidence of inputs, such as number of faculty, salaries, classes taught, and the like, represents good evidence that can be useful in judging institutions. However, what is implied by the concept of accountability is evidence regarding outputs, such as the quality of professional performance after education, contributions graduates make to the society, or evidence as to the quality of life lived by graduates of collegiate institutions. First, obtaining information about such matters is enormously expensive and technically extraordinarily difficult to accomplish. Further, in view of the typically ambiguous objectives of higher education, even specifying what sorts of outputs are desired probably transcends the capabilities of institutions.

EIGHT

ฟฟฟฟฟฟฟฟฟฟฟฟฟฟฟฟ

Significance
and Prospects

During the late 1960s and early 1970s, radical changes in American higher education were either seriously suggested or were actually adopted on a reasonably large scale. While being so close to actual or proposed changes does not allow adequate perspective and hence might be somewhat premature, nonetheless even a partial appraisal is needed, to help administrators and policymakers arrive at reasonable decisions. Some evaluation of a few major changes, even if impressionistic, seems wise, as do an elaboration and judgments of some of the major issues that those developments have produced.

Summarizing the 1970s

If actual changes and those strongly urged were combined, a profile of American higher education would emerge that would

293

be distinctly different from the profile of, say, 1965. While both public and private institutions of higher education operated throughout the period, the public sector enrolled a substantial majority of all students (approximately 70 percent, compared to 30 percent in the private sector). The large majority of public institutions were organized into statewide systems for coordination or control and multicampus universities and their complex systems educated the majority of students. This development of supracampus systems resulted in a diminution of authority and prerogatives allowed to local campuses and transferred those powers to more centralized state or suprainstitutional agencies. Accompanying this increased centralization was an increased bureaucratization, and many of the critical decisions concerning education were made by individuals not generally known either to the public or to wider professional educators.

Overall, there was a net gain in the number of private institutions, as compared with the early 1960s. However, those private institutions enrolled a steadily decreasing proportion of the college-attending population and also encountered rather severe financial difficulties. Although Bowen and Minter (1975) have indicated that the majority of private institutions are in reasonably good financial shape, as many as 300 are running operating deficits or are being forced into serious efforts for retrenchment. These private institutions continue to receive a substantial proportion of their operating budgets through tuitions. However, a significant change of the 1970s is the fact that private institutions in thirty-one states are now entitled to receive some form of state scholarship funds or state aid. In an effort to reduce costs and to enrich programs private institutions are entering into new and somewhat complex multi-institution arrangements similar to the state systems and multicampus institutions in the public sector. While there is a great deal of experimentation, for the most part consortial arrangements in the private sector (partly because they lack the sanctions of law) have been less effective and efficient and have less visibility and impact than the multiinstitution arrangements in the public domain.

Both public and private institutions of higher education began seeking new clientele to replace what is expected to be a rather sharp decline in enrollments of the traditional college-age group by the end of the decade. It does not appear that the public nor the private institutions are partial to any particular new clientele or technique for recruiting them. Both public and private institutions have engaged in colonizing and establishing centers far from the home campus. Both public and private are seeking new students, whether they be older adults, minority-group members, or the economically underprivileged—always provided that tuition or fulltime equivalent appropriations are or can become available through links with state and federal programs. And both public and private institutions are seeking new vocational programs that can appeal to the various new clients. This tailoring of curricula to emerging student demands is in some respects one of the more significant changes. Prior to the late 1960s, institutions did modify programs if they began losing substantial numbers of applications for enrollments. Colleges of engineering have been notably sensitive to application trends. However, there did not seem to be the willingness to create radically different vocational programs, just to attract students. For example, a Jesuit university with a strong tradition of the liberal arts and sciences is now offering programs in public safety; a former state teachers college is offering off-campus programs in public administration and urban affairs; and a private liberal arts college is creating a law school stressing public service practice of law. Should this quest for new markets continue, it could very well result in collegiate institutions almost becoming brokers of whatever kind of educationally related services for which there was a market and demand.

Although no American collegiate institution (with the one possible exception of Wesleyan University in the early 1960s) would ever publicly admit to having enough money, during the late 1950s and 1960s collegiate institutions typically did experience a golden economic age characterized by expanding incomes and financial ability to do more than ever before. However, by 1968 conditions had changed, and public and private institutions and systems of institutions alike began systematic and frequently frenzied searches for ways to cope with deteriorating financial conditions. These searches involved slowing down plant maintenance, eliminating nonprofessional services, restricting travel expenditures, restricting communications, and, finally, reducing (typically through attrition) actual professional appointments. In one way or another, all institutions tried to develop some form of management information systems and more precise ways of budgeting than the incremental line item budget that had previously been typical. An important motivation for moving to complex systems of institutions was to effect economies of scale. With varying degrees of intensity, institutions experimented with educational technology as a possible means for reducing costs. Also, in both public and private institutions, there was increased interest in using part-time faculty and in replacing senior faculty members with junior faculty members whenever vacancies occurred. A related development has been the rather general attempt to reduce the proportion of faculty members holding permanent tenure, which at the same time reduces costs and ensures greater program flexibility.

Then there were the concerted and formal efforts on the part of faculties to become more intimately involved in governance. The pattern is only partially perceptible, but the first effort was to create representative senates with specifically delegated powers to advise or to legislate. These senates either failed to involve faculty sufficiently or failed to protect economic interests. Then came the widespread movement toward unionism and collective bargaining. And there was also a rather general proclivity on the part of faculty members to have recourse to the courts to protect appointments and civil and constitutional rights and to define more precisely roles and prerogatives of various campus constituencies. This has clearly been a time of constitutionalism on campus, in which faculty rights and responsibilities were specified in legally binding documents. Negotiated and specific contracts became prevalent, and specified formulas were created to govern such things as tolerable amounts of outside faculty consulting and work expected by institutions of faculty members. In some respects quite different was the general interest on the part of institutions systematically to facilitate faculty development. Earlier there had been such attempts as a few centers for the improvement of instruction, interinstitutional workshops such as the Danforth Workshop on Liberal Arts Education or the North Central Association Study of Liberal Arts Education, and the ubiquitous fall faculty conference. However, giving the rationale that faculties during the 1970s would stabilize and that faculty renewal would come less from new appointments than from changing attitudes and practices of existing faculty, states, the federal government, foundations, and institutions themselves began to experiment with faculty renewal. The federal Fund for the Improvement of Postsecondary Education made substantial grants for faculty renewal; states such as Florida appropriated funds specifically earmarked for faculty renewal; systems of institutions such as the University of California budgeted small faculty grants to assist renewal; foundations such as the Lilly Foundation and the Hazen Foundation gave high priority to faculty development; and individual institutions budgeted modest amounts for faculty renewal and/or created agencies to assist faculty particularly to improve their teaching practices. Even the policy commissions such as the Carnegie Commission on Higher Education and its successor, the Carnegie Council on Policy Studies in Higher Education, advocated high priority for formal, systematic, and funded attempts to encourage faculty development.

Collegiate finance is such a complex phenomenon that it is difficult to describe in the sense that a faculty involvement in governance can be described. A few salient features can be enumerated, however. Institutions have sought to generate new income through serving new groups of students. Federal programs, as exemplified by the higher education amendments of 1972, have sought to extend opportunity for access to higher education by providing various forms of support for students. This contrasts sharply with the earlier characteristic form of federal assistance, exemplified by the National Defense Education Act, which sought to foster academic excellence and the preparation of highly technical and scholarly people. The states have sought to utilize the capacity of the private sector through state scholarship programs or limited direct aid to institutions. At the same time, the states have sought to effect economies through demanding greater accountability. One of the potentially most distinctive developments, should they ever mature, are the so-called 1202 commissions, mandated by Section 1202 of the Education Amendments of 1972 and charged with the distribution and control of funds emanating from various federal programs.

Curricular and instructional changes are like financing—so complex as to defy epitomizing. There is continuation of such earlier attempted reforms as new groupings of students, new temporal arrangements, modified ways of assessing student performance, increased use of field or clinical experience, and experimentation with interdisciplinary work. Institutions continue to explore such possibilities. However, the principal efforts of the 1970s take one or both of two principal forms. There is a considerable interest in nontraditional learning, which makes great use of independent study, life experience, educational potentialities of noneducational institutions, and many types of part-time study or interrupted periods of study. The other thrust is a resurgence of the traditional, with major and cognate fields increasing in significance for student programs; the restoration of more rigorous and specified kinds of evaluation of student performance; and a reconsideration of the values of graduation requirements, such as general education requirements.

To these salient factors can be added a cluster of other matters, not necessarily less important, yet less visible. Except in the most highly selective institutions, admissions requirements in the form of aptitude test scores and rank in high school graduating class appear to have become less rigorous during the 1970s. A related development has been the steady decline in measured aptitude test scores from approximately 1968 to 1976. There continues to be much discussion of the values of counseling and guidance, but with relatively little new in practice except for the limited experimentation with computer-assisted guidance and the availability of more guidance information. An example of the latter would be the consistently made recommendation that students should be provided indices of their likelihood of success at institutions to which they apply. An important outcome of the student protest period was the involvement of students in academic governance, as members of senates, boards of trustees, board committees, and various faculty committees and departments. Residence halls during the 1970s appear to be considerably more popular with students than they were from approximately 1965 to 1970, although the significance of this shift is difficult to gauge. A matter that seemingly preoccupies higher education is the affirmative action movement, by which more women and minorities are actively recruited as undergraduate students, graduate students, and faculty members. Certainly between 1970 and 1976 affirmative action commanded a great deal of administrative time. Whether this trend will continue is unknown. A California Supreme Court decision in 1976 overturning a University of California racial quota for minority students in the Davids Medical School may have been a harbinger of a retreat from affirmative action of the quota sort.

Major changes in graduate education have not taken place in the well-established schools whose institutions are members of the Association of American Universities. The significant changes have come about in new kinds of graduate institutions, such as the free-standing professional schools and the nontraditional graduate programs offered by some of the established but still developing institutions. The powers of departments apparently have been less affected than the powers of central administration in public institutions administered through a system. One change, however, should be noted—an increased willingness on the part of central administration in faculty oriented and nonunionized institutions to exercise position control and to exercise definite vetoes over recommendations for appointment, promotion, and tenure. In institutions such as Stanford or the University of California, during the 1960s, departmental recommendations were typically followed, and departments assumed the right to fill any vacancy. As financial problems worsened during the late 1960s, this gradually changed, and the office of the president or provost assumed the right to recall positions as they became vacant and to reallocate them only on the basis of demonstrated need.

The magnitude of these proposed or generally adopted changes, may be underscored by comparing a typical student in 1964 or 1965 with one in 1975 or 1976. In 1964 a typical student in American higher education was between seventeen and twenty-one years of age, was attending a publicly supported institution governed by a single board and a single administration, and had enrolled in a degree program on the assumption that he or she would proceed straight through to receipt of a degree. Actually, of course, only about half of such students did proceed systematically to a degree, but, regardless of whether the institution was a two- or four-year institution, the assumption was that of regular progress toward a degree in an academic field or in one of a relatively few professional programs. This student had been admitted on the basis of performance on a test of academic aptitude and prior high school performance, and expected to receive letter grades ranging from A to F, established on the basis of test performance and performance in writing papers or doing laboratory work. The student assumed that the institution, its administration, and its faculty were responsible for maintaining and creating an academic program and establishing the rules governing student relationship to the program. Student participation in governance was limited to participation in student government and, to a lesser extent, in the governance of residence halls. The typical student would be aware of some experimental programs, such as an honors program, a house plan, or a theme residence hall, but only a few students would actually be participating in such innovative efforts. Whether or not the student lived on campus, the expectation was that instruction would be carried on in classrooms or laboratories on a single campus and that it would be the student's responsibility physically to attend at least the regularly scheduled class meetings. Student tuition, while varying from state to state, represented less than a fifth of the cost of instruction provided, the rest being appropriated on an annual or biannual basis by the respective states.

By academic year 1975–76, that situation had altered considerably. The typical student then was older and attended either a campus of a multicampus university or a branch or center maintained in a location remote from the principal campus. The student attended part-time or in the expectation of taking substantial time off from attending school to work, travel, or engage in other activities. While students seeking a degree continued to emphasize a major in an academic or vocational subject, a greater variety of vocational majors were available, and the student would receive academic credit for off-campus activities, either obtained while enrolled or credit for prior life experiences. The relatively small proportion of the student body interested in social action could participate as voting members of departmental committees or could serve on an institution senate. Student life was for the most part under the individual control, but processes for adjudication of differences were specified in considerable detail. In the event institutional procedures proved inadequate, the student recognized that he or she had access to courts and was willing to utilize them for redress of grievances. The model student was still unaffected by most of the various curricular or instructional innovations. However, he or she had learned to use a computer, had undertaken some off-campus activities for academic credit, and had received at least a sprinkling of pass-fail grades rather than the traditional letter grades.

Significance of Changes

Given these proposed, attempted, or adopted changes, individuals, institutions, and policymakers are presented with a number of questions and issues. Is nontraditional learning likely to last as a major component of American higher education? If it is, should established institutions undertake major nontraditional offerings? Again, if it is, will credits and credentials earned in nontraditional programs in the long run be judged as comparable to those earned in more traditional ways? At a time when the capacity of established institutions of higher education is likely to exceed demand, what is the future of new kinds of institutions for the ambitious individual? Where lies wisdom: in attending an established law school or a new one providing more convenient schedules and assignments? What should be the attitude of an institutional president faced with growing faculty sentiment for a union? Should the attitude be to accept the inevitable, to strongly resist, or to adopt some middle position? Similarly, what should the institutional posture be in the face of growing centralization of authority in public institutions: acceptance, resistance, or compromise? Or, another matter: Is there some optimum amount of institutional or state resources that should be devoted to educational technology and systems of educational technology? Put crassly, should an institution faced with a stabilized or even declining budget attempt a major conversion of the campus to provide for computer-assisted or computer-managed instruction? A broader sort of issue is the matter of expanding access to higher education on the part of many new groups of students. Should institutions seek to provide whatever kind of service any group of potential students wish, or should a more parsimonious view of institutional purpose be adopted?

There are no easy answers to such questions, and there is precious little evidence or information available on which to base answers. There is, to be sure, a great body of opinions, and there are strong feelings regarding every reasonable proposed set of changes. But there is no real evidence as to how many people actually desire nontraditional educational programs enough to pay reasonable amounts to participate in them. There is currently no generally available and acceptable means for establishing the validity of educational outcomes of either traditional or nontraditional study. There is no evidence that systems of institutions either contribute to or detract from efficiency or equity in higher education. Nor is there solid evidence as to the impact of unionism on educational programs, academic governance, or traditional academic values. What evidence there is regarding educational uses of technology provides no basis for acceptance or rejection of television, computers, or other media. Nor, given the complexity of research problems in education and the typical lack of articulation between research findings and policy decisions, is there likely to be warrantable evidence. Yet decisions must be made, and so some interpretation of the significance of these new developments must be attempted.

Despite the complexity of such questions and the lack of conclusive evidence needed to answer them, a reasonably strong tentative position seems warranted and should be expressed, if for no other reason than to make clear the author's bias. Nontraditional learning, in the sense of a full-blown movement, quite properly should come to an early end. This does not mean that the separate elements should not from time to time be used in appropriate situations. It does argue that the logical extension of the nontraditional movement in aggregate so expands the concept of education as to render it meaningless. Relatedly, it makes better socioeconomic and educational sense to use existing institutions likely to have excessive capacity than to create a plethora of new institutions possessing for the most part an extremely precarious base. It was discovered, for example, that during a brief six- or seven-year period existing medical schools were able to expand entering classes sufficiently so that the earlier called-for creation of many new medical schools proved unnecessary. Given the nature of legal education, class size expansion is preferable to creating new colleges, especially when the quality of those institutions overall appears to be questionable.

Given the fact that unions in publicly supported institutions have really not improved the economic condition of the professoriate as compared to the condition in nonunion public systems and given the potential threat of adversarial arrangements to traditional collegiality, it probably would be better if widespread unionization of faculty did not take place. This does not imply catastrophic results from unionization and collective bargaining, nor does it massive destruction of academic values. Academic values can be and have been maintained in a union situation; it is just that maintaining them would be somewhat easier without the legalization of the always latent cleavage between faculty and administration. In a similar vein, in the best of all possible worlds the centralizing tendencies would be slowed and even reversed, and the large state systems and multicampus universities would be dismantled. Centralized systems for the most part have not achieved the fundamental roles of economy and equity that they were intended to play, and they do possess the potential for external intrusion in essential academic matters properly the concern of individual campuses. Again, it should be pointed out that academic freedom and the essential activities of faculty members have been and can be maintained on campuses within centralized systems, but they are maintained through greater effort and with greater friction than would be necessary if individual campuses were the primary locus of administrative and policymaking authority. Limited statewide coordination is probably desirable, if for no other reason than to provide an arena for the discussion and consideration of statewide educational needs and/or the education and edification of state government and the public generally. But the movement from coordination to control carries with it greater dangers than possible benefits are worth.

The question as to whether collegiate institutions should seek to provide educational services to many new groups of students is somewhat more complicated. Historically, collegiate institutions have followed a gradual egalitarianism, extending educational services first to the agricultural and industrial classes, then to other groups of the economically disadvantaged, and finally to racial and ethnic minorities. This gradual egalitarianism is consistent with fundamental American democratic premises and values and should not be rejected. However, the almost frenzied efforts on the part of institutions to find new clients and to provide them whatever kind of service they wish, although the individual institution may lack the necessary capacity to render that service, should be restrained. The school of agriculture, engaging in agriculture experimentation and agricultural extension and linked to county agents and 4-H Club representatives, exhibits an ideal pattern for rendering service. Experimentation provided the data used in the curriculum in the school of agriculture, which prepared people to disseminate that information throughout a state. Thus there was an indigenous critical mass of people, and there were principles that assigned validity to the services rendered. This is actually quite different from the picture presented by a small liberal arts college with no tradition of research and graduate education that offers a Ph.D. program in educational administration or the local community college that offers programs to upgrade sophisticated management in a nearby corporation. In neither situation does the existing faculty possess the requisite expertise, and it can be questioned whether the academic administrators possess the sophistication in evaluation to recruit and supervise a specifically recruited new faculty.

While the evidence concerning the cost-benefit effectiveness of educational technology still is confusing and inconclusive, the clear educational potentiality of such things as the computer, videotape cassettes, and television is so great that continued experimentation should be urged. However, experimentation should not be undertaken with the idea that immediate favorable economic consequences are likely to accrue. It is distinctly possible that by the twenty-first century existing educational technology or less expensive and more sophisticated variants of it could become as significant educationally as was the printed word. However, until that time comes institutions would be better advised not to jeopardize the financial pace of traditional forms of education by precipitously embracing the new technology.

These observations are related to several overarching generalizations. The first of these is that, historically, different kinds of collegiate institutions and different sorts of educational practices have tended to regress toward a mean or a generally perceived archetypal institution or practice. Thus technical institutions, teachers colleges, liberal arts colleges, and special-purpose institutions have tended to grow to resemble complex multipurpose institutions operating in an ethos of continued growth. Similarly, innovations in educational practice such as interim terms, ad hoc courses, nondirective teaching, and intensified clinical experience have tended to move toward structured terms or semesters, scheduled classes, lecturing, and abstracting the essence of field experience into casebooks, books of readings, and, finally, textbooks. To the extent that this generalization continues to have force, one would expect similar regression in the future as nontraditional learning changes toward orthodoxy and as new kinds of institutions take on the characteristics and practices of traditional ones.

And this regression is a useful phenomenon for something as complex as an educational system in a developed and technological society. All collegiate institutions properly share a limited number of transcendent purposes needed throughout the society. Hence, considerable comparability is desirable. Thus junior colleges, liberal arts colleges, state colleges, state universities, and private universities all participate in the socialization and induction of youth into the adult world. As that world becomes more complex and varied, so do the commonly shared tasks of different kinds of collegiate institutions. It is desirable for new sorts of institutions to appear periodically to serve new groups in new ways. If the need that prompted the creation of a new institution proves valid, the entire higher educational system will be leavened by it and will in turn assimilate the new institution into the mainstream of educational practice. Thus it is probably good, overall, that the creation of new kinds of institutions do appear, and it is also probably good that most of them as quickly disappear, while those that persevere take on more and more of the characteristics of the long-existing institutions. It is argued that a system of higher education that consisted of many institutions, each uniquely tailoring its efforts to specific clientele, would fail in its essential normative role.

A second and related generalization is that educational theory and practice, in the United States at least, have changed periodically in a pendulumlike fashion; thus prescription and tight requirements and free election of courses replace each other periodically. Similarly, education for vocation and education for character alternate as being the most generally accepted purpose of collegiate education. Other polar types can be mentioned: scientific versus humanistic orientation, elitism versus egalitarianism, student centered versus subject centered, or protectiveness of students versus a laissez-faire attitude. If this pattern, which can be demonstrated historically, persists, then one can now expect a swing away from intensive academic use of life experience, student participation in evaluating their own performance, and use of independent study as a predominant mode of instruction.

Such a reaction is to be desired, because of the abuses that have become too painfully apparent. A bachelor's degree program that grants three quarters of the needed credit for various sorts of life experience, the relevance of which is established by student testimonial alone, and grants the remaining quarter of credit for thirty three-hour class meetings and independent study (and this is quite typical) is a travesty of the essential nature of education. Higher education is an important but limited instrument for the development of certain kinds of human behavior. It uses words, numbers, and abstract conceptualizations to develop reasonably sophisticated skills of cognition and insight and to help students cope with and eventually control a complex culture and society. The development of those skills requires immersion of the individual into a situation allowing for continuous interaction between the mentor and the student. This is not to say that other traits or skills are trivial or unimportant. Character traits such as a sense of honor or an optimistic spirit may be more important for an individual's well-being than the ability to calculate mathematically. Such traits are for the most part unaffected by formal collegiate education—they are developed much earlier in life. It seems wise to interpret the concept of education parsimoniously and to utilize those techniques and instrumentalities most likely to achieve the limited set of objectives. A caveat must be added: Approving a swing away from excessive educational reliance on experience, self-evaluation, or independent study does not imply rejecting them as having no formal educational significance. They do have significance, as clinical practice, some free election of courses, and independent and solitary research and scholarship demonstrate. Rather, what is suggested here is the desirability of retreat from extremes.

A third, somewhat more tenuous generalization is that the

major social institutions, such as the family, education, formal religion, or commerce, are so complex and so derived from the history of the people that they defy analysis of how they actually work. Applied to higher education, this point of view says that we really do not know how people learn or what the college experience actually does. There is, of course, evidence (limited to be sure) that college graduates appear to lead somewhat different lives than do people who did not attend college, but there are so many variables, such as socioeconomic levels of families, ethnic and religious background, or even sibling position, that it has proven impossible to base educational practice on knowledge. To the extent that this is true, then the acceptance or rejection of any of the salient developments of the 1970s will depend on what people feel or have faith is effective, rather than what is known to be effective. This notion has a stoical charm to it. Education has been characterized as being an organized anarchy with unclear objectives and uncertain technology, lacking means for evaluation of its performance. Yet it is an important organization within which people can work and engage in interesting activities. The ultimate viability of the organization is determined by the degree to which people find and savor the opportunities and activities the organization provides. That traditional forms of higher education have proven satisfying is demonstrated by the amazing consistency of the form and substance of collegiate institutions in Western civilization. For the last 1,100 years, Bologna, Paris, Oxford, Cambridge, and Edinburgh of the twelfth and thirteenth centuries were amazingly similar to Harvard, Stanford, and the universities of Michigan and California of the late twentieth century.

The Nontraditional Movement. The major developments of the 1970s must be examined in the context of such generalizations or at least hypotheses. The first of these developments, in order of theoretical or philosophical, if not actual, importance, is proposed or adopted changes in curriculum and instruction. By far the most widely publicized such development has been the nontraditional movement and its concern for new kinds of students. While the literature describing the nontraditional continues to grow and radiate hope, it seems highly possible that the movement has reached its zenith and that forces are operating to slow it. Nontraditional learning emphasizes, among many things, interpreting life experiences for formal educational purposes, independent study, educational uses of many different social institutions and agencies, new kinds of delivery systems, and use of part-time and nonprofessional faculty.

The awarding of academic credit for life experience seems to be encountering such resistance as to force the conclusion that the practice will be considerably attenuated in the relatively near future. Regional and specialized accreditation agencies are developing policies regarding credit for life experience that will require institutions to present persuasive evidence of educational validity if life experience is to be acceptable. Obtaining persuasive evidence, however, is extraordinarily expensive. Ideally, student portfolios annotating life experience should be verified and validated, both by examining the detailed nature of the life experience and determining what particular skills or traits have actually been developed. This requires a great deal of professional faculty time devoted to studying portfolios and examining students, as well as the use of valid instruments to measure educational outcomes. After examining a number of institutions making great use of life experience, it appears that the awarding is done quite casually, either by clerical staff or after cursory review by faculty members or administrators. As soon as more rigorous methods of appraisal are used, administrative costs rise to intolerable levels. Similarly, when assigned field or clinical experiences are made an essential part of a degree program, the question of supervision and appraisal arises. In providing adequate supervision—as is done, for example, in the cooperative work-study program of Northeastern University—costs mount. Institutions seeking to provide acceptable levels of supervision and appraisal are forced either to accept high costs (justified because of the values, as in the case of clinical work in nursing or medicine), to provide supervision by relatively inexpensive professional help (as in the case of employing, on a part-time basis, professionals who at the same time are employed in other institutions), or to reject widespread use of clinical and field experience (on the ground that it is simply too costly for an institution to provide in view of the anticipated benefits). To these factors must be added the attitude of traditional institutions, especially of established graduate and professional schools, which tend to be skeptical of academic credit acquired outside of formal and recognized courses, and the expanding attempts throughout established higher education to slow down the accidental grade inflation that took place during the 1960s. There are, of course, elements of academic credit awarded for effort outside of the classroom and laboratory that probably will persist. Clinical experience in the health fields, some clinical experience in legal education, practice teaching, and field work in engineering are examples. But the awarding of academic credit for military service, for service on the job while enrolled for courses, for individually contrived off-campus activities, and for participation in foreign travel, social welfare activities, and personal development activities seem likely to decline and probably disappear.

The ideal way to handle this matter of academic credit would be to identify those skills, traits, and attributes that are of primary concern to the limited mission of higher education and that might also be directly affected by noneducational activities. The possession or lack of possession of them could then be determined through the same kinds of examining procedures used in colleges and universities and, when appropriate, actual academic credit could be awarded. This ideal is reflected in the general education programs in the college of the University of Chicago during the 1940s and 1950s, in the Basic College of Michigan State University, and in the College of Basic Studies at the University of South Florida. All students were required to take and pass comprehensive examinations over broad fields of study. Students could prepare for those examinations by taking courses, by studying independently, or by already possessing the requisite skills and knowledge developed by other means. Such an ideal is expensive, because the examinations, to be valid, must be carefully prepared and evaluated. Starkly stated, the choice presented institutions would be either to develop rigorous means to examine for desired knowledge, skills, traits, and abilities developed in noneducational study or to refrain from awarding academic credit.

Similar forces operate with respect to independent study. Independent study has typically and ironically taken either of two major directions. The first has been presenting students with highly structured courses and modules, individualized by allowing each student to proceed to mastery at his or her own rate of speed. Experiments with the Keller Plan, individually paced learning systems, computer-assisted courses and games, and programmed texts have demonstrated power to produce measurable educational gains. But such structured experiences are costly to prepare, and they require specific technical competencies on the part of instructors. For these two reasons, while there is much experimentation with structured, individually paced courses and modules, relatively few have been adopted and maintained over a long period of time within a single institution, and even fewer have been adopted by enough institutions so that an economically sound critical mass of users is obtained. The other direction it recently took is a highly unstructured situation. Students, singly or in groups, have been told to discover a problem for themselves and then to set about solving it, using resources wherever available to help them do so. A typical example is the Unified Science Program offered at MIT. Students registered for as much as a full semester of credit and then set about discovering something that interested them and then organizing their own activities to examine the phenomenon in detail. Some students did seem to enjoy the freedom to set their own goals, but the majority experienced considerable frustration, floundering about to find a problem and procedure. That same floundering characterized other such organized attempts. Further, the typical evidence of educational success has been expressions of student feeling, frequently on the ground that other kinds of evidence would be irrelevant to the gains that come about through independent study. This does not mean that unstructured approaches to independent study are invariably ineffective. Institutions such as Evergreen State College or the University of Wisconsin at Green Bay have made such independent study an essential part of degree programs. However, both of those institutions have also budgeted for sufficient faculty time to counsel and supervise student activities.

Independent study, as interpreted in the nontraditional movement, exhibits several additional characteristics worthy of skepticism. Students working on their own for much of an academic program experience loneliness and lose motivation unless they perceive a very tangible and valuable outcome. While solid evidence is not available, the experience of the open university in England suggests that those students who persevere are most likely to be teachers seeking an upgraded credential. To provide carefully and professionally developed portable modules, as is being attempted in the University of Mid-America, is proving so costly as to attract legislative criticism and too costly for students to pay the full cost of instruction. The relatively unsupervised independent study is proving difficult to validate in terms of recognized educational outcomes. In the 1950s, Bonthius, Davis, and Drushal (1957) examined the many variations of independent study then in vogue and reached the conclusion that independent study carefully supervised was a highly effective but also the most expensive form of instruction available. The situation does not seem to have changed since. If this description is accurate, the matter of adequate financing must be solved if this form of nontraditional learning is to persist. Public funds could, of course, be devoted to such a purpose, but there can be serious question as to whether they will be.

Given the firm belief that some well-supervised and guided independent study has high educational value, the cost problem should be solved as it is in established residential campuses. The solution is to provide a range of modes of instruction and learning, from relatively low-cost large lecture courses to the very high-cost independent study. The high enrollment low-cost courses help subsidize tutorials, independent study, and doctoral research. No institution can afford to base its entire curriculum on the independent study mode and do it properly. Thus the nontraditional institution that charges reasonable tuitions and expects its students to do most of the work independently is properly suspect. The nontraditional institution that offered a range of high-cost and low-cost activities would be much less vulnerable to valid criticism.

Related to, and even an essential part of, independent study is the nontraditional interest in new delivery systems. These include televised programs, videotape modules, computer-assisted or -managed programs, carefully programmed texts and workbooks, miniaturized and portable laboratory kits, distribution of educational material through newspapers, and various kinds of linking and networking arrangements. Some of the more carefully prepared examples of new delivery systems are ingenious and seem to be educationally valuable, but they all are more expensive per student credit hour produced than are orthodox, formal, classroom arrangements. Moreover, there is no evidence that those systems yield sufficiently greater educational benefits to warrant the increased costs. Despite this lack of conclusive evidence, experimentation with new delivery systems and actual utilization of them in significant ways should not be rejected. The Television College of the Chicago City Junior Colleges has long been a worthwhile undertaking, as has more recently been the offering of engineering courses via television from the Stanford University School of Engineering. But the cost factor is still present, and institutions cannot rely on more or less complete reliance on the media as the major mode of instruction. Like independent study, media-based instruction should be offered alongside of other styles of instruction.

Another key tenet of nontraditionalism is the use of part-time faculty and the use of people in other kinds of organizations and activities for educational purposes, for it is assumed that a nontraditional student living some distance from a campus can obtain professional services from a part-time professional living in his or her own area. The nontraditional movement also assumes that public librarians, business executives, penal officials, social workers, or any of a variety of personnel can and should be available to help students achieve their educational goals. There is an appealing logic to such a position. However, there are several vexing issues. Formal accreditation, while not rejecting the use of part-time faculty, has typically insisted that an accredited institution should have a reasonably sized full-time administrative and instructional core of people to provide coherence to the program, to maintain program continuity, and to provide the administrative services, such as committee work, necessary for an educational institution. Thus, on ideological grounds, it does limit the proportion of the faculty that can be part-time. Secondly, there is an emerging problem of parasitism. Nontraditional programs frequently employ an adjunct professor who also holds a full-time appointment in another institution, generally in the field related to that being offered by the nontraditional program. The adjunct professor assumes his nontraditional role as an overload, for which he receives extra compensation. Under proper constraints, this is not to be criticized, for it is not unlike professors taking on consulting activities or research activities for which extra compensation is received. However, the nontraditional program, as for example, the University Without Walls, Nova University, or the Union for Experimenting Colleges graduate program are obtaining professional services from adjunct professors at less than full cost, since the adjunct professors' home institutions pay for such things as retirement, health insurance, and other fringe benefits. When nontraditional programs also expect to use library services of other institutions and classroom space, paid for at less than full cost, they are in part existing parasitically on other institutions. There can be question as to how great this parasitism can become before host institutions begin to resist. Just to illustrate a potential situation, Laurence University opened a nontraditional doctoral program in higher education administration in Santa Barbara, California. It planned to grow to a steady enrollment of 250 doctoral students who would be on the campus for five weeks each summer. Laurence made no provision for a core library but assumed that its students could use the collection of the nearby University of California at Santa Barbara. Now, a specialized professional collection of books is created in a university library to support the university's own students. The collection can probably tolerate some additional use, but the sudden intrusion of 250 doctoral students into a collection designed to support perhaps no more than 10 or 15 doctoral students overuses that collection and could rather quickly destroy it.

Another potentially significant problem is the growth of unionism. Should unionism and collective bargaining become the prevailing means of assuring job security in collegiate institutions, it is quite conceivable that the use of nonunionized part-time faculty and nonprofessional faculty could very well become the subject for contract limitation. As a general rule, the use of part-time or adjunct faculty should be limited. Appropriately experienced part-time faculty can bring significant new points of view to the program, but they cannot maintain the continuity of interaction and the administrative integrity of complex educational programs. Any major program, such as a law curriculum or degree program in business administration, that draws more than 25 to 30 percent of its instructional staff from the part-time or adjunct ranks should be suspect and should be advised by such agencies as accreditation associations to desist or present persuasive evidence as to the validity of greater use of part-time or adjunct personnel. Similarly, institutions should by and large refrain from offering programs, either on campus or in the external mode, unless they can ensure the easy availability to all students of an essential core of library holdings. Reliance on library holdings of other agencies or expecting that students from remote locations will use such resources as the ERIC collection should be proscribed as not fulfilling essential educational responsibilities.

Several other complexities should also be mentioned. A substantial number of newer private institutions offering nontraditional programs assume tuition as the principal income and at the same time assume serving people unable or unwilling to pay full-cost tuition from their own sources. For students to afford tuition, they must rely on funds provided by various federal or state programs, such as the GI Bill of Rights. In several California institutions, for example, over 80 percent of students are supported with veterans' entitlements. There can be serious question as to the survival of those programs once GI benefits are terminated. And should other financial assistance programs terminate, one can wonder about the long-term financial liability of any nontraditional efforts. This is a most vexing matter. The various federal programs, including veterans' benefits and Basic Education Opportunity grants and various state scholarship programs, represent sound social policy. Furthermore, it would be inappropriate intrusion into academic matters for the federal or state government to insist on some ratio, at a given institution, of students receiving and not receiving educational benefits; yet institutions that cater to students eligible for a particular kind of external support are living so dangerously as to jeopardize institutional longevity if that one source of funding dries up. A case in point is a California-based institution whose various federal funds were impounded by the federal government, resulting in immediate discharge of all faculty and administrators and leaving in limbo those students who had been matriculated and were working toward a degree. As a general rule, institutions should not be created if they have no firm endowment base and if they assume that a majority of the students will receive external support with which to pay tuitions. Regional accrediting associations properly should take this matter into consideration, even to the point of awarding or not awarding candidacy. The overall implication of this point of view is that necessary educational services to the poor and previously excluded should probably be the chief responsibility of the financially secure institutions rather than of those which are financially precarious.

The last complex problem has to do with the receptivity of established institutions to educational innovations such as nontraditional study. In the past, innovations such as the free elective system, general education, or comprehensive examinations became generally acceptable only after pacesetting institutions had adopted them. The available literature regarding nontraditional programs seems to indicate that the most activity is taking place in a relatively few, recently created state institutions or in the quite atypical and small private institutions. Nontraditional programs, when they exist in such places as the University of Minnesota or the Madison campus of the University of Wisconsin, tend to be relatively small and invisible. One can at least theorize that until the major private and public universities seriously embrace the nontraditional it will probably remain peripheral to the mainstream of American higher education. This is as it should be. The network of reasonably large and adequately financed institutions in the United States represents the primary way by which educational services can best be delivered. There is room and need for other kinds of institutions to demonstrate new patterns that might subsequently be adopted by mainstream institutions and to serve continuously if securely financed and organized. The United States is a pluralistic society, and different people need somewhat different educational settings—however, not too different. Thus, in the past, denominational colleges provided both a normative education function comparable to nondenominational institutions and a condition supportive of specific religious beliefs. While the need for such institutions probably continues to exist, it should be pointed out that the rapid expansion of departments of religion in secular mainstream institutions exemplifies assimilation of educational effort whose validity has been established.

Complex Structure. A critique and assessment of the newer organizational and structural features of American higher education is in some respects much easier than assessment of curricular and instructional developments. Such things as statewide coordinating and controlling bodies are in existence, and, while it is difficult to determine whether they have achieved fundamental goals, nonetheless patterns for the future can be inferred. There is the observation that no state has eliminated statewide agencies once they were created. Similarly, unionism is in being, and its continued existence, if not its fundamental impact, can be discussed. The quality of academic life in collegiate institutions in the United States would probably be somewhat better in the absence of complex suprainstitutional structures and unionism, both of which manifest somewhat divisive characteristics and tend to limit needed autonomy of academic organizations. Yet one cannot responsibly urge turning the clock back and trying to eliminate agencies becoming well established. The policy posture should be for institutions to try to remedy the conditions that stimulate interest in unionism and to act responsibly and for the public good, to such an extent that apparent need for suprainstitutional control is substantially attenuated.

New Institutions. Much more difficult to critique and gauge are the new institutions—especially the private ones that sprang up during the early 1970s. One important reason for this difficulty is the fact that so many of the newer institutions have been based on definite ideologies concerning which people have strong emotions. Proponents of egalitarian ideals have difficulty not writing or speaking about institutions such as DQU, Nairobi, or Portland Community College in rhapsodic terms. Similarly, proponents of maintaining rigorous academic and scholarly standards have difficulty not writing about such places with critical, or even invidious and pejorative language. This emotional problem is confounded by the fact that there is no real evidence available as to the educational effectiveness of newer institutions, either in terms of achievement of unique institutional goals or in comparison with the effectiveness of more established and traditional institutions. This problem will require an extraordinarily long time to solve, if it ever will be solved. After all, long-established institutions also base much of what they do on faith rather than on evidence.

Recognizing the possibility of all sorts of exceptions, examination of many new institutions allows for some overall general impressions. The first of these is that they are characterized by considerable opportunism. Fairhaven College and Nova University shifted from a highly academic and scholarly orientation to a completely new posture when support and enrollment for the original programs did not materialize. New College of California, originally created to offer a humanistic undergraduate education, created a law school and investigated the possibility of creating a school of recording arts and a school of architecture when it appeared that there was potential student interest in those fields and a potential faculty that would staff the programs on a part-time basis. New York Institute of Technology, while created earlier in 1955, nonetheless illustrates this opportunism. It had originally been founded with a gift of equipment and property, but, like most institutions of higher education, it had to struggle to make financial ends meet. Seeking out clients to keep its facilities going full strength therefore became, during the 1970s, an economic necessity. Thus it worked out arrangements with the military, business, industry, and some professional associations to offer the sorts of programs those organizations wished and would help support.

Related to this opportunism is the tendency for new institutions to seek to attract students by offering quite definite advantages, many of which are economic in character. Thus degree programs are offered in shorter than usual time by awarding academic credit for previous and concurrent experiences or by concentrating academic work in intensive periods of instruction. They also offer programs at times or in places presumably more convenient to students. Thus evening law schools and degree programs are frequently offered at places of work.

More so than during previous periods of institution building, the new institutions of the late 1960s and 1970s have used a supporting rhetoric sharply critical of traditional modes of higher education. Thus the Wright Institute and the California School of Professional Psychology have severely criticized the behavioristic trends in psychology departments in established institutions and have claimed to offer needed programs in counseling and personality psychology not available elsewhere. Fielding Institute, Walden, and Laurence University point out the evils of excessively long doctoral programs and promise that by means of nontraditional methods the time required to obtain a degree can be sharply attenuated. La-

Verne College, pointing out the abstract nature of doctoral programs in educational administration, promises a program that is based firmly on actual practice and the study of practical means of management and administration. Several of the institutions that cater to minority groups, such as Malcolm King College or Nairobi, argue that existing institutions have not met the essential needs of minorities and offer a program that promises to do so. This reaction to presumed existing deficiencies is even found in new public institutions; thus the president of Evergreen State College says he constructed the program to rectify all of the things that he had found wrong in existing institutions of higher education.

The fourth impression is the financial precariousness that typifies the new institutions, especially the private ones. The typical financial base for new institutions is a combination of federal and private foundation grants, student fees, volunteer or marginally remunerated faculty, and programs tailored to allow student access to various kinds of federal and state student support programs. Illustrative of the financial precariousness and also of the means used to cope with it is the frequent use of temporary facilities for the adaptation of facilities originally designed for other purposes but that could be purchased with relatively low down payments, the price to be amortized over a long period of time out of tuition-based operating funds. And they also rely on resources such as libraries operated by other institutions or agencies.

The leadership of so many new institutions seems somehow uniquely motivated to an unusual degree. The leaders appear to be individuals who found themselves quite out of step with patterns and processes found in older, more established institutions and who sought, by creating a new institution, to provide themselves with a more comfortable environment in which to function. Several real, but for obvious reasons nameless, examples are illustrative. The president of one doctoral degree-granting institution taught in an established but experimental college; moved from there to a more extremely experimental college; then assumed the presidency of a new, nontraditional institution that encountered difficulties with accreditation; and finally created a brand new institution conforming to his own educational beliefs. The president of another doctoral degree-granting institution, who has impeccable academic credentials, nonetheless fits the same pattern, having resigned from a major university over a matter of conscience; subsequently having returned and then resigned from that same university over intellectual differences with his colleagues; having accepted a new appointment in a major private university but then leaving that because of intellectual differences; and ending up creating a new institution. A third president, who became disenchanted with a doctoral program in which he was enrolled, then created a new doctoral degree-granting institution designed to rectify all of the deficiencies that he believed characterized his previous academic home. Still another president had previously presided over a well-established institution; left that post for a professorial one; was drawn back into administration in another established institution as a vice-president; and found himself disenchanted with the way things were being conducted, but at the same time powerless to change them. Creating a new institution seemed to him a possible way toward an intellectual utopia.

A last impression, which unfortunately cannot be well documented because so many of the quite new institutions have not established solid statistical data, is that the student bodies reflect extreme positions with respect to satisfaction with the institutions and their educational programs. On the one hand, rather high attrition rates seem to be produced when students find their somewhat idealistic expectations not being fulfilled. At the same time, those students who find the new institution comfortable are almost rhapsodic regarding their experiences, even concerning conditions that could be judged inadequate or deficient on any objective basis.

A serious question is what the long-term significance of these new institutions is likely to be and what the likelihood is that particularly the private institutions can long survive. Many of them were created in order to produce genuine diversity in an increasingly homogenized American higher education. New institutions were not only to offer diverse programs themselves but were also to stimulate other institutions to create more options for students of differing backgrounds and interests. They take their lead from sentiments frequently expressed by Frank Newman that "What is needed now is a genuinely new dimension for our diversity—schools with differing structures of teaching and learning" (Hall and Associates, 1974, pp. ix–x). Thus far the number of students accommodated in new institutions is relatively small. Even in the new nontraditional public institutions, aggregate figures are unavailable, but indicative figures can be presented: Nairobi College in 1971, approximately 300 students; DQU (1974), 1,000 students; Nova University (1976), 4,000 students; California School of Professional Psychology (1976), 500 students; Pima College (1971), approximately 100 students; New College of California (1976), 80 students; and Evergreen State College (1975), approximately 2,500 students. Thus the numbers actually served are not great. While the more visible programs have been more widely publicized, they do not appear to have been emulated in larger or established institutions. Here and there small alternative colleges have been created in existing institutions to provide diversity, but enrollments have been typically small, and practices have not been emulated by other units within the university.

It seems reasonably clear that new public institutions are likely to remain in existence, except in a few unique situations, such as New York City, where fiscal problems forced the closing of several institutions and the collapsing of several to form one institution. However, the private institutions appear to be in much greater jeopardy. As the application rate for law schools declines—as it began to do in 1976—the newly created law schools are likely to experience substantial income loss. As the GI Bill of Rights ends, institutions that have enrolled disproportionately large numbers of veterans are likely to find themselves in difficulty. Since neither the federal government nor the foundations appear willing to provide sustaining funds for new institutions, that source of support does not appear to be promising. In view of the anticipated overall decline in college enrollment by the late 1970s, the prognosis for continued existence of the new private institutions does not appear particularly good. Some undoubtedly will remain, particularly if they offer needed degree programs in vocational fields for which sustained demand is likely. The California School for Professional Psychology (since accredited) is one such, since the demand in California for various kinds of credentialed counselors seems insatiable. As for the other new private institutions that typically offer some variant on the liberal arts and sciences and some kinds of professional work in religion, education, business or law, frequently in a nontraditional mode, the future appears to be quite uncertain. As long as the founding leadership remains, as long as there are some public programs providing funds that can be funneled into the institution in the form of tuition, and as long as enrollments in the majority of public four-year institutions do not plummet, a fair number of these new institutions are likely to persist. However, changes in one or two variables could produce widespread demise of these new institutions, since few, if any, have endowments or even modest reserves.

Educational Brokering. Closely related to the development of new institutions is the rather interesting and quite recent development of established institutions contracting with noneducational and frequently for-profit organizations to deliver academic services for which the educational institution awards academic credit, credentials, and degrees. Educational institutions have long contracted with public and private agencies for services. Examples are residence hall systems contracting for food services, departments contracting to offer degree programs for school systems, libraries contracting with remainder houses to make acquisitions, and universities contracting with computer centers for computing services. A recent quick check of institutional annual reports in the region of the Western College Association revealed over eighty organizations with which institutions claimed to have contracted to receive services. However, as was indicated earlier, the financial plight of institutions deepened during the 1970s, and, as institutions sought new clientele, the idea of contracting for academic services associated with academic credit emerged. What seems to be involved is that an outside organization, frequently using part-time staff can organize courses and programs, prepare instructional materials, recruit students, recruit faculty, arrange for space, and actually conduct academic credit-earning degree programs at considerably less expense than an established accredited educational institution can do itself. The contracting organization does not require the expensive and diversified physical plants that educational institutions need. It does not need to deploy some of its resources to support service and research activities. By using part-time staff, it is not obligated to pay for retirement, health benefits, and other fringe benefits. By conducting programs in school facilities during periods of the day schools are not in operation, rentals can be kept either quite low or eliminated completely. Properly organized, a contracting agency can pay for all expenses, generate a profit, and still allocate as much as 25 percent of gross revenues to the educational institution in return for its awarding academic credit and degrees. This is such a recent phenomenon that no serious predictions are possible. However, it can be noted that established institutions and regional accrediting bodies have begun to take cognizance of the phenomenon, and some definite actions seem likely. It seems likely, for example, that regional accrediting associations will be forced by constituent members or by the accrediting officers themselves to prohibit such arrangements. A plausible arrangement that does seem to be attracting interest is for accrediting associations to acknowledge the right of institutions to contract for whatever services they wish but to announce that contracting with an unaccredited organization or institution to offer educational services for which academic credit will be granted will be grounds for withdrawal of accreditation from the contracting institution. Some who agree that such a development is likely feel that it reveals rigidity and unwillingness to innovate on the part of accrediting agencies. Without entering into that debate, contracting for educational services is potentially so threatening to the economic well-being of the majority of established institutions that no action less than prohibition of the practice seems possible. This development seems eminently desirable and fundamentally not at all rigid. It places the responsibility for the granting of academic credit squarely with the institution awarding the degrees. If a brokering agency wishes its services to be accompanied by academic credit, it can seek and gain accreditation itself. Then a valid basis for cooperation between the brokering agency and educational institution would be established, as obtains for the exchange of academic credit between different collegiate institutions.

   Consortia. The earlier discussion of cooperative and consortial arrangements between institutions, particularly between private institutions, stressed that the idea of cooperation is appealing and that the matters concerning which cooperation could theoretically be attempted quite extensive. Further, those who are professionally involved with consortia are enthusiastic, professional, and

quite convinced that interinstitutional cooperation represents one of
the most significant structural forms for the future. The Council for
Interinstitutional Leadership meets frequently, and consortial arrangements have been studied by doctoral students, with results
published in at least thirty-seven doctoral dissertations.

Any overall assessments must first distinguish between types
of consortial arrangements. Certainly fund-raising arrangements
such as the United Negro College Fund have demonstrated genuine
economic values to member institutions, so that their continued
existence can almost be taken for granted. Statewide associations of
private institutions symbolize the private sector, and, especially if the
1202 commissions created by Section 1202 of the Higher Education Amendments of 1972 become important, the statewide associations will likely become the most important connection between a
private sector and those commissions dealing with federal funds.

The multipurpose consortia that have attempted to deal with
a range of cooperative arrangements, from common purchasing to
cross-listing of courses offered by member institutions, present the
most complexities. Their future will likely depend in large measure
on the impact of several developing or even crescendoing forces.
The first of these is the historic competition between American collegiate institutions. In the United States, with the exception of the
years 1958 to 1970 and, of course, the brief period of World War
II veteran enrollments, there have always been more spaces available than applicants to fill them. In the past, collegiate institutions
did compete mightily for students and for financial resources. Although enrollments overall do continue to rise and can be expected
to rise throughout the 1970s, competition for students is increasing,
and overall there is space available for more than the supply of
traditional students (relatively young, relatively able, relatively
successful, and economically relatively comfortable). This surplus
capacity is one important factor in the quest for new students. If, as
is predicted, there is an actual decline in enrollments of one or two
million students in the early 1980s, thus producing intense competition, what will be the attitudes of individual institutions toward
multiprogram cooperation between natural competitors?

A second force, although probably considerably more trivial
than competition, is the unknown potential impact of unions on

private institutions and cooperative arrangements between them. Thus far unionism has taken deepest hold in specific types of institutions within the public sector. With few exceptions, private institutions have not yet embraced collective bargaining. In the public sector, unions seek to negotiate with the most centralized center of power, the system headquarters for multicampus universities or state government itself, as in the case of the Pennsylvania state colleges. Should faculties in private institutions that are members of multipurpose consortia opt for a union, the relationships between the union and consortial headquarters could very well become the subject for contract provisions. This is especially likely if the consortium attempts to provide for differential curricular responsibilities between institutions. One can imagine jurisdictional disputes as to which institution should offer specific academic programs if faculties in several of them have the requisite training and interest.

A third factor or force is even more abstract and conjectural. It can be argued that consortia have come into existence for many reasons, including the transcendent reason of absorbing some of the surplus of professionally qualified academics that began to appear by the end of the 1960s. For example, there is an interesting parallel between the growth of consortia and consortial activities and the growth in the number of people being graduated with doctoral degrees from programs in higher education. But the potential for absorbing excess professionals in the entire American system of higher education is obviously limited. When the absorbative limits of the entire system have been reached and the number of available professionals continue to pour out of graduate schools, as probably will happen, the pressures in all parts of the system will certainly intensify. Will faculty members in Institution A tolerate that institution's support of Institution B, which is employing professionals, when Institution A is faced with possible professional staff cutbacks?

Until such forces are acutely encountered, it seems reasonable to expect continuation of those multipurpose consortial arrangements not exclusively reliant on specific federal funding programs to continue and to provide valuable but not essential services to member institutions. However, when the core purpose of an individual institution appears seriously threatened or the core group of professionals jeopardized, then the consortium will probably be abolished.

The ideal of consortial arrangements is so appealing that it is to be hoped that many clusters of institutions can continue cooperative efforts. Not only can arrangements provide some enrichment for faculty and students alike but they may also, in years to come, produce a new organizational structure that would allow for cooperation and autonomy at the same time. However, in the absence of external funding, such as that provided by federal titlements (which actually do generate income for institutions), consortial arrangements are an added expense. If the institution can absorb that expense, the potential is at least modestly positive.

Unions and Senates. Unions and senates should be treated together, because there is strong reciprocal relationship between the two. Senates, as previously noted, came into existence when total faculty assemblies proved to be too cumbersome for decision making, when demands on the part of faculty for greater responsibility became pronounced, and when the historic administration-centered organization broke down under the onslaught of dissenting students and faculty. In a sense, the failure of senates to cope with the economic condition of the professoriate was one of the contributing forces to the rise of unions, and there is strong presumptive evidence that, as unions become deeply established on the campus or in a system, the influence of senates declines. The imponderable, of course, is the prognosis for unionism and collective bargaining throughout the American system. A possible model can be suggested that may suggest that prognosis. In California, if application rates of traditional students stabilize and begin to decline, and at the same time the community colleges are required to charge full-cost tuition for extended day, evening, and adult education programs, and at the same time the state adopts legislation permitting teachers to unionize and bargain collectively, then a domino phenomenon would seem plausible. The nineteen state campuses of the state university and college system appear to be ripe for unionization. On the campuses, there appears to be widespread faculty discontent with the centralized powers of the system headquarters. There is also considerable discontent over the second-class citizen status as compared with the faculties of the University of California, and there are marked salary differentials between the university system and the state college system. In the event that permissive legislation were enacted, unionization would quickly follow and would produce substantial increases. At the same time, the public junior colleges would convert their unionlike organizations and would begin to bargain collectively with the sanction of law. Now, should those two systems generate, through collective bargaining, economic benefits for teachers comparable or even superior to those in effect for the University of California, the stage would be set for intensive unionizing efforts on the university campuses. It is instructive here to note that Temple University faculty adopted a union after it became apparent that the salary increases for the fourteen state colleges were exceeding those received by the Temple University faculty. If public higher education in California became unionized (and this is a distinct possibility), then the rest of the states probably will quickly follow. Similarly, it seems reasonable to expect that if the University of California at Berkeley should become unionized the concept will become markedly more acceptable for the private sector. That is how the status system in American higher education operates. It should be pointed out that unionization can be prevented on a given campus if the central administration has the will and is willing to exert the strong leadership necessary in a struggle against unionism. The president of Michigan State University and his associates did just that and defeated a drive to elect a collective bargaining agent. But very likely, once momentum is established, as is suggested by the California model, the movement will come rather quickly to dominate the entire American system.

Centralization. Although the values claimed for centralization of public higher education through coordinating counsels, statewide boards, and tigthly organized systems of institutions have as yet not been demonstrated, the movement is so thoroughly under way and so appeals to governors, legislators, and the general public, all of whom are concerned with controlling expenditures, that it cannot be resisted. The particular form this centralization has taken or will take will, of course, vary from state to state, based on state characteristics, history, and tradition. However, some form of statewide control seems to be inevitable. The question is, What sort of structure can be suggested that will be least damaging to individual campuses and the educational programs for which they exist? Voluntary coordination has not proven workable, and legislated coordinating counsels and commissions typically have not been able to control program development or reduce expenditures. On the other hand, single statewide boards for all of higher education, such as in Wisconsin, are vulnerable to pressures to establish parity of status and remuneration for faculties of all types of institutions, with the collateral possibility of producing a decline in the educational and research quality of the distinguished senior universities. The 1975–1977 budget bill of the state of Wisconsin, for example, contained a section creating a study committee to examine differences in cost per student on the various campuses in Wisconsin. The clear implication was that costs should be comparable, but the critical question was not addressed: How does a Ph.D.-granting internationally renowned research university make itself comparable to two-year and four-year campuses in the same system? It may well be that the drive for comparability in the City University of New York system emphasized by the collective bargaining agreement produced intolerable financial strains and at the same time reduced the possibility of the senior institutions achieving great national reputation.

There are three models from which it might be possible to abstract some more generally appropriate principles and structures. The first of these is New York, with a statewide board of regents, with broad powers, including fiscal and programming over all high education in the state, both public and private. Then there are two multiuniversity campuses based on geographic location, each with institutions of different types and serving different clientele. Both the State University of New York and the City University of New York, although the central administration of each possesses complete power, have exercised considerable self-restraint and have allowed a great deal of campus autonomy. Faculty members on various campuses of the State University of New York, for example, are aware of the chancellor's office and its prerogatives, but they also reflect a great deal of satisfaction in their ability to conduct their own affairs without excessive infringement from Albany. The second model is that of Illinois, in which there are two multicampus universities, each with their own boards and a number of state colleges. There is a strong coordinating body, which does exercise review and recommending power over budget and program requests from the systems and individual institutions, and those recommendations appear to be highly regarded by the legislature and the governor's office. There does, however appear to be considerable dissatisfaction on the various campuses with the exercise of power by the Board of Higher Education, and there are continuous efforts to evade or negate its recommendations. The third model is that of California, which maintains a second-generation coordinating agency called the Commission on Post-Secondary Education. There are, then, three systems: one highly centralized (the state universities and colleges), one somewhat decentralized (the University of California), and one highly decentralized (the state system of junior colleges, each of whom has its own board of trustees with complete budgetary power). The chancellor's office of the junior college system is a relatively weak, data-generating and coordinating body that does not appear to intrude overly much in the internal affairs of the individual colleges or junior college districts. Faculty members on the campuses of the state universities and colleges complain a great deal about intrusion of the central administration into campus affairs, including into the making of appointments and the granting of tenure. There is modest complaining of intrusion on the campuses of the University of California.

Based on quite impressionistic evidence, the Regents of the State of New York, which have a constitutional basis for existence, appear to have been an effective force throughout their long history. In California, the constitutional status of the University of California has similarly given it a degree of autonomy that beyond doubt has contributed to the enormous reputation of that institution. Thus a model could be proposed: The statewide agency could have constitutional existence with clearly specified powers, individual institutions could be divided either by function or by geographic location (it appears really to make very little difference how divided), and each system could be governed by the board of trustees, which could also have a constitutional basis for existence and having specified powers. Such an arrangement allows higher education to deal effectively with the legislature and the governor and also prevents a statewide agency from becoming oppressive with respect to the various institutions. The Carnegie Council has pointed out that state governors increasingly are becoming the most powerful voice in public higher education and that in some respects that development ought to be constrained. The use of the constitutional provision appears to be a distinct possibility.

These structural changes imply an increase in the size of administrative and bureaucratic offices and a possible quite radical change in the role of campus chief executives. Many of the new institutions offering nontraditional programs are forced to expand central office staff, even if they utilize primarily part-time faculty. The sheer administration of programs delivered away from a campus and the monitoring of asymmetrical registrations and programs, to be done properly, thus require substantial administrative and support staff. Campus administrative staffs increased in size partly because of load factors but also to comply with requirements of increasingly large system and state-wide headquarters. To those must be added additional administrative supportive support to cope with the growing role of the courts and the growing amount of administrative law applicable to institutions of higher education. If such concepts as accountability become general, this again would increase administrative staffs in order to generate and order the needed information on which to base accountability reports. Very likely nothing much can be done to effect significant reductions in administrative and bureaucratic staffs throughout the American system, but careful review of the cost benefit of changed services, such as gathering information and adopting new delivery systems and nontraditional modes of instruction, may suggest ways of retarding the growth of administrative staffs or of refraining from offering some kinds of services if on further analysis the costs of administration exceed potential educational benefits.

The role of a campus chief executive could very well prove to be one of the biggest derivative changes, coming about as a result of the other developments of the late 1960s and 1970s. Although the early development of systems of institutions during the early 1960s had begun to erode campus presidential prerogatives and the strengthening of departments at the same time had a similar effect, presidents were still relatively the most powerful and influential individuals on the campus and took considerable pride in contributing to the growth and enrichment of their institutions. By the 1970s, however, statewide systems offices were growing stronger, senates had begun to share more in administrative power, negotiated contracts had begun to specify and limit management responsibilities, and the courts and legislation had also begun to limit the domain of presidential discretion. Of course, the impact of such legislation as affirmative action also exerted a limiting pressure. By the end of the 1960s, a number of writers had urged a restoration of presidential leadership, and even some faculties that had acquired considerable responsibility began to ask that presidents again assume greater prerogatives. Although the situation of the 1970s could make it theoretically desirable that presidential power, prerogatives, and leadership increase, the congruence of these other developments may preclude the redressed balance of institutional power that was being urged. Thus, as of 1976, the dimensions of the campus chief executive's office are undetermined and subject to quite capricious fluctuations, and even the direction of likely evolution is unknown.

Of all the possible developments for the improvement of American collegiate education, none is more important than the restoration of presidential power and prerogatives to the campus chief executive. Historically, major developments in higher education typically have come about as a result of presidential leadership. Significant innovations significantly succeed or fail, depending on the degree of presidential commitment. The tone and sense of movement or lethargy on a campus is related to the role played by the president. Institutions that have experienced serious financial difficulties have then experienced restored economic equilibrium when presidents exerted strong influence. This is not to argue for the return to the autocratic president that has existed in the past, but it is to urge the president to govern with sufficient power.

A Summing Up

These observations point to an overall judgment that structural and financial changes initiated or accelerated after 1968 are likely to persist and become part of the higher educational tradition. At the same time, the radical curricular and instructional changes suggested by the nontraditional movement, the rationale of some new institutions, and the egalitarian reformers are not likely to become deeply imbedded or particularly influential. If this is so, it then becomes necessary to determine why. A major reason for questioning the long-term significance of the nontraditional movement is that it seems to rest on a conception of higher education as an agent for reforming society. Providing new services for many different groups of people seems to assume a breakdown in other social institutions that have previously been expected to provide service. Thus higher education is seen as a surrogate for the family, by providing day-care centers; a surrogate for elementary and secondary education, by providing basic education; a surrogate for industry and unions, by providing apprentice kinds of training; a surrogate for churches, recreation departments, and social welfare agencies, by providing leisure-time activities; and a surrogate for the entire knowledge industry, by attempting to provide whatever information or knowledge any individual wishes. Now, colleges have always served a surrogate role to some extent. They have taken custody of a portion of the nation's youth for several years, and they have provided some housing and some entertainment. But the claimed domain of activity during the 1970s is so broad that, if all-out efforts were made to service everyone, resources would be drawn away from the traditional collegiate functions of enculturating the young and providing some vocational and professional training. Collegiate institutions are essentially conservative, as indeed are all educational institutions. They are created by the powerful in a society to preserve that society and not to produce significant social change. The more far-reaching curricular and instructional changes of the 1970s seem destined to be rejected by most college boards, administrators, and faculty members as being at variance with the historic mission of collegiate institutions.

The new private institutions that have come into existence since 1968 are not likely to last very long, for many reasons, including the fact that they for the most part have violated too many principles involved in institutional survival. First, they seek to appeal to transitory constituencies rather than to well-established constituencies with a definite tradition of supporting the institution. These new institutions seek to serve those who wish to become lawyers but who cannot be accepted into established law schools, those who want advanced degrees but do not have time to attend established programs, those who need longer than average time to mature, and those who wish the personal satisfaction that comes from possessing a credential or degree. New private institutions created earlier sought to serve members of a particular religious denomination, or a specific, distinctive, geographic community.

Relatedly, the newer private institutions for the most part do not reflect a reasonably firm and established intellectual or ideological base in the sense that Protestantism or Catholicism provided an intellectual base for institutions created earlier. Rather, the intellectual base seems to be a rather diffuse social meliorism, permitting the offering of all kinds of different services, or to be angry irritation and frustration with the status quo. Neither of these, especially in the absence of a firm financial base, seems sufficiently strong to permit long and stable growth.

Thirdly, many of the new private institutions assume the continuation of a somewhat questionable financial base. They assume that tuition will provide principal income, and they seek to keep tuition within the reach of potential students, either through the continued availability of state and federal student aid programs or through reducing time requirements so that full tuition would be substantially less than if students were required to spend additional amounts of time gaining a degree. As inflation continues, this trade-off of time against dollars could very well produce absurdities. Then too, they seek to keep costs down by using part-time faculty or faculty members who, for one reason or another, will accept less than average salaries. For both of these subsidies, limits are clearly visible.

Educational institutions and educational practices require nurture and support from powerful elements in the society. Land-grant colleges eventually obtained the support from the agricultural interests in the society and grew increasingly strong as agriculture emerged as a mainstay of an expanding economy. The Flexner report (1910) on medical education received immediate support throughout the country from many different segments of society that had also come to realize the inadequate quality of medical practice and medical education. As suggested earlier, the junior college movement was broadly supported because it was democratic in tone but still preserved prestige. The more radical curricular instructional and institutional changes in the 1970s do not seem to possess a sufficiently powerful set of constituencies to maintain them. A few reforming academics, some minority and disadvantaged groups, and officials in a few foundations comprise the base. At the same time, these elements have encountered apathy, resistance, or outright opposition on the part of strong, existing institutions, accreditation agencies, the major professions, and political leaders who have yet to be convinced of the economic values.

Certainly the conservatism of academics with respect to the core function of colleges and universities is involved in obstacles raised against widespread adoption of quite new educational practice. College faculty members, depending to some extent on disciplinary affiliation, tend to be somewhat to the social, economic, and political left of the general population. However, with respect to the curriculum methods of teaching or grading and the other elements of an institution's educational program, faculty members do tend to resist change particularly, and professors in large, prestigious, departmentally organized, pacesetting institutions may be expected to ignore key tenets of nontraditional education, or, if seriously suggested, to deny adoption of them. For example, there was a West Coast controversy over the fact that the Western College Association (WCA) granted regional accreditation to a two-campus proprietary institution that had, among other things, a rather open admissions policy and a supportive counseling program. The less well-known western law schools that had only recently acquired accreditation by the American Bar Association violently opposed the WCA act on the ground that it was diluting the quality of legal education. Deeper probing suggested that an important objection was fear of competition from the somewhat nontraditionally organized law school. Officials of the major prestigious law schools in California, however, remained unconcerned. One remarked that the controversy was a tempest in a teapot and in no way affected what the prestigious law schools do or care about.

While difficult to prove conclusively, several assertions seem plausible. The first is that the professoriate that is organized into departments is inclined to resist most suggested educational changes.

Further, the higher the prestige of a university, the more resistant to innovation its faculty is likely to be. To illustrate, 500 institutions were studied. Over a ten-year period, each had sent at least one team of four faculty members to the Danforth Workshop on Liberal Arts Education. The purpose of the workshop was to help institutions make educational changes and to help faculty members improve their professional attributes. Most institutions that sent a team subsequently adopted proposals the team made for change, and the adoptions persisted. However, when analyzed according to type of institution, the higher-prestige institutions invariably demonstrated a lower rate of adoption than did the lower-prestige institutions. The typology used was the Carnegie Commission on Higher Education classification scheme, positing Level 1 and Level 2 of research universities, doctoral-granting universities, comprehensive colleges, and liberal arts colleges. The second level of each type adopted significantly more of the proposals than did the higher level.

What appears during the late 1970s is an American system of higher education in which a substantial body of literature emerged urging major new educational practices. A few of the professional societies, such as the American Association for Higher Education, lent their weight to publicizing the new. Yet overall the number of students actually affected remains relatively small. A similarly growing body of literature also deals with structural and organizational changes and these, especially in the public sector, are rapidly being put into effect. However, it is difficult to discover solid evidence that these changes are in any way significantly modifying how students and professors go about their educational tasks and responsibilities. Education, including higher education, is a social institution designed to enculturate people into the society and to acquaint them with the constantly expanding number of things they must know in order to cope with that society. It operates on the basis of tradition, partly because so little is really known about how people learn and develop and partly because traditional ways of doing things have not proven unsuccessful. People attend college, graduate, assume adult roles, and live out their lives with varying degrees of satisfaction or dissatisfaction. Until persuasive evidence is obtained that clearly superior ways of inducting youth into adulthood can be found, the practice of higher education is likely to proceed as it has in the past.

Personal Credo

This book violates a fundamental premise of historical research—that the perspective of time is essential to gauge the significance of events. The book was written in 1976 and 1977 and has tried to assess the likely importance of developments beginning less than a decade earlier. It is entirely possible that such an assessment might more clearly reflect hopes rather than objective appraisal, although an attempt has been made throughout to be dispassionate about developments and their likely outcomes. However, there comes a time in writing contemporary history, particularly history undertaken as a basis for policy, to set aside recording and analyzing and to express a position with respect to the many issues discussed. The concluding paragraphs of the concluding chapter seem the appropriate place to express a personal credo. An ideal system (or more precisely a nonsystem) of higher education in the United States should consist of many different types of institutions to serve the many kinds of students desiring it. There should be junior colleges, liberal arts colleges, church-related colleges, regional universities, comprehensive universities, and comprehensive universities polarized around such things as science and technology. At the same time, it should be recognized that all of these collegiate institutions share important purposes and values in common, and so, while there will be important differences between a small liberal arts college located in Appalachia and a research-oriented university in California, both will share the important goal of inducting and socializing youth into American civilization and society. Institutions that reject that fundamental goal should properly find themselves outside of the pale of formal higher education. Given the history and conditions of the United States, it is good that there are publicly and privately controlled institutions, and the proportionate balance of students attending each should, if at all possible, be stabilized around 70 percent public and 30 percent private, the current proportions. The private institutions can provide more easily different

programs for different students, manifest more intensely fundamental principles of academic freedom, and, above all, prevent the
educational monopoly of publicly controlled institutions. This last
is based on the belief that monopolies are inherently bad.

The federal government has an important stake in higher
education, and the significance of that stake should be symbolized
by creating a Cabinet-level secretary of education who could ensure
that the voice of education is heard in the highest council along
with the voices of diplomacy, war, commerce, and labor. However,
such a position should not become a ministry of education, in the
French sense, with power for direct influence over academic programs throughout the country. Those academic programs and
practices are best determined by constituencies on a single campus,
and any efforts to transfer those responsibilities should be resisted
intensely. In this same connection, it is probably too late to reverse
the tendencies in the several states to create coordinating and controlling agencies above the campus level. However, it is not too late
for individual campuses in many different ways to reassert campus
responsibility and autonomy and to resist extension of centralizing
tendencies from coordinating agencies to statewide systems with
statewide boards and administrative structures. Perhaps the best
arrangement would be moderately strong coordinating committees
or commissions whose activities would be legally constrained by specific expressions of domain of purely campus responsibility.

This system or nonsystem of higher education continues to
serve educational, service, and research purposes. However, the core
mission of all institutions, regardless of type, has been the educational mission of preparing the young for entry into the adult society. This primary mission should be continued, and if individual
institutions have departed substantially from it they should be
encouraged to return to an emphasis on the core responsibility. This
does not mean that some programs for adults should not be offered,
but they should not be offered if they jeopardize the core function
or if they are offered by institutions that do not possess the intellectual traditions and resources needed for extending programs to
many different groups of students. Thus the tendency for institutions
to broker services for which the institutions are really not qualified
should be criticized and gradually eliminated.

Modern collegiate institutions do properly offer a variety of programs and activities that include many different preparations or vocations; preserving the culture through libraries, museums, and galleries; and serving as a community intellectual resource. However, collegiate institutions are important but limited institutions that cannot and should not attempt to do too many things. Colleges and universities, for example, can have little effect on fundamental character traits such as honesty, optimism, or a sense of humor. Those are formed much earlier and through different media. Colleges and universities are at their best when they develop skills and abilities resting on the uses of words, numbers, and abstract concepts. Institutions organized to emphasize other things, such as the joys of gardening, the cultivation of spiritual serenity, or therapeutic self-expression, are not institutions of higher education, even though they may be quite laudable institutions that improve the human condition. Relatedly, in accomplishing principal purposes, collegiate institutions properly make use of many different techniques, including field work, collection of artifacts, and even remunerated work closely related to academic work. However, the basic techniques should continue to consist of reading and writing, numerical calculations, and practice in developing and using abstract concepts, which are best developed through sustained and intensive interaction between teacher and student and through closely supervised independent effort, so that constant evaluation is done by informed individuals to help students perfect their cognitive skills. Counseling, self-services, group therapy, recreational facilities, and the opportunity to live with others are all important but limited activities designed to facilitate or remove barriers from student development of those intellectual traits that are the chief responsibility of higher education. To adopt a more expansive view and to conceive of as educational the many activities that change human behavior is to so extend the meaning of higher education as to render it meaningless.

Higher education should be viewed as contributing both to individual worth and satisfaction and to the social good. This means that individuals and society should contribute to the financing of higher education in the United States and that a reasonable tuition should be expected from those who can afford it, while a reasonable subsidy should be provided for those who cannot. Institutions are more likely to prosper when their funds come from a variety of sources, including public subsidy, tuition, gifts, grants, and earnings from education-related activities. Probably the ideal arrangement for privately controlled institutions would be 50 percent of the budget coming from tuition and benefaction and 50 percent from public sources of all sorts, which might include capitation provision (direct payment per degree conferred), some direct institutional support, or overhead support connected with students whose tuitions come from public sources. Within the public sector, possibly 70 percent of the budget should come from tuition and direct state appropriations and the remaining 30 percent from other public sources and from private benefaction. Whatever the precise arrangement adopted, there should be a reduction in the tuition gap between the privately controlled and publicly controlled institutions, but the gap should not be eliminated completely. To achieve a goal properly means that public tuition should go up the same time public support to private institutions is provided.

Within the system of higher education in the United States, there should be constant experimentation with methods of instruction, learning, and operations. Most of these experiments should be expected to fail or prove inconclusive, for the practices and processes of higher education change slowly. Out of the welter of experimentation and attempted innovation may come a synthesis of new developments that can change the face of higher education. This has happened in the past, and it is always possible in the future. However, while experimentation should be encouraged, it should also be viewed skeptically, the burden of proof ultimately resting on demonstration of achievement rather than on promise of potential achievement. During the early 1970s, there was far too much embracing of new ideas, such as the nontraditional movement, on the basis of promise rather than careful assessment of realistic performance.

Historically, from the medieval universities on to the present (with some notable aberrations from time to time), the transcendent values in colleges and universities have been intellectuality, collegiality, civility, and the tranquility necessary to study and ponder the human condition in the abstract. These are sound values and should be preserved at all costs. This means that institutions that wish to substitute experience in the day-to-day conduct of affairs for intellectuality should be viewed as something other than higher education. In connection with these values, it should be noted that unionism can be tolerated and that a unionized campus very likely would not destroy academic vitality. The processes of higher education have gone on under many different conditions, ranging from war to religious excesses, and will undoubtedly continue to do so in the future. However, the unionized campus would seem to weaken the values of collegiality and civility, and, if one treasures those, as this author does, it would be better if unionism and collective bargaining were not adopted.

Bibliography

American Association for Higher Education. *Faculty Participation in Academic Governance: Task Force Report.* Washington, D.C.: American Association for Higher Education, 1967, p. 20.

ARROWSMITH, W. "The Future of Teaching." In C. B. T. Lee (Ed.), *Improving College Teaching.* Washington, D.C.: American Council on Education, 1967.

ASHBY, E. *African Universities and Western Tradition.* Cambridge, Mass.: Harvard University Press, 1964.

ASTIN, A. W. "Undergraduate Achievement and Institutional Excellence." *Science,* 1968, *161,* 661–668.

BERDAHL, R. O. *State Coordination of Higher Education.* Washington, D.C.: American Council on Education, 1971.

BIRD, C. *The Case Against College.* New York: McKay, 1975.

BLACKBURN, R., and OTHERS. *Changing Practices in Undergraduate Education.* Berkeley, Calif.: Carnegie Council on Policy Studies in Higher Education, 1976.

BLOOM, A. "The Failure of the University." *Daedalus,* Fall 1974, p. 64.

341

BONTHIUS, R. H., DAVIS, F. J., and DRUSHAL, J. G. *The Independent Study Program in the United States.* New York: Columbia University Press, 1957.

BOTH, O. L. *A New Curriculum for a New Generation.* Unpublished paper, Kansas Wesleyan University, February, 1976.

BOWEN, H. R. "Teaching and Learning: 2000 A.D." In C. T. Stewart and T. R. Harvey (Eds.), *New Directions for Higher Education, no. 12.* San Francisco: Jossey-Bass, 1975.

BOWEN, H. R. *Financing Higher Education: Current State of the Debate in Higher Education, Human Resources and the National Economy.* Washington, D.C.: Association of American Colleges 1974.

BOWEN, H. R., and DOUGLAS, G. K. *Efficiency in Liberal Education: A Study of Comparative Instructional Costs for Different Ways of Organizing Teaching-Learning in a Liberal Arts College.* New York: McGraw-Hill, 1971.

BOWEN, H. R., and MINTER, W. J. *Private Higher Education.* Washington, D.C.: Association of American Colleges, 1975.

BOYER, E. L. "Changing Time Requirements." In D. W. Vermilye (Ed.), *Learner-Centered Reform: Current Issues in Higher Education 1975.* San Francisco: Jossey-Bass, 1975.

BROWN, J. D. *The Liberal University.* New York: McGraw-Hill, 1969.

BROWN, J. W., and THORNTON, J. W., JR. *New Media in Higher Education.* Washington, D.C.: National Education Association, 1963.

BROWN, J. W., and THORNTON, J. W., JR. *New Media and College Teaching.* Washington, D.C.: National Education Association, 1968.

Carnegie Commission on Higher Education. *The Capitol and the Campus: State Responsibility for Postsecondary Education.* New York: McGraw-Hill, 1971a.

Carnegie Commission on Higher Education. *Less Time—More Options.* New York: McGraw-Hill, 1971b.

Carnegie Commission on Higher Education. *The Fourth Revolution: Instructional Technology in Higher Education.* New York: McGraw-Hill, 1972a.

Carnegie Commission on Higher Education. *The More Effective Use of Resources: An Imperative for Higher Education.* New York: McGraw-Hill, 1972b.

Carnegie Commission on Higher Education. *Governance of Higher Education: Six Priority Problems.* New York: McGraw-Hill, 1973.

Carnegie Council on Policy Studies in Higher Education. *Low or No*

Tuition: The Feasibility of a National Policy for the First Two Years of College. San Francisco: Jossey-Bass, 1975.

Carnegie Foundation for the Advancement of Teaching. *More than Survival: Prospects for Higher Education in a Period of Uncertainty.* San Francisco: Jossey-Bass, 1975.

Carnegie Foundation for the Advancement of Teaching. *The States and Higher Education: A Proud Past and a Vital Future.* San Francisco: Jossey-Bass, 1976.

CARPENTER, C. R. "Instructional Functions of New Media." In J. W. Thornton, Jr., and J. W. Brown (Eds.), *New Media and College Teachers.* Washington, D.C.: National Education Association, 1968.

CARTTER, A. M. "Future Faculty Needs and Resources." In C. B. T. Lee (Ed.), *Improving College Teaching.* Washington, D.C.: American Council on Education, 1967.

CARTTER, A. M. *Ph.D.s and the Academic Labor Market.* New York: McGraw-Hill, 1976.

CHALMERS, G. Unpublished speech presented at the meeting of the American Council on Education, Washington, D.C., 1950.

CHAMBERS, M. M. *Appropriations of State Tax Funds for Operating Expenses of Higher Education, 1971–72.* Washington, D.C.: National Association of State Universities and Land-Grant Colleges, 1972.

CHEIT, E. F. *The New Depression in Higher Education—Two Years Later.* New York: McGraw-Hill, 1971.

CHEIT, E. F. *The Useful Arts and the Liberal Tradition.* New York: McGraw-Hill, 1975a.

CHEIT, E. F. "Managing Financial Resources in Higher Education During a Period of Rising Costs." Unpublished doctoral dissertation, University of California, Berkeley, 1975b.

CLARK, B. R. *The Open Door College.* New York: McGraw-Hill, 1961.

COHEN, M., and MARCH, J. G. *Leadership and Ambiguity.* New York: McGraw-Hill, 1974.

College and University Bulletin, 1972, 25 (1, entire issue).

Commission on Non-Traditional Study (Samuel B. Gould, Chairman). *Diversity by Design.* San Francisco: Jossey-Bass, 1973.

CONANT, J. B. *Education and Liberty.* Cambridge, Mass.: Harvard University Press, 1953.

CORSON, J. J. *The Governance of Colleges and Universities.* New York: McGraw-Hill, 1960.

CORSON, J. J. *The Governance of Colleges and Universities* (rev. ed.). New York: McGraw-Hill, 1975.

CREMIN, L. A. *The Transformation of the School.* New York: Vantage Books, 1961.

CRAIG, G. A. "Green Stamp or Structured Undergraduate Education." *Daedalus,* Fall 1974, p. 144.

CROSS, K. P. "New Forms for New Functions." In D. W. Vermilye (Ed.), *Lifelong Learners—A New Clientele for Higher Education: Current Issues in Higher Education 1974.* San Francisco: Jossey-Bass, 1974.

CROSS, K. P. *Accent on Learning: Improving Instruction and Reshaping the Curriculum.* San Francisco: Jossey-Bass, 1976a.

CROSS, K. P. "Commitments to Improve the Quality of Learning." Speech presented to the 75th annual meeting of the College Entrance Examination Board, New York, October 25, 1976b.

CROSS, K. P., VALLEY, J. R., and ASSOCIATES. *Planning Non-Traditional Programs: An Analysis of the Issues for Postsecondary Education.* San Francisco: Jossey-Bass, 1974.

CROW, M. L., and OTHERS. *Faculty Development Centers in Southern Universities.* Atlanta: Southern Regional Education Board, 1976.

DRESSEL, P. L. *College and University Curriculum.* Berkeley, Calif.: McCutchan, 1968.

DRESSEL, P. L., and DELISLE, F. H. *Undergraduate Curriculum Trends.* Washington, D.C.: American Council on Education, 1969.

DRESSEL, P. L., and MAYHEW, L. B. *Critical Analysis and Judgment in the Humanities.* Dubuque, Iowa: W. C. Brown, 1954a.

DRESSEL, P. L., and MAYHEW, L. B. *Critical Thinking in Social Sciences.* Dubuque, Iowa: W. C. Brown, 1954b.

DRESSEL, P. L., and MAYHEW, L. B. *Science Reasoning and Understanding.* Dubuque, Iowa: W. C. Brown, 1954c.

DRESSEL, P. L., and THOMPSON, M. M. *Independent Study: A New Interpretation of Concepts, Practices, and Problems.* San Francisco: Jossey-Bass, 1973.

DUNHAM, E. A. *Colleges of the Forgotten Americans: A Profile of State Colleges and Regional Universities.* New York: McGraw-Hill, 1969.

DUPIN, R., and TAVEGGEA, T. *The Teaching-Learning Paradox.* Eugene: Center for the Advanced Study of Educational Administration, University of Oregon, 1968.

DURYEA, E. D., and FISK, R. S. *Collective Bargaining, State University and the State Government in New York.* Buffalo: State University of New York at Buffalo, 1975.

DURYEA, E. D., FISK, R. S., and ASSOCIATES. *Faculty Unions and Collective Bargaining.* San Francisco: Jossey-Bass, 1973.

"Education Amendments Act of 1972 to Higher Education Act of 1965." Public Law 92318.

ENARSON, H. L. "University or Knowledge Factory." *Chronicle of Higher Education,* June 18, 1973.

FLEXNER, A. *Medical Education in the United States and Canada.* Boston: Merrymount Press, 1910.

FRANKEL, C. "Reflections on a Worn-Out Model." *Daedalus,* Fall 1974, p. 25.

FREDERIKSEN, N., and SCHRADER, W. B. *Adjustment to College,* Princeton, N.J.: Educational Testing Service, 1951.

FREEMAN, R., and HOLLOMAN, J. H. "The Declining Value of College Going." *Change,* 1975, *7,* 24–31, 62.

FRENCH, S. J. *Accent on Teaching.* New York: Harper & Row, 1956.

FROOMKIN, J., and PFEFERMAN, M. "A Computer Model to Measure the Requirements for Student Aid in Higher Education." In *Proceedings of the Social Statistical Association.* Washington, D.C.: American Statistical Association, 1969.

GARBARINO, J. W. *Faculty Bargaining: Change and Conflict.* New York: McGraw-Hill, 1975.

GIRARD, D. P. "How Should We Prepare American Students, Graduates, and Faculty to Benefit Most from Their Study, Travel, or Residence Abroad and to Make the Foreign Experience Further International Understanding?" In F. H. Horn (Ed.), *Current Issues in Higher Education 1953.* Washington, D.C.: National Education Association, 1953.

GLENNY, L. A. *The Anonymous Leaders of Higher Education.* Berkeley: Center for Research and Development in Higher Education, University of California, Berkeley, 1971.

GLENNY, L. A., and KIDDER, J. R. *State Tax Support of Higher Education.* Denver: Education Commission of the States, 1974.

GOLLATTSCHECK, J. F., and OTHERS. *College Leadership for Community Renewal: Beyond Community-Based Education.* San Francisco: Jossey-Bass, 1976.

GOULD, S. B., and CROSS, K. P. (Eds.). *Explorations in Non-Traditional Study.* San Francisco: Jossey-Bass, 1972.

GREENBERG, D. S. *The Politics of Pure Science.* New York: New American Library, 1967.

GROSS, E., and GRAMBSCH, P. V. *Changes in University Organization, 1964–1971.* New York: McGraw-Hill, 1974.

HALL, L., and ASSOCIATES. *New Colleges for New Students.* San Francisco: Jossey-Bass, 1974.

Harvard Report. *General Education in a Free Society.* Cambridge, Mass.: Harvard University Press, 1947.

HEISS, A. *Inventory of Academic Innovation and Reform.* New York: McGraw-Hill, 1973.

HODGKINSON, H. L. *The Campus Senate.* Berkeley: Center for Research and Development in Higher Education, University of California, Berkeley, 1974.

HOFSTADTER, R. *Anti-Intellectualism in America.* New York: Vintage Press, 1966.

INNES, J. T., JACOBSON, P. B., and PELLEGRIN, R. J. *The Economic Returns to Education.* Eugene: Center for the Advanced Study of Educational Administration, University of Oregon, 1965.

JACOB, P. E. *Changing Values in College.* New Haven, Conn.: Edward W. Hazen Foundation, 1957.

JAFFE, A. J., and ADAMS, W. "Two Models of Open Enrollment." In L. Wilson (Ed.), *Universal Higher Education: Costs, Benefits, Options.* Washington, D.C.: American Council on Education, 1971.

JELLEMA, W. W. *From Red to Black? The Financial Status of Private Colleges and Universities.* San Francisco: Jossey-Bass, 1973.

JENCKS, C., and RIESMAN, D. *The Academic Revolution.* Garden City, N.Y.: Doubleday, 1968.

Joint Committee on the Master Plan for Higher Education. *Report of the Joint Committee on the Master Plan for Higher Education.* Sacramento: California State Legislature, 1973.

KEETON, M. T. "Reform and Red Tape." In D. W. Vermilye (Ed.), *Learner-Centered Reform: Current Issues in Higher Education 1975.* San Francisco: Jossey-Bass, 1975.

KEMERER, F. R., and BALDRIDGE, J. V. *Unions on Campus: A National Study of the Consequences of Faculty Bargaining.* San Francisco: Jossey-Bass, 1975.

KENNEDY, T. "Removing the Barriers to Educational Opportunity." In F. H. Horn (Ed.), *Current Issues in Higher Education 1950.* Washington, D.C.: National Education Association, 1950.

LANG, P. D. "Expectations for Accountability in Higher Education." In B. F. Doenges (Ed.), *Accountability: Proceedings.* Corvallis: Oregon State University Press, 1971.

LEE, C. B. T. (Ed.). *Improving College Teaching.* Washington, D.C.: American Council on Education, 1967.

LEE, E. C., and BOWEN, F. M. *The Multicampus University: A Study of Academic Governance.* New York: McGraw-Hill, 1971.

LEE, E. C., and BOWEN, F. M. *Managing Multicampus Systems: Effective Administration in an Unsteady State.* San Francisco: Jossey-Bass, 1975.

LICKLIDER, J. C. R. "Potential of Networking for Research and Education." In M. Greenberg and others (Eds.), *Networks for Research and Education—Sharing Computer and Information Resources Nationwide.* Cambridge, Mass.: M.I.T. Press, 1974.

LINDQUIST, J. "Strategies for Contract Learning." In D. W. Vermilye (Ed.), *Learner-Centered Reform: Current Issues in Higher Education 1975.* San Francisco: Jossey-Bass, 1975.

MCCOLLUM, S. G. "College for Prisoners." In D. W. Vermilye (Ed.), *Learner-Centered Reform: Current Issues in Higher Education 1975.* San Francisco: Jossey-Bass, 1975.

MCGRATH, E. J., and MEETH, L. R. "Organizing for Teaching and Learning: The Curriculum." In S. Baskin (Ed.), *Higher Education: Some Newer Developments.* New York: McGraw-Hill, 1965.

MCKEACHIE, W. J. *Teaching Tips.* Lexington, Mass.: Heath, 1969.

MAGAZINER, I. "Draft of a Working Paper for Education at Brown." Mimeograph. Providence, R.I.: Brown University, 1967.

MARCH, J. G. "Commitment and Competence in Educational Administration." In L. B. Mayhew (Ed.), *Educational Leadership and Declining Enrollments.* Berkeley, Calif.: McCutchan, 1974.

MAYHEW, L. B. (Ed.). *General Education: An Account and Appraisal.* New York: Harper & Row, 1960.

MAYHEW, L. B. "The New Colleges." In S. Baskin (Ed.), *Higher Education: Some Newer Developments.* New York: McGraw-Hill, 1965.

MAYHEW, L. B. *Long-Range Planning for Higher Education.* New York: Academy for Educational Development, 1969.

MAYHEW, L. B. *The Carnegie Commission on Higher Education. A Critical Analysis of the Reports and Recommendations.* San Francisco: Jossey-Bass, 1973a.

MAYHEW, L. B. Unpublished report to the Exxon Foundation. New York: Exxon, 1973b.

MAYHEW, L. B. *Computerized Networks Among Libraries and Universities: An Administrator's Overview.* Stanford, Calif.: ERIC Clearinghouse on Information Resources, 1975.

MAYHEW, L. B., and FORD, P. J. *Changing the Curriculum:* San Francisco: Jossey-Bass, 1971.

MILLETT, J. *Financing Higher Education in the United States.* New York: Columbia University Press, 1952.

MILLETT, J. D. *Campuswide Governance 1966–1976.* Washington, D.C.: Academy for Educational Development, 1977.

MOOD, A. M. *The Future of Higher Education: Some Speculations and Suggestions.* New York: McGraw-Hill, 1973.

MUELLER, K. H. *Student Personnel Work in Higher Education.* Boston: Houghton Mifflin, 1961.

National Association of State Universities and Land-Grant Colleges. *1976–77 Student Charges at State and Land-Grant Universities.* Washington, D.C.: National Association of State Universities and Land-Grant Colleges, 1976.

National Education Association. "Educational Policies Commission Report." National Education Association, 1964.

OGILVIE, W. K., and RAINES, M. R. *Perspectives, the Community Junior College.* New York: Appleton-Century-Crofts, 1971.

O'NEIL, R. M. "Pros and Cons of Learner-Centered Reform." In D. W. Vermilye (Ed.), *Learner-Centered Reform: Current Issues in Higher Education 1975.* San Francisco: Jossey-Bass, 1975.

PATTERSON, F. *Colleges in Consort: Institutional Cooperation Through Consortia.* San Francisco: Jossey-Bass, 1974.

PETERSON, V. T. *Renewing Higher Education: The Competency-Based Approach.* Toledo, Ohio: Center for the Study of Higher Education, University of Toledo, 1976.

President's Commission on Higher Education. *Higher Education for American Democracy.* Washington, D.C.: U.S. Government Printing Office, 1947.

ROBINSON, A. L., and OTHERS. *Black Studies in the University.* New Haven, Conn.: Yale University Press, 1969.

ROSSMAN, J. E., and OTHERS. *Open Admissions at City University of New York.* Englewood Cliffs, N.J.: Prentice-Hall, 1975.

REYNOLDS, J. W. *The Comprehensive Junior College Curriculum.* Berkeley, Calif.: McCutchan, 1970.

RUML, B. *Memo to a College Trustee.* New York: McGraw-Hill, 1959.

RUSK, D. "What Developments in the Next Ten Years Will Change the Conditions Under Which Higher Education Works?" In F. H. Horn (Ed.), *Current Issues in Higher Education 1953.* Washington, D.C.: National Education Association, 1953.

SANFORD, M. (Ed.). *The American College.* New York: Wiley, 1961.

SCHULTZ, T. W. *Investment in Education.* Chicago: University of Chicago Press, 1972.

Southern Regional Education Board. *Priorities for Postsecondary Education in the South.* Atlanta: SREB, 1976.

TAUBMAN, P., and WALES, T. E. *Higher Education and Earnings.* New York: McGraw-Hill, 1974.

TAYLOR, C. H., JR. "Introduction." In A. L. Robinson (Ed.), *Black Studies in the University.* New Haven, Conn.: Yale University Press, 1969.

THOMPSON, R. *The Impending Tidal Wave of Students.* Washington, D.C.: American Council on Education, 1954.

Universal Higher Education. Washington, D.C.: National Education Association, 1964.

University of San Francisco External Degree Programs. San Francisco: University of San Francisco, 1976.

VERMILYE, D. W. (Ed.). *Lifelong Learners—A New Clientele for Higher Education: Current Issues in Higher Education 1974.* San Francisco: Jossey-Bass, 1974.

VERMILYE, D. W. (Ed.). *Learner-Centered Reform: Current Issues in Higher Education 1975.* San Francisco: Jossey-Bass, 1975.

VEYSEY, L. R. "The Emergence of the American University." Unpublished paper, 1965.

WALTON, W. W. *Productive Delivery Systems for Non-Traditional Learning.* Stanford, Calif.: ERIC Clearinghouse on Information Resources, 1975.

WIDNER, E. W. *The World Role of Universities.* New York: McGraw-Hill, 1962.

WILLINGHAM, W. W. *Free-Access Higher Education.* New York: College Entrance Examination Board, 1970.

WOLANIN, T. R., and GLADIEUX, L. E. *Congress and the Colleges: The National Politics of Higher Education.* Lexington, Mass.: Lexington Books, 1976.

Index

Mayhew, Lewis B
    Legacy of the seventies / Lewis B.
Mayhew. -- 1st ed. -- San Francisco :
Jossey-Bass, 1977.

    xvi, 366 p. ; 24 cm. -- (The Jossey-
Bass series in higher education)
    Bibliography: p. 341-349.
    Includes index.

    1. Education, Higher--U.S.
    I. Title.